AGING

THE PASTORAL PSYCHOLOGY SERIES,
NUMBER 8

AGING:

ITS CHALLENGE TO THE INDIVIDUAL AND TO SOCIETY

Edited by

WILLIAM C. BIER, S.J.

FORDHAM UNIVERSITY PRESS · NEW YORK

Printed in the United States of America

Table of Contents

PREFACE   vii

I. AGING IN PERSPECTIVE: HISTORICAL, CULTURAL, RELIGIOUS   1

Aging in Preindustrial and in Contemporary Industrial
    Societies   3
      Charles F. O'Donnell
The Aged in Chinese and Japanese Cultures   14
      Gino K. Piovesana, S.J.
The Challenge of Aging for Contemporary Religion   26
      William F. Hogan, C.S.C.

II. THE BASIC SCIENTIFIC DIMENSIONS   35

Demography of Aging   37
      Leon F. Bouvier
Physiology of Aging   47
      Nathan W. Shock
Sociology of Aging   61
      Howard A. Rosencranz

III. THE PSYCHOLOGY AND PSYCHOPATHOLOGY OF AGING   71

Psychology of Aging   73
      M. Powell Lawton
Individual Differences in Aging   84
      Anne Anastasi
Psychopathology of Aging   96
      Robert J. Campbell

IV. RETIREMENT: CENTER OF THE AGING CHALLENGE   117

Retirement: The Emerging Social Pattern   119
      Ruth G. Bennett

Pre-Retirement: Planning and Programs   134
    Vito A. Giordano
Retirement Among Priests and Religious   145
    Rose Mary Strain, R.S.M.

V. THE EXPERIENCE OF RETIREMENT   165

The Experience of a Retired Priest   168
    Benjamin L. Masse, S.J
The Experience of a Retired Businessman   172
    Samuel Scheiber
The Experience of a Retired Nun   174
    Marie Laurette Lovely, S.C.
The Experience of a Retired Business Executive   175
    Harry A. Schwartz
The Experience of a Retired Religious Educator   180
    Rae Bragman

VI. THE CHALLENGE FOR THE AGING INDIVIDUAL   185

The Challenge of Aging for Married Partners   187
    Seymour B. Jacobson
Aging and Career Development   195
    Tom Hickey
The Prospect of Death   212
    Leo J. O'Donovan, S.J.

VII. THE CHALLENGE FOR SOCIETY   225

The Older Person and his Family   227
    Mary Scholastica Handren, R.S.M.
Community Services to the Aging   236
    Clare J. Kagel
Creating Homes for the Aged   247
    John B. Ahern

VIII. SUCCESSFUL AGING: THE ULTIMATE CHALLENGE   255

A Sociological Viewpoint   257
    Maria Mercedes Hartman, S.S.N.D.
A Psychological Viewpoint   265
    Comilda S. Weinstock
A Religious Viewpoint   282
    Rosaria Buesching, O.P.

Preface

A series of Pastoral Psychology Institutes, sponsored by the Psychology Department of Fordham University, was begun in 1955. With the single exception of 1967 when no Institute was presented, they have been offered in alternate years since their inception. The volumes in the Pastoral Psychology Series are an outgrowth of the Institutes, with the current volume containing the papers presented in the 1973 Institute.

These Institutes, intended originally for the clergy and initially open only to them, began with a series of topics in which, it was judged, the behavioral sciences were in a position to make a contribution to clergymen in their attempt to deal with problems encountered in pastoral work. In more recent years the Institutes have been opened to other professional persons in addition to clergymen, and the topics selected for treatment have been broadened accordingly.

The first two Institutes, those of 1955 and 1957, dealt rather briefly with a series of topics which were combined for publication into a single volume, the first in the Pastoral Psychology Series, entitled: *Personality and sexual problems in pastoral psychology.* Subsequent Institutes were devoted to single topics which received more extenstve treatment. The 1959 Institute concerned itself with addiction, before the drug problem assumed the proportions found today, and the proceedings appeared as volume two in the series: *Problems in addiction: Alcohol and drug addiction.* The 1961 Institute focused on the teenager and provided the material for volume three: *The Adolescent: His search for understanding.* Marriage was the topic of the 1963 Institute and of volume four in the series: *Marriage: A psychological and moral approach.* The 1965 Institute concerned itself with the topic of woman in the Church and in the modern world, and the proceedings appeared as volume five under the title: *Woman in modern life.* The 1969 Institute addressed itself to the question of conscience because of the central position which this topic had come to assume both in the Church and in the world. This Institute provided the material for volume six in the series with the title: *Conscience: Its freedom and limitations.* The last previous Institute, that in 1971, turned its attention to the topic of alienation as one of the pervasive characteristics of modern man, and the proceedings appeared as volume seven: *Alienation: Plight of modern man?*

A consistent feature of the Institutes has been their interdisciplinary approach. From the beginning of the series there has been a significant emphasis on the contributions of the behavioral sciences, including, in addition to psychology, particularly psychiatry and sociology. Frequent contributions have also been made by such disciplines as theology, philosophy, political science, and social work. More limited contributions, depending usually upon the particular topic under consideration, have been made to the Institute series by anthropology, economics, the legal profession, and the judiciary.

All the Institutes have conformed to the same overall pattern of arrangement. They have been conducted from a Monday through a Friday of a week in the latter half of June. The Institute reported in the present volume ran from the 18th to the 22nd of June 1973. This time was initially selected and has been adhered to because it fits, with a minimum of inconvenience to both contributors and participants, between the end of the academic year and the start of summer school or other summer commitments. It also has the not-inconsiderable advantage of being held at a time when the academic facilities of the campus are not taxed, and hence are available for the Institute.

The Institutes have provided a concentrated week-long experience focused on a pre-selected topic, and the interchange in both formal discussion and informal conversation between the contributors, who gave the papers, and the participants, who attended, has consistently emerged as a particularly valuable feature of the Institutes. Invaluable, however, as discussions of this kind are for those who are present, experience with them indicates that their significance is greatly—one is inclined to say almost entirely—conditioned by the immediate context in which they occur. They represent a face-to-face situation, where expression, gesture, and tone of voice are important elements, and where the atmosphere of spontaneous interchange is all-important. All of this is lost in the printed word. It is virtually impossible to recapture this atmosphere afterward, and consequently this volume, like its predecessors, regrettably forgoes the attempt to do so. This experience, which is a living one, is the bonus which is reserved for those who are able to spend the week required to attend the Institute, as opposed to those who must be content with the reading of the published volume. We believe, however, that the published proceedings have a contribution to make to a far larger group than those present at the Institute sessions, especially since the topics of the more recent Institutes have been broadened beyond the problems encountered in pastoral work. The reception accorded previous volumes in the Pastoral Psychology Series would seem to attest the validity of this conviction.

The topics chosen for the Institute series have combined an attention to the perennial, as for instance personality and sexual problems in pastoral work, and to the contemporary. With the continuation of the series, more attention has been given to immediately current problems. Thus it can be said that the topics chosen for the more recent Institutes have been timely, even in a period of rapidly changing times. It has been the aim of the planners of the Institute series to select topics which not only are current, but lend themselves to, and indeed require, the kind of interdisciplinary approach which the Institute series is in a position to provide.

In selecting *Aging* as the topic for the 1973 Institute, the planning Committee believed that it had achieved both the above-mentioned objectives. Quite evidently, aging is one of the topics which have come very prominently into national focus in recent years. This is the result, of course, of the extraordinary increase in the number of elderly people in the population. In this century, the *percentage* of the United States population aged 65 and over has more than doubled (from 4.1% in 1900 to 9.9% in 1970), while the *number* increased more than sixfold (from 3 million to 20 million). To put the same basic fact slightly differently: a child born in 1900 could expect to live to an average age of about 48 years; a child born in 1969 could expect to live 22 years longer, to an average of 70 years. The major reason for this increase has come from reduced death-rates for children and young adults, with the consequence that many more people now reach old age.

These are the basic facts: their implications are manifold, and create a challenge both for the aging individual and for society-at-large. It was the purpose of the Institute, as the sub-title indicates: *Aging: Its challenge to the individual and to society,* to point up some of these challenges and to call attention to certain useful and productive responses to them. The kind of treatment thus envisioned could clearly be provided only in an interdisciplinary context.

An additional focus in the Institute was upon the *religious* aspect of aging. Beginning with the first National Conference on Aging in 1950, and continuing through the 1961 and the 1971 White House Conferences on Aging, increasing attention has been given to this problem in its multiple aspects. The medical, biological, and behavioral aspects of aging have been impressively researched, and the research is continuing, even at an accelerated pace. Many of the facets of aging have been carefully studied, such as employment and retirement, physical and mental health, housing, income, nutrition, transportation, and so forth. The religious approach to aging, however, has received disproportionately little attention. It was gratifying, in this connection, to note that one of the 14 subject-matter sections in the 1971 White House Conference on Aging was devoted to spiritual well-being. The delegates from this section spoke as follows in their final recommendation:

> As delegates to the White House Conference on Aging in the section concerned with spiritual well-being, we call attention to this fact of life: to ignore, or to attempt to separate the need to fulfill the spiritual well-being of man from attempts to satisfy his physical, material, and social needs is to fail to understand both the meaning of God and the meaning of man.*

The planning Committee for the Institute agreed with the above statement and attempted to put it into practice in preparing for the Institute. Thus, a conscious effort was made in the Institute to redress to some extent the imbalance found in so many conferences on aging and in so much of the literature, and to give rather particular attention to the religious dimensions of aging. The Committee suggested that these be cast in the form of religious challenges, challenges both to the aging individual and to the churches—committed, as they are, to reach in their ministry *all* their people.

A glance at the table of contents reveals that the material presented in this volume is divided into eight sections. Section I attempts to provide some background by considering aging in historical, cultural, and religious perspective. Sections II and III present the scientific dimensions of aging, as seen by modern science. It seemed to the planning Committee that retirement was a focal point in the aging process as experienced in contemporary Western culture, and consequently Sections IV and V were allocated to a consideration of this topic. Section VI deals with selected challenges presented to society by the presence of large numbers of aged people in its midst, while Section VII looks to the challenges presented by aging to the individual involved. Finally, Section VIII presents what the Committee called the ultimate challenge for anyone who lives long enough: namely, the challenge of successful aging, the finding of the gift of added years of life to be a period of reward and satisfaction.

As editor of the Proceedings and Chairman of the Institute Committee, I am pleased to pay grateful tribute to my fellow Committee members, all of whom are or were connected with Fordham University and all of whom shared with me the responsibility for the planning and the conduct of the Institute out of which these Proceedings came. They are: Rev. Alfons Deeken, s.J., at the time of the Institute a doctoral student at Fordham University, and now a faculty member at Sophia University, Tokyo; Rev. Joseph G. Keegan, s.J., Associate Professor of Psychology; Rev. Gerald J.

---

* 1971 White House Conference on Aging. *Toward a national policy on aging: Proceedings of the 1971 White House Conference on Aging.* Washington, D.C.: Government Printing Office, 1973. 2 vols. Vol. 2, p. 57.

McCool, S.J., Professor of Philosophy; Rev. Edwin A. Quain, S.J., Professor of Classics and Editorial Associate of Fordham University Press; and Rev. Daniel J. Sullivan, S.J., Assistant Professor of Biology. Among the Committee members mentioned, a particular debt of gratitude is owed to Fr. Deeken, who, shortly before the Institute, saw published his brief but widely-circulated volume: *Growing old, and how to cope with it* (Paulist Press, 1972), and who proved to be an indispensable asset in preparing for the Institute. Another person to whom I most willingly acknowledge my indebtedness is Sister Rose Mary Strain, RSM, Director of Pre-retirement and Retirement for the Sisters of Mercy of the Province of New York, with headquarters at Dobbs Ferry. With her knowledge of the field of aging she served as consultant to the Committee in charge of the Institute, and was an indispensable support to its Chairman.

July, 1974   WILLIAM C. BIER, S.J.

I
AGING IN PERSPECTIVE: HISTORICAL, CULTURAL, RELIGIOUS

Aging in Preindustrial and in Contemporary Industrial Societies

CHARLES F. O'DONNELL

Charles F. O'Donnell received his A.B. degree from Iona College in 1960, his M.A. in economics from Fordham University in 1962, and his Ph.D., also in economics, from Fordham University in 1970. In his professional career, Dr. O'Donnell has been associated entirely with Iona College, as Lecturer (1961–1962), as Instructor (1962–1966), as Assistant Professor (1966–1970), and as Associate Professor (1970——). Currently, in addition to his position in the Economics Department, Dr. O'Donnell is Dean of the School of Arts and Sciences. He is a member of the Association of Social Economics, the American Economics Association, the Economic History Association, and the Eastern Association of College Deans and Advisors of Students.

This paper will confine itself primarily to the economic status of the aged in preindustrial and in industrial societies. Since other papers will cover the sociological, psychological, and physiological aspects of aging, I will devote myself to a discussion of the way in which different societies have provided for the aged, with particular emphasis on the income-maintenance programs of the United States.

PREINDUSTRIAL SOCIETIES

In most preindustrial or traditional societies, there has generally been a strong family relationship, one the sociologists refer to as the extended family or the multigenerational family (or the consanguine family). In these societies, the family provided the basic economic and social support for the aged (both in the immediate and in the more distant family). These traditional societies were characterized by low life-expectancy and high infant-mortality rates so that relatively few reached a really old age (Baerwald, 1970). As Simmons pointed out, this intergenerational responsibility was a cultural factor prevalent in preindustrial societies:

> Intergenerational responsibility was the keynote of the family, and it embraced all age groups, the waxing and the waning alike. Such a family system guaranteed probably the greatest sense of security that aging persons have yet known [Simmons, 1960, p. 82].

> Perhaps, the most significant range of contrast to be observed in the adjustments to aging from very primitive to highly industrialized societies is that in the former the "terms" or conditions for aging were imbedded in the cultural developments as by-products of broad societal interests, while in the latter the trend has been toward a breakdown in the traditional types of adaptions to aging and the growth of planned and legislated forms of old age security as specific objectives and through the instrumentality of group-action programs. Such *planned* social provisions for the aged in primitive societies were extremely rare. The social provisions for the aged were more nearly "automatic" and traditional in form [Simmons, 1960, pp. 66–67].

In preindustrial societies, especially in agrarian ones, the aged performed light tasks both in the home and in the occupational area of the family, and were useful, productive members of society. This was especially true in the periods when the prevalent form of industry was the domestic putting-out system or the handicraft system. The extended family was not so prevalent during the nineteenth and early-twentieth centuries in the United States as in Europe because we were a nation of immigrants and could easily settle land in the West. But rural America approximated the typical model: as families grew, wings were added to the farmhouse to provide for the newlyweds or the grandparents, and the aged performed the usual tasks around the farm.

For those individuals who were outside a family structure, private charity, sponsored by religious communities, was available to aid them. Begging was also quite common in traditional societies. In seventeenth-century England the earliest of the poor laws were passed to regulate begging by the poor. Eventually, the poor laws established concepts of settlement, local responsibility, the means test, and the work house which persist to the present (Baerwald, 1970).

INDUSTRIAL SOCIETIES

With the Industrial Revolution came major changes in the economic, political, and social fabric of societies. With the growth of the factory movement, industry moved out of the home, and the urbanization of society intensified. Shifts occurred in the role of the family and in the care of the aged.

In the late-nineteenth and twentieth centuries, the technological changes in the productive process, advances in the medical sciences, and demographic changes caused increased concern for the plight of the aged. While the life expectancies of the population rose as did the percentage of the population over age 65, the increased urbanization and industrialization of societies contributed to the development of the nuclear family or conjugal family and made the aged the victims of progress. Where once the skill of the experienced craftsman was required and sought after, the assembly line made his skills obsolete and placed an emphasis on speed and muscle, which generally are youthful attributes.

In response to the changing position of the aged, nations began to develop social-security or social-insurance programs to provide societal means of protecting the aged against the vicissitudes of life. In 1889, Germany established the first program of old-age insurance, which originally covered only production workers, but was extended in 1911 to white-collar workers. This marked the beginning of the institutionalization of the support for the aged and of the transferral of such support from a family responsibility to a societal one. Many other nations established social-security programs in the first third of the twentieth century.

When the United States established its program in 1935, it was the last major Western industrialized nation to do so. Perhaps it is appropriate to consider why. Before the 1930s, there was no public demand for such a program, for several reasons. Americans believed that the individual should provide for his old age through savings, and many opposed Social Security because they saw it as a dole system, which, they were convinced, would be "detrimental to American ideals and traditions, destructive of individual character and personality, ruinous to family traditions and subversive of the basic principles of our government" (Epstein, 1933, p. 63). Americans considered it "the duty of the children, and not of the State, to take care of the old. It is assumed that if the State relieves the children of this responsibility, family ties are loosened, and since the family is one of our most highly valued institutions, this danger is to be avoided at all costs" (U. S. Committee on Economic Security, 1935, p. 158). Furthermore, if there were poverty among the aged, it could be handled by local governments or by the excellent system of private charitable agencies which had developed.

The prevalent view that the individual or family unit could provide for the aged, already buffeted by industrialization and urbanization, was shattered by the Great Depression. Unemployment soared—especially among the older workers—and workers lost their ability to earn, the basis of their security. Personal savings were wiped out by the virtual collapse of the banking system and security markets after the fall of 1929 and by the wave of bank failures. From 1929 to 1933, one-third of the banks failed (9,765 bank suspensions), with losses to depositors of $1.4 billion (U. S. Bureau of the Census, 1960). The value of stocks and bonds declined drastically. Thus, persons who had attempted to follow the American tradition of providing for their own retirement by accumulating personal assets watched as these assets were destroyed by forces outside their control. At the same time, the private pension system suffered from the economic malaise. Forced to turn to private charity, millions found these agencies incapable of handling the flood of applicants, and they turned to state and local governmental welfare agencies. These, too, proved incapable of handling the massive amount of relief needed, and people looked to the federal government as the source of funds for public assistance and for the establishment of a comprehensive program of economic security, especially old-age insurance.

TYPES OF OLD-AGE INSURANCE

In a recent study (U. S. Department of Health, Education & Welfare, Social Security Administration, 1972), it was found that 101 of the 133 independent nations have some program of old-age, invalidity, and survivors' insurance. This paper will consider only the Old-Age and Survivors' Insurance programs (OASI). This section will discuss some of the major characteristics of these programs and then will consider the American system.

The programs have been established by statutory law, which specifies benefit and contribution levels, conditions for qualification, etc. Most are financed by contributions from employees and employers paid into a special trust fund and by some contributions from general revenue funds. The programs are generally compulsory in nature, with all covered workers required to participate in the system. Social insurance systems differ from public assistance programs in that the former pays benefits as a matter of right. If a person meets the conditions of the law, the statutory benefits are given to him without the means test so characteristic of the welfare system.

In addition to the social insurance program, some nations (Canada and Sweden, for example) provide a universal pension. This is a pension paid to all permanent residents over a specified age without any conditions. About a dozen nations, including the United States, have established supplemental public assistance programs (Old-Age Assistance) to augment the OASI benefits for the needy aged.

The American OASI was established in 1935 and amended most recently in 1973. It is financed currently by a tax on both employees and employers of 3.75% of the first $10,800 of earnings. The proceeds from the contributions go into the OASI trust fund (currently about $36 billion). The law establishes the criteria for eligibility for benefits. The benefit level (or the primary insurance amount) is calculated for most workers on the average monthly covered earnings for the period from 1956 to the time of retirement. Benefits are determined by the benefit formula which pays a higher percentage at the lower levels of income. In 1971, for instance, the payment formula was: 81.83% of the first $110, plus 29.76% of the next $290, plus 27.81% of the next $150, and so forth.

Let us now compare several aspects of the American system with those of other nations. Because benefits are calculated for the period from 1956 to the time of retirement, the American beneficiary suffers from the fact that his benefit is affected by years when the maximum covered earnings were low (e.g., the maximum earnings credited from 1956 through 1958 were $350 a month, or $4,200 a year). If we assume that a person retiring at the end of 1972 always earned the earnings maximum, his average monthly covered earnings would be only $490 even though in his final years his earnings were $750 a month. This failure to adjust for changes in earnings adversely affects the individual. Nine nations (Algeria, Austria, Belgium, Canada, France, West Germany, Norway, Sweden, and Yugoslavia) revalue actual earnings so that they can be more comparable to current earnings levels.* "Basing pension computations on revalued earnings, rather than on actual wages earned in the past, adjusts newly awarded pensions for the general rise in economic levels while retaining the differentials between the pensions of higher and lower paid workers" (U. S. Department of Health, Education & Welfare, Social Security Administration, 1972, p. xvi). The method for the calculation of benefits varies. A number of programs provide some form of basic pension to which is added an increment of 1% to 2% for years of coverage beyond a certain minimum. Others pay a stipulated percentage of earnings for each year of coverage. The American program uses a bracket formula which allows a progressive element to enter into the calculation. The 1972 amendment, however, provides a special minimum benefit which recognizes length of coverage, and is computed by multiplying $8.50 by the years of coverage beyond 10 years and less than 30 years. Thus, the special minimum would be $170 for a worker with 30 years of coverage.

Once the initial benefit is awarded, it must be adjusted regularly if the beneficiary is not to suffer from the erosion of his purchasing power because of inflation. Until recently, OASI benefits were adjusted on an *ad hoc* basis. Frequently, beneficiaries suffered losses in real purchasing power in the intervals between the *ad hoc* adjustments. The 1972 amendment introduced an automatic adjustment of benefits (and the contributions base). After 1974, benefits will be increased whenever the Consumer Price Index rises by 3% or more. A number of countries (e.g., Germany and Canada after 1975)

* For a detailed discussion of the German program see my dissertation (O'Donnell, 1971a, pp. 247–262).

adjust benefits for changes in earnings rather than in prices, which, I believe, is preferable to price adjustment since it preserves the benefit–earnings relationship, an integral part of the OASI. Adjustment for wage changes would normally result in more adjustments than would the price adjustments. Currently about 20 nations provide for some form of automatic or quasi-automatic adjustment of benefits (O'Donnell 1971b, pp. 48–51).

The majority of the OASI programs require retirement, or reduce benefits, if earnings are above a certain level, e.g., the retirement test in the United States is $2100. If a worker earns more than $2100, his benefit is reduced approximately a dollar for every $2 he earns. Approximately 15 nations pay full benefits regardless of earnings (U. S. Department of Health, Education & Welfare, Social Security Administration, 1972).

POVERTY AMONG THE AGED IN AMERICA

I should like to discuss briefly poverty among the aged. The OASI program has two basic objectives: one is to prevent destitution in old age by providing a minimum level of income or floor of protection, and assumes that OASI will be supplemented by personal assets and private pensions; the other is to provide a level of benefits for a retired couple which would replace "at least 50 percent of his average wages under the social security system" (U. S. House of Representatives, Committee on Ways and Means, 1967, p. 22).

The OASI has failed to prevent poverty among the aged. In 1971 an aged couple with an income less than $2,424 or an individual with $1,931 or less was below the low-income threshold or the poverty level.* Even under this Spartan definition of poverty, 4,273,000 elderly, or 21.6% of the aged, were classified as poor. The aged constitute 16.7% of the 25,559,000 poor Americans.

I believe that a major reason for this high level of poverty among the aged is that the American OASI program assumes that there is a tripartite system of income maintenance for the aged, with OASI as the base to be supplemented by private pensions and personal assets. Studies over the years have consistently indicated that the vast majority of OASI beneficiaries do not receive a second pension to augment their OASI benefit. A recent study (Bixby & Reno, 1971) found that only 30% of the couples and 14% of nonmarried persons received a second pension. The 1963 Survey of the Aged (Epstein & Murray, 1967) and the 1968 Survey (Bixby, 1970) have demonstrated that the aged have very limited personal assets. The 1968 Survey found that while 60% of the couples and 45% of the nonmarried persons had some income from personal assets, this income amounted to only 13% of the incomes of the couples, 14% of the income of nonmarried

* For a description of the way the poverty index was developed, see Orshansky, 1965a; Orshansky, 1965b).

men, and 19% of the income of nonmarried women. If the retirement income of the aged from all sources other than OASI is examined, the evidence is that over 40% of the couples and almost 60% of the individuals had incomes of less than $150 from such sources.

Because of the dearth of supplemental pensions and the limited personal assets of the aged, most such persons are virtually dependent upon OASI. In 1967, OASI benefits accounted for 38% of the income of its beneficiary couples and 47% of an individual's income. In the lower income groups, OASI was the major source of income (Bixby, 1970).

The 1972 amendment of the Social Security law established a supplemental security-income program for the aged, blind, and disabled, effective 1974. The Old Age Assistance program will be terminated. Under the new plan, an aged person with no other income will be guaranteed a monthly income of $130 ($195 for a couple). The law exempted the first $20 of Social Security or of any other earned or unearned income except income based on need. This is a guaranteed income for the aged, but the levels are even below the poverty levels of 1971 and are much less than what is needed in 1974.

Other factors have contributed to the magnitude of poverty among the aged. Because of the continuing technological changes in the production function, we are able to produce a much greater output with a smaller labor force. For example, in agriculture the number of workers has declined from 7,891,000 in 1947 to 3,472,000 in 1972 (from about 13% of the labor force in 1947 to about 4% in 1972), while the index of output rose from 71.1 to 97.5.* The index of farm employment decreased from 216.5 to 89.4. In manufacturing, the index of output rose from 44.7 in 1947 to 115.9 in 1972 while the employment index rose only from 72.6 to 108.2. The overall private output index rose from 45.6 to 118.0 while the employment index rose only from 80.6 to 107.1 (U. S. Department of Labor, 1973). Similar changes are occurring in other industrialized nations.

Structural changes have continued to occur in the labor force. We shifted from an agricultural economy in the nineteenth century to a goods-producing and then to a service-producing economy in the post-World War II period. In spite of very high levels of economic growth, we currently have a substantial number of unemployed workers (an annual unemployment rate of 5.6% in 1972).

Although in employment it is generally unlawful to discriminate against a person because of age, the law accepts 65 as the age at which compulsory retirement is not unlawful age-discrimination. Studies indicate that 60% of the pension plans and 44% of workers covered by pensions are subject to compulsory-retirement features. These generally require retirement at

* 1967 = 100 in all cases

65 (Reno, 1972). A recent survey of newly entitled beneficiaries (Reno, 1971) found that, of those filing for OASI at age 65, 36% had left their employment because of compulsory retirement. The next most frequently cited reason was health (23%). Of those forced to retire, 41% felt that they had no work-limiting health conditions and would have preferred to continue working.

Many workers are retiring before the age of 65 even though they will receive an actuarially reduced OASI benefit. The earliest age at which a man may retire and receive a benefit is 62. It has been found that, of those retiring at 62, 54% had retired because of health and 13% because their jobs had been discontinued. Many had been unemployed for substantial periods. Forty-one percent of those unemployed at the time of filing had been out of work for 6 months or more, one-third had not worked for a year, and 17% had not been employed for more than 3 years.

Because of structural changes, compulsory retirement, and limited employment opportunities for those over 65, the labor-force participation-rate of men over 65 has decreased from 47.8% in 1947 (2,376,000) to 24.4% in 1972 (1,085,000). For elderly women the rate has risen slightly from 8.1% (445,000) to 9.3% (1,085,000), and reflects the overall change in the female labor-force participation-rates (from 31.8% in 1947 to 43.9% in 1972) (U. S. Department of Labor, 1973). Similar changes have occurred in other industrialized nations where the labor-force participation-rate of those over 65 is substantially lower than it is in agricultural economies (Kreps, 1971).

Thus, the aged cannot rely on earnings as a source of income since old age is increasingly becoming a period of nonemployment. But their retirement income from OASI, private and public pensions, and personal assets is inadequate to prevent their living in poverty. As the President's Commission on Income Maintenance Programs stated:

> Millions of hardworking Americans, accustomed all their lives to paying their way, find themselves becoming unalterably and unavoidably poor in old age. . . . The poor will remain poor once they retire, and others who retire may become poor in their old age. Opportunities for the aged poor to make any improvement in their own lives are remote and unrealistic. Only public programs can make a difference in their incomes [The President's Commission on Income Maintenance Programs, 1969 pp. 23–24].

However, unless we reassess our basic concept of OASI as merely a floor of income to be supplemented by second pensions and personal assets, our income-maintenance programs for the aged will continue to fail to meet the needs of the elderly. We must face up to the fact that, for most of the aged, the tripartite system is a myth. The Swiss program of social insurance was, until recently, also based on the philosophy of a tripartite system; but when the program failed to meet the income needs of its recipients, the Swiss moved to strengthen the tripartite system and to augment it by establishing a program of supplementary payments. When the pension income of a person is less than a national minimum standard, the supplementary payment would make up the difference. To reduce the need for supplemental support, the basic OASI pension was substantially increased, company pensions were made mandatory, and tax incentives were developed to encourage the accumulation of personal assets (Kirkpatrick, 1972).

We must undertake similar efforts to make the tripartite system a reality. Those workers fortunate enough to have private pension coverage must be assured that they will receive the pensions at retirement age. Thus, vesting rights and portability must be established, and there has to be proper management and insurance of the more than $150 billion in pension reserves. Coverage must be extended to that half of the private labor force not currently covered by pensions. If the private pension system is to remain a part of our income-maintenance program, it must provide benefits in the future for far more of the aged than it currently does. Only about one-fifth of the aged currently receive private pensions. Tax laws must encourage savings.

The basic OASI benefits must be substantially increased. Changes must be made in the method of calculating the primary insurance amount so that it will more realistically reflect the earnings level at the time of retirement. A continuation of the *ad hoc* repairing and patching up of an inadequate system is not what is needed now. We must have a fundamentally new approach to our income-maintenance program, especially OASI, if it is to meet the needs of its beneficiaries.

CONCLUSION

This paper has briefly traced the changes in the economic status of the aged from preindustrial societies to the contemporary period. It must be realized that the social insurance programs are relatively new and are still evolving. Although the form of providing for the aged has changed from the family-centered system to the institutionalized social insurance system, there remains a link between the two. Both are based on intergenerational transfers and relationships. In the extended family, the relationship was direct and personal. Today, it is impersonal and indirect, but, nonetheless, real. Our present OASI is an intergenerational transfer. OASI taxes are levied upon the workers. The proceeds from these contributions flow into the OASI trust.

Because OASI is operated primarily on a pay-as-you-go basis with a limited reserve of about a year's benefits, most of the current receipts are used to fund the benefits of the current recipients. While the OASI taxes reduce the disposable income of the covered workers, its benefits add to the income of the aged and its other beneficiaries. Thus, the working population is still contributing to the support of the aged as has been man's custom since time immemorial. Today, we have greater opportunities and challenges than our predecessors had. With the increases in productivity in the industrialized nations, we have been able to overcome the age-old problem of scarcity. In this time of affluence, we have the capacity and resources to ensure that the years of retirement will truly be the "golden years." The question is: do we in America have the will to eliminate poverty, especially among the aged?

REFERENCES

Baerwald, F. *Economic progress and problems of labor.* (2nd ed.) Scranton: International Textbook, 1970.

Bixby, L. E. Income of people aged 65 and older: Overview from 1968 survey of the aged. *Social Security Bulletin,* 1970, *33* (4), 3–25.

Bixby, L. E., & Reno, V. Second pensions among newly entitled workers: Survey of new beneficiaries. *Social Security Bulletin,* 1971, *34* (11), 3–28.

Epstein, A. *Insecurity: A challenge to America.* New York: Smith & Haas, 1933.

Epstein, L. A. & Murray, J. H. *The aged population of the United States: The 1963 Social Security Survey of the aged.* (Social Security Administration Research Report, No. 19). Washington, D.C.: Government Printing Office, 1967.

Kirkpatrick, E. K. Switzerland changes social insurance philosophy. *Social Security Bulletin,* 1972, *35* (4), 24–26.

Kreps, J. M. *Lifetime allocation of work and income: Essays in the economics of aging.* Durham: Duke University Press, 1971.

O'Donnell, C. F. *Old-age and survivors insurance benefits in a macrodynamic context.* (Doctoral dissertation, Fordham University) Ann Arbor, Mich.: University Microfilms, 1971. No. 71-8732. (a)

O'Donnell, C. F. A critique of the old-age and survivors insurance program of the United States. *Review of Social Economy,* 1971, *29,* 39–54. (b)

Orshansky, M. Counting the poor: Another look at the poverty profile. *Social Security Bulletin,* 1965, *28* (1), 3–29. (a)

Orshansky, M. Who's who among the poor: A demographic view of poverty. *Social Security Bulletin,* 1965, *28* (7), 3–32. (b)

President's Commission on Income Maintenance Programs. *Poverty amid plenty: The American paradox.* Washington, D.C.: Government Printing Office, 1969.

Reno, V. P. Why men stop working at or before age 65: Findings from the survey of new beneficiaries. *Social Security Bulletin,* 1971, *34* (6), 3–17.

Reno, V. P. Compulsory retirement among the newly entitled workers: Survey of new beneficiaries. *Social Security Bulletin,* 1972, *35* (3), 3–15.

Simmons, L. W. Aging in preindustrial societies. In C. Tibbitts (Ed.) *Handbook of social gerontology: Societal aspects of aging.* Chicago: University of Chicago Press, 1960. Pp. 62–91.

U. S. Bureau of the Census. *Historical statistics of the United States: From colonial times to 1957.* Washington, D.C.: Government Printing Office, 1960.

U. S. Committee on Economic Security. *Social security in America: The factual background of the Social Security Act as summarized from staff reports to the Committee on Economic Security.* Washington, D.C.: Government Printing Office, 1935.

U. S. Department of Health, Education & Welfare, Social Security Administration.

Social security programs throughout the world, 1971. (Office of Research and Statistics, Research Report No. 40). Washington, D.C.: Government Printing Office, 1972.

U. S. Department of Labor. *Manpower report of the President, March 1973.* Washington, D.C.: Government Printing Office, 1973.

U. S. House of Representatives, Committee on Ways and Means. *Social Security amendments of 1967.* (Report of the Committee on Ways and Means on H. R. 1280). Report No. 544. 90th Congress, 1st session, 1967.

The Aged in Chinese and Japanese Cultures

GINO K. PIOVESANA, S.J.

Father Gino K. Piovesana, S.J. was born and educated in Italy, part of his studies being taken at the Oriental Institute in Rome. He joined the staff of Sophia University in Tokyo in 1951, where he taught philosophy until 1957. He was then made Librarian of the University and Head of the Russian Section on the Faculty of Foreign Languages and Affairs. He was also Superior of. the Jesuit Community of Sophia from 1960 to 1965, and Chairman of the Board of Trustees of Sophia University from 1965 to 1968. He has been in this country since 1969. A member and Chairman (1964–1968) of the Board of Editors of Monumenta Nipponica, Father Piovesana holds, in addition to his Ph.D. degree in philosophy, a degree of Doctor of Literature from Keio University, Tokyo. Father Piovesana has had published five books in Japanese dealing with Philosophy, Soviet Union Intellectual Trends, and Historical Materialism. His recent Japanese philosophical thought (3rd edition, Tokyo, 1968) has been translated into three foreign languages. Father Piovesana has contributed 17 articles on Japanese philosophy and Japanese thinkers to The Encyclopedia of Philosophy, of which he is also a member of the Editorial Board. Currently, Father Piovesana is on the staff of the John XXIII Ecumenical Center at Fordham University.

"The Orient" and "Oriental" are primarily geographical terms, and when speaking of the civilization of the East one has to use the plural form because there is no such thing as Oriental culture. Nakamura Hajime has rightly pointed out the superficiality of generalizations such as the "Oriental mind" or the "mystico-intuitive" Oriental soul. Indians, Chinese, Tibetans, and Japanese reveal very distinct characteristics in their ways of thinking and their attitudes even within some common religious background, which, it may be remarked in passing, appears to be common only because it is not analyzed in detail and depth (Nakamura, 1964, pp. 623–644). This paper comprises a discussion of traditional attitudes toward aging only in China and Japan where the common background of Confucianism has enhanced the position of the old man in both societies (no attempt has been made to discuss the changes caused by recent developments). It is mostly within the family that old age receives special consideration in China and Japan. Yet because the family structure of both societies far transcends the limits of the family, reverence toward the aged has been a distinct characteristic of China and Japan. Notwithstanding their differences, both societies possess this feature in common, as we shall see.

AGING IN CONFUCIANISM

Chinese thought and attitudes on aging are expressed in three books of the Chinese classics of Confucianism. In the best known of these, the *Confucian analects,* Confucius characterizes his own progress in sagacity in the following manner, giving at the same time the rationale why aging deserves our unqualified respect:

> At fifteen, I had my mind bent on learning. At thirty, I stood firm. At forty, I had no doubts. At fifty, I knew the decrees of Heaven. At sixty, my ear was an obedient organ for the reception of truth. At seventy, I could follow what my heart desired, without transgressing what was right [*Chinese classics,* I, *Confucian analects,* Bk. II, Ch. 4].

The strict correlation between aging and progress in wisdom could not be better indicated. Age meant accumulation of wisdom, and a man at seventy was considered to have reached almost a blessed stage of moral learning and practical conduct. Later commentators of Confucius' sayings had some difficulties with this passage. When Confucius was almost divinized in later centuries, it was said of him that "he was born with knowledge, and did what was right with complete ease." Thus the above quotation was explained as if Confucius were speaking not of himself but of the common man in search of knowledge. Yet Confucius and his early followers who compiled the *Confucian analects* thought differently, and, commentators' casuistry aside, the belief that only age warranted progress in wisdom has been the characteristic of every Chinese sage and writer and the cardinal tenet of Confucian morals.

Although age as such is considered a necessary condition of moral progress, it is in the context of family relationships that it received most detailed explanation, aged parents deserving most consideration. Our quotation from the *Confucian analects* is soon followed by the teaching on filial piety, which does not mean merely supporting one's parents: "Dogs and horses likewise are able to do something in the way of support—without reverence; what is there to distinguish the one support given from the other?" (*Chinese classics* I, *Confucian analects*, Bk. II, Ch. 7). In Confucianism, reverence is a technical term and is akin to a religious feeling combined with awe and respect. Filial piety, however, is dealt with in another well-known Confucian classic which bears the specific title *Classic of filial piety*. There it is stated that "Filial piety is the root of all virtues, and the stem out of which grows all moral teaching" (*Sacred books of the East*, III, *Hsiao Ching* [*Classic of filial piety*], p. 466). This general principle is explained in several short chapters in which filial piety is taught to the Son of Heaven—the emperor—to princes, and to major and minor officials of the empire, down to the common man, for "nothing is greater than filial piety." The ruler and the ruled, the rich and the poor, the literati and the ignorant peasant— all had to profess this virtue. It was not only a private virtue, but a civic norm upon which rested the well-being of the realm. More practical norms to fulfill the obligations of filial piety were prescribed in another classic, *The book of ritual*, which also deals with the care of old people in general (*Sacred books of the East*, Li Chi [*The book of ritual*], XXVII–XXVIII, pp. 464–468; 229–230).

Because of the overwhelming role of Confucianism in shaping Chinese society, Chinese civilization has been characterized as a family culture and a culture of the old man (Lang, 1968, p. 10). China's heroes were neither the knights of medieval Europe nor the samurai of Japan, but literati and officials. Their qualifications increased with age because long years of study and experience were required to master the intricacies of Confucian learning and to acquire expertise in affairs of the empire—all based on preserving ancient traditions and regulated by meticulous procedures. To old age was attached a special sanctity also because only the aged could have the sense of the golden mean, another cornerstone of Confucian wisdom. Realistic and practical as the Chinese have always been, they were obviously aware of senility problems. Therefore, to avoid any excess and to reach a reasonable balance in everything without which no virtue could exist, *The doctrine of the mean* was taught in another sacred book of China (*Chinese classics*, Chung Yung [*The doctrine of the mean*] I, Pt. 2).

ANCESTOR WORSHIP AND AGING

Confucianism is a very broad term which embodies many cultural traits of ancient China. Not all of what commonly passes as Confucianism was initiated by Confucius: ancestor worship antedates Confucius, who, moreover, is known to have lacked interest in discussions concerning the condition of spirits after death. Confucius was concerned with an earthly-bound social ethic and not with transcendental beings and truths. He wanted to bring peace and order to a country divided by fighting lords. Priding himself on being a restorer of old traditions and not an innovator, Confucius retained ancestor worship, which, after all, canonized filial piety. To pay due respect to one's ancestors was considered very beneficial for the living, too, for it fostered the stability and the continuity of the family. For the common man, ancestor worship constituted the main component of Chinese religious life which was always centered in rites and ceremonies for the dead. Ancestor worship was likewise incorporated by Buddhism and Taoism —religious beliefs in China, as well as in Japan—since none of these religions found ancestor worship antagonistic to its religious tenets. Different names are used for the spirits of the dead, called in Japan *hotoke* by Buddhists and *kami* by Shintoists. However, to respect both the *hotoke*s and the *kami*s is a basic virtue of every Japanese. In China a very common name for Buddhist monasteries was *Kuan Hsiao Suu* or Monastery for the Glorification of Filial Piety, and filial piety headed the ten Taoist virtues. The incorporation of ancestor worship into other religions was facilitated by the fact that it itself was not an "institutional" religion such as Buddhism, Taoism, and Shintoism, all of which have an independent theology, worship, and priesthood of their own. Ancestor worship is a "diffused" religion which relies upon other social structures to communicate its basic ideas and cult (Yang, 1967, Ch. XII, p. 294ff.). Ancestor worship was naturally centered in the family, and from the family it drew its main vitality, with institutional religions giving it ritualistic support.

Both aspects of ancestor worship, the religious and the earthly, were prominent features of Chinese and Japanese societies. This worship certainly redounded to improving the condition of the family on earth, in some cases keeping the family tradition alive for centuries. Japanese military families have left interesting historical records in the so-called *kakun,* or family instructions (laws), willed by the founder of the family. They were strictly followed by descendants and kept alive by retainers as well. When in the eighteenth century merchant families reached great prosperity and even political power, they were guided by "family instructions" in which the spirit of Japan's incipient capitalism can easily be read. They were faithfully transmitted to the modern *zaibatsu* or the large-scale family concerns, the backbone of Japanese modernization.

Reports to the ancestors on important decisions the head of the family had to make constituted another side of ancestor worship which served to keep the tradition of the family alive. It is a custom even now in Japan that the emperor and the prime minister report to the ancestors of Japan at the Ise Shrine on important events of the country. The head of even a modest family never fails to obtain the blessing of the departed on occasion of a marriage, a long trip, and the like. In the family *butsudan* ("the altar of the Buddhas") or in the *kamidana* ("the altar of the Shinto gods"), tablets bearing the ancestors' names are preserved. But even in the absence of an altar in the house, family temples keep the tablets, where at least once a year special rites are performed. How much all this is a religious duty is a moot question into which it is not necessary to enter here. What is clear is that by honoring the ancestors a link is kept with the past, and the living too are more respected—the older members of the family being considered on the threshold of ancestor worship.

THE CONFUCIAN TRADITION IN JAPAN

Japan as a cultural entity is like Korea and Annam a "cultural variant" of the East Asian tradition mothered by China. Although Japan belongs to the Chinese sphere of cultural influence, she was never wholly captured by the Confucianism imported from the mainland around the fifth century of the Christian era. Japan was politically never conquered by China, and Confucianism was juxtaposed with nativist traits and did not alter the political structure of Japan. The warrior–aristocratic structure of Japanese society was never challenged by Chinese political ideas evolved by Chinese Confucianists. In this sense Japan was less receptive than Korea. In respect for the aged, however, the Japanese were not inferior to the Chinese. Filial piety took, as we shall see, a distinctive Japanese character—an adaptation to Japanese conditions of the original Confucian belief.

The Confucian classics were brought into Japan as early as A.D. 404–405, although it is only with the Taiho code (702) that we are able to assess the impact of Confucianism on Japan.* A Confucian Academy was established, and books like the *Confucian analects* and the *Classic of filial piety* became mandatory texts. The Taiho legislation codified filial piety in more than one article. An official, for example, had to leave office during the period of mourning for parents (three years), and also when the sickness of parents required his presence near them. In the case of an official living far from home, a leave of absence was provided every three years to allow him to perform his duties which included preparing his parents' bed for a restful night and inquiring about their health in the morning. The part of

---

* Before the Taika Reform (645) and the use of the Chinese calendar, Japanese chronology is very approximate.

the Code which deals with criminal offenses lists six cases of unfiliality to be met by measured punishment. Offensive words and deeds top the list, followed by failure to support parents and lack of proper behavior during the mourning period, ending with crimes of adultery with concubines of a grandfather or father.

The part of the Code dealing with civil matters is prefaced by an injunction to governors of provinces to make a tour of their districts once a year to acquaint themselves with people who had become distinguished as a dutiful son, an obedient grandson, a righteous husband, or a virtuous wife. The reward for the meritorious was exemption from taxes. Many examples of such virtuous deeds are given in ancient Japanese chronicles. The *Zoku Nihongi, The ancient chronicle of Japan,* for instance, records ten cases of dutiful sons for the years 714–722 (Sakamoto, 1965, pp. 47–49). In March 757, Fujiwara no Nakamaro, following the example of the T'ang dynasty Emperor Hsuan-tsung, published an edict whereby all subjects had to provide themselves with a copy of the *Classic of filial piety,* almost a dream then in Japan considering the level of literacy even among aristocrats. Fujiwara no Nakamaro is, however, an interesting case because he deposed Crown Prince Doso who allegedly behaved impolitely during the period of mourning. Filial piety was also the reason why Oi, the new Crown Prince, was chosen, and the same rationale was used by the Empress Koken when in 758 she handed over the throne to Crown Prince Oi. The empress could take her leave to observe the period of mourning only by abdication.

Political expediency aside, it is obvious from the above examples how respect for parents was held in high esteem in ancient Japan. Japanese Buddhism in this did not compare with Confucianism. Shinran (1173–1262), the founder of a popular Buddhist sect, said, for instance, that he had never recited his *Nembutsu* prayer with his parents in mind. Buddhist books used to praise a man who left his elderly mother to become a monk, certainly a mortal sin for any Confucianist and a crime in the eyes of most Japanese. Buddhism, although it gave the Japanese consolation in time of death, never offered a social ethic which was based solely on Confucian norms. Confucianism, moreover, in the course of becoming accepted, was modified to fit the Japanese political structure. Thus, for example, the theory of dynastic changes by revolution when the emperor was no longer fulfilling the Mandate of Heaven was never accepted in Japan. To be sure, military rulers were demoted, but emperors (who had no political power) were left unscathed by warring lords fighting for political supremacy. Filial piety, too, underwent some adaptations in Japan, coming in second best after loyalty to the lord or the ruler of the land.

The China envisioned by Confucius was not a land of warriors. His perfect gentleman was not a samurai, and martial virtues were not fostered by Confucianism. As the Chinese saying goes: "Good iron is not used for nails; a good man does not become a soldier." Japanese society was different, however, and conflicts between duties toward parents and the lord were bound to arise. To settle the matter as early as 827, the *Keikoshu* (a collection of prose and poetry) stressed (in the 20th *kan* or "book") the priority of loyalty over filial piety. With the developing of feudalism in medieval Japan and during the Tokugawa period (1600–1867), warrior bravery prevailed over the Confucian civic virtues. Yet, if we exclude cases of obvious conflict, the samurai spirit blended well with Confucianism, and certainly did not lessen respect toward parents and elders in general. As a matter of fact, the warrior spirit and Confucianism formed what is called the modern *kazoku seido* or "the familial structure" of the prewar Japanese state centered in the emperor.

However, before we discuss modern Japan, the best known and most respected Tokugawa Confucianist, Nakae Toju (1608–1648) must be mentioned. Nakae, the "Saint of Omi," as he is often called from the name of the province from which he came, wrote the popular and widely read *Dialogues with an old man* (*Okina mondo*). In this book as well as in more learned works, Nakae extolled the virtue of filial piety and the respect due to parents in particular. The very title of the book clearly indicates the Confucian belief that only men advanced in age could impart wisdom. Naturally, this prestigious source was often used by other Confucianists. Some quotations from Nakae's *Dialogues* have so permeated Japanese society that they cannot be passed over in silence:

> Filial piety is the root of man. When it is lost from one's heart, then one's life becomes like a rootless plant, and if one does expire instantly, it is nothing but sheer luck. . . . Filial piety is what distinguishes men from birds and beasts. When men are not filial, Heaven will visit upon them the six major punishments. It was said in ancient times that a man without filial piety turned into a man with a dog's head, clearly indicating that he was a beast. . . . Filial piety is the summit of virtue, and the essence of the Way in the three realms of heaven, earth, and man. What brings life to heaven, life to earth, life to man, and life to all things, is filial piety [Tsunoda, 1958, pp. 383–384].

It is clear, especially from the last sentence, that for Nakae filial piety was an eternal and universal principle, the origin of everything, the underlying moral power in the universe. Nakae is usually credited with spreading the notion that the duties of filial piety were but a reciprocal payment for the debt children had toward parents who had brought them into the world and cared for them during their helpless infancy. It was an obligation "higher than the heavens and deeper than the seas," as Nakae himself wrote, which naturally meant that it was limitless and by definition incapable of repayment. Tsuda Sokichi, a great authority on Chinese and Japanese Confucianism, has maintained that to equate filial piety with this basic sense of obligation is more characteristic of Japanese than of Chinese moralists. Be that as it may, it is obvious that Japanese Confucianists cultivated filial piety as much as their colleagues in China. Chinese and Japanese societies were, however, quite different, which explains why filial piety took different forms.

AGING AND FAMILY IN CHINESE AND JAPANESE SOCIETIES

China by 2000 B.C. passed from a tribal organization to feudalism which ended with the Warring States Period (fifth to third century B.C.). By the middle of the third century B.C., the Chinese empire began to take shape, and Confucianism, which had been born during the Warring States Period, was to become the ideological backbone of the empire. It was almost a thousand years later that the neo-Confucianism of Chu Hsi became the official learning of the empire, as a result of the enforcement of the examination system for Chinese officials, with examinations based upon Chu Hsi's new commentaries on the Confucian classics. Yet the basic tenets of the most popular classics such as the *Confucian analects* and the *Classic of filial piety* molded Chinese society well before Confucianism became the official learning.

Much is made of the ideological nature of Confucianism. Imperial China was an agrarian society, which needed a large peasant class and a centralized government with a powerful bureaucracy to solve the problems of land irrigation and flood prevention by means of large-scale public works. Confucianism was, no doubt, a viable ideology to uphold the structure of the empire. "The root of the empire is in the State; the root of the State is in the family; the root of the family is in the individual." This famous saying by Mencius well epitomized the basic political philosophy of Confucianism, which postulated an individual brought up to respect the father, obedient to the authorities outside the family, and, ultimately, to the emperor. In the *Classic of filial piety* it is hinted that "the filial piety with which the superior man serves his parents may be transferred as loyalty to the ruler" (*Sacred books of the East*, III, *Hsiao Ching* [*Classic of filial piety*], p. 483). Yet this point cannot be stressed too much, because in China filial piety was never identified with loyalty as was the case in Japan. In this sense Confucianism was made an ideology much more in Japan than in China, as we shall soon see in more detail.

First, however, some general considerations on aging and family relations in China. As a sociologist says: "Since Chinese society in general has placed strong emphasis on age considerations, as well as those of kinship, it is not odd that age considerations play a considerable part in role differentiation within the family" (Levy, 1949, p. 48). Both "absolute" and "relative" age groupings have been emphasized in China. According to the same expert "Chinese society's orientation to age is one which invests increasing age with increasingly higher status" (Levy, 1949, p. 48). This is in marked contrast with the industrial West, in particular the United States, which is a youth culture. In the West honor to aged people is a "matter of sentimentality. In China extreme age lends to judgment a weight of validity which is lacking in the West" (Levy, 1949, pp. 63–64). The word *lao* (old) was an honorific term used as a prefix for persons who at times were, absolutely speaking, not aged at all. The prefix "old" gave the honor of age to what followed. Thus the father of a friend was referred to as "old elder brother of my father" although old age and family relationship were both non-existent. In China as well as in Japan there is no single term for brother or sister. The terminology of the family was carried over to denote the relationship between friends (a friend of considerably older age being also called "uncle" or even "father"), while in the West, especially in the United States, close relationship between father and son tends to take over the terminology of friendship and business, as manifested by terms such as "pals" and "partners." In China the reverse process is characteristic, family relationship determining all the others (Levy, 1949, pp. 134ff.).

Experts on Japanese society emphasize even more the use of "displaced" terminology. As one says, "the habit of modelling the structure of social groups outside the family . . . on the pattern of the family, has been developed [in Japan] with a consistency rare in other societies" (Dore, 1958, p. 94). Even today and despite Japan's modernization which demands more impersonal forms of association, the *oyabun–kobun* ("father-part and son-part") system or organization exists in business, trade unions, political parties, academic institutions, athletic teams, and even among criminals. The elder person, accorded the title father, is naturally not related in terms of kinship to his followers, and the *aniki-bun* ("elder-brother-part") is only metaphorically attributed to older members of the group. But what cements these social units is not so much filial duty, or younger- toward older-brother relationship. Loyalty is the real bond, a derivation of the feudal fealty which has been characteristic of much of Japan's history.

The Chinese family was a self-contained unit, but in Japan the family was part of a larger grouping. At the top was the feudal lord, and loyalty toward him came first. A typical anecdote about Confucius tells the story of a feudal lord (still extant at the time of Confucius) who boasted of the loyalty of his subjects, instancing as proof the fact that a son would not fail to report his father if the latter had committed a crime. Confucius replied that in his state citizens were more virtuous because there no son would ever accuse his father. Japan's history is, however, the story of military rulers, of warring barons, and of Tokugawa feudalism which lasted to very recent times. Loyalty to the feudal lord was essential to a society of samurai, who lived by the sword and were in constant danger of death. Japanese Confucianists never had the prestige and the authority which the Chinese literati had. Japanese Confucianists rationalized their warrior society by advocating *chuko ippon*, "unity of loyalty and filial piety."

This unity was not orthodox Confucianism but it certainly helped Japan's modernization. Industrialization directly sapped the solidarity of Chinese society, based exclusively as it was on the family unit. The modernization of Japan instead was fostered by a family structure which extended to the political realm, making the emperor the head of what was called a *kazoku kokka* or the "family structure of the state."

Feudalism in Japan ended officially in 1868 when the power of the Tokugawa military rulers was restored to the emperor; fiefs were abolished, and local lords renounced their privileges in favor of the new state. The Emperor Meiji and more so his new ministers, the so-called oligarchs, launched Japan into a rapid and superimposed modernization. The Japanese family was not subverted in the process because its cohesion was sublimated into the great family which was the new Japanese nation. Divided feudal loyalties were unified under the aegis of the emperor who became the new symbol of national unity. The family–state system was undoubtedly artificially fostered by the oligarchs for it was a very convenient tool for Japan's rapid development.

Some early-Meiji-period intellectuals tried to reject the traditional family system and Confucian ethic in general. Fukuzawa Yukichi in particular distinguished himself by his attacks on Confucianism and its ideas on the family (Blacker, 1964, pp. 67ff.). Others, however, thought differently, especially those in government service like Motoda Eifu. They succeeded in 1890 in having promulgated the Imperial Rescript on Education which sanctioned the new morals for Japanese youth, a "teaching bequeathed" from ages past, "infallible for all ages and true in all places." The imperial house represented the direct descendants from the divine progenitors of Japan, and since the other families were somewhat related to and dependent upon such lofty ancestors, the whole nation formed a great family.

This ideology took more explicit shape in 1910 when new textbooks on Japanese morals were prepared. Scholars in government service, such as the philosopher Inoue Tetsujiro and the constitutionalist Hozumi Yatsuka, worked out the details of the family–state concept of national polity. Jurists had previously (1890–1898) debated the new Civil Code which was then in preparation. Traditionalists opposed innovators who wanted to change the customary family laws under the impact of French civil codes. Hozumi Yatsuka published in 1891 an article, typical of the conservative viewpoint, bearing the title: "The Emergence of the Civil Code and the Destruction of Loyalty and Filial Piety" (Rabinowitz, 1968, pp. 17–43). The dispute centered mainly on the headship of the family—the head of the family, according to Japanese tradition (which was much stricter than in China), having all parental rights.

Behind the dispute was the thesis that the rights of the head of the family were but representative of the power and authority of the head of the great family which was the nation. To tamper with the former was to impugn the latter. In the 1930s when militarist nationalism took over Japan, the family–state concept reached its climax. In a book published by the Ministry of Education which in a few years sold more than two million copies the following is stated:

> Filial piety directly has for its object one's parents, but in relationship toward the emperor finds a place within loyalty. . . . Our country is a great family nation, and the Imperial Household is the head family of the subjects and the nucleus of national life. . . . In China, too, importance is laid on filial duty, and they say that it is the source of a hundred deeds. In India, too, gratitude to parents is taught. But their filial piety is not a kind related to or based on the nation. Filial piety is a characteristic of Oriental morals; and it is in the convergence with loyalty that we find a characteristic of our national morals, and this is a factor without parallel in the world [Tsunoda, 1958, p. 789].

The book in question was the *Kokutai no Hongi* or *The fundamentals of our national polity* published in 1937. In 1941, the *Shimin no Michi* (*The way of the subject*) reinforced and carried to its ultimate conclusions the loyalty due to the state on the part of Japanese subjects. Until the defeat of Japan in World War II, the family–state concept, referred to as the unique "national polity" (*kokutai*) of Japan, was extolled by politicians and schoolmasters, and in countless publications. After 1945, a natural reaction set in, and progressive intellectuals in particular attacked the family–state ideology as the source of all evils which had brought upon Japan the miseries of war and defeat. Now a much more sober evaluation of the family structure of Japanese society is in the offing—Japan's rapid modernization and even her postwar economic miracle being connected with the family system.

A return to the good points of a family system, which has always linked the present family with past and future generations, seems to be a quest of contemporary China and Japan, notwithstanding their great cultural and social changes. This would appear to be a lesson for the West, where the past or the traditional tends to be disconnected with the present and the future. But a national identity cannot exist without a link with a traditional past.

REFERENCES

Blacker, C. *The Japanese enlightenment: A study of the writings of Fukuzawa Yukichi*. London: Cambridge University Press, 1964.

Chinese classics (trans. by J. Legge). London: Oxford University Press, 1893–1895. 5 vols.

Dore, R. P. *City life in Japan*. Berkeley: University of California Press, 1958.

Lang, O. *Chinese family and society*. Handon, Conn.: Archon Books, 1968.

Levy, M. J., Jr. *The family revolution in modern China*. Cambridge: Harvard University Press, 1949.

Nakamura, H. *Ways of thinking of Eastern peoples: India–China–Tibet–Japan*. Honolulu: East–West Center, 1964.

Rabinowitz, R. W. Law and the social process in Japan. *Transactions of the Asiatic Society of Japan* (3rd series) 1968, *10*.

Sacred books of the East (trans. by J. Legge). London: Oxford University Press, 1879–1885. (Republished: Delhi: Motilal Banarsidas, 1968.)

Sakamoto, T. *Nihon ni okeru rinri shiso no tenkan (The development of ethical thought in Japan)*. Tokyo: Yoshikawa Kobunkan, 1965.

Tsunoda, R. *et al.* (Eds.) *Sources of Japanese tradition*. New York: Columbia University Press, 1958.

Yang, C. K. *Religion in Chinese society: A study of contemporary social functions of religion and some of their historical factors*. Berkeley: University of California Press, 1967.

The Challenge of Aging
for Contemporary Religion

WILLIAM F. HOGAN, C.S.C.

Father William F. Hogan, C.S.C., received his A.B. degree from the University of Notre Dame in 1952 and his J.C.D. from the Gregorian University, Rome, in 1960. His previous positions include those of Chairman of the Theology Department, Stonehill College, North Easton, Massachusetts; Superior of the Holy Cross International House of Studies in Rome; and Assistant Provincial. Currently, Father Hogan is Provincial of the Eastern Province of the Holy Cross Fathers. He is the author of three books: No race apart, Reflections for renewal, *and* One and the same Spirit. *Father Hogan has also contributed to the* New Catholic Encyclopedia; *has edited a series of paperbacks on religious life, published by the Stonehill College Press; and is a contributor to many periodicals.*

For some people, the title of this paper might immediately evoke thoughts of programs which should be started to meet current needs. Certainly, there is validity to and need for this approach, and by no means should there be disparagement of church-affiliated programs of building residences for the elderly, sponsoring educational programs and special ministries to the aged, and so on. But it seems that there is a much deeper issue than mere programs, and to devote attention solely to programs would be to remain only on the surface and to restrict ourselves to remedies rather than face the core problem. Moreover, programs without other efforts

26

might very well prove harmful to the elderly because some well-intended endeavors serve only to help the aged become children; though these efforts keep the senior citizens from boredom, they do not contribute to any inner growth and may be conducive to the trivialization of existence (Heschel, 1966, p. 73). Really to meet the challenge of the aging, religion must address itself more deeply to the process of life and the development of a life-vision because "the vast majority of mankind look upon the coming of old age with sorrow or rebellion and it fills them with more aversion than death itself" (de Beauvoir, 1972, p. 539).

There appears to be widespread pessimism about old age on the part of too many of our fellow-men; the attitudes expressed in Psalm Thirty-one are all too common:

> For my life is worn out with sorrow,
> My years with sighs;
> My strength yields under misery,
> My bones are wasting away.
> To everyone of my oppressors
> I am contemptible.
> Loathsome to my neighbors,
> To my friends a thing of fear.
> Those who see me in the street
> Hurry past me.
> I am forgotten, as good as dead in their hearts,
> Something discarded [Ps 31:10–13].

The reverence for the aged among the Japanese and Chinese is well known. But we perhaps are not so aware of how much the scriptures praise the aged and instruct people to honor them. Not only is youth considered worthy of esteem, but also old age: "The glory of young men is their strength, and the beauty of old men is the grey head" (Pr 20:29). The elders played a special role in Old Testament religion and in the early period of Christianity; they were the chief teachers, the judges, the leaders (Brown, 1964, ch. 1). If there is a change today, if reverence for the aged is lacking, if the aged feel such a lack, then religion must address itself to the cause. Therein lies the challenge.

THE FUNCTIONAL VALUES OF AMERICAN SOCIETY

America's value system has been basically oriented toward youth and unfavorable to old age because it has been characterized by an occupational-achievement-and-success mentality which emphasizes activity and work, practicality and efficiency, and progress (Kent, 1968, p. 5). All these values are of a "functional-having" outlook rather than of a "being" dimension. They do not take into account the achievement of serenity and inner peace in the midst of an upset world; they overlook the wisdom which can develop over a long life. So widespread a tone in society's values fosters the attitude that the elderly are inferior to the young, and that new developments are preferable to the old and traditional. Yet, strangely enough, youth today rather generally reject these values as shallow and superficial. Nonetheless, they are the values and goals to which today's older person was exposed during his lifetime; his early socialization occurred amid the value orientation of the latter part of the nineteenth century and the early part of this century.

As a result of this past emphasis on functional values, many of those approaching old age today develop a concept of it as a time of darkness, uselessness, ostracization; and surely the overall picture of society's reactions gives them little reason for thinking otherwise. Witness the discrepancy between the funds allocated to alleviate the needs of the elderly and the amount spent on luxury items and gadgets (Townsend, 1971, ch. 1). As Henri Nouwen has observed, too many people give the impression that our world does not have room for the elderly, and thus the fear of old age as a time of excommunication has replaced the fear of death (McNeill, 1972). For many, this feeling is very real, and it is based on the factors of apparent segregation from earning power, desolation through the breaking of familiar ties, and loss of self-worth through non-productivity. It results in the self-concept of "I am who I was." "Who I am now" has no meaning.

OLD AGE AS A POTENTIAL FOR GROWTH

Aging should not be the way to darkness, but the way to light, as the psalmist states: "[The virtuous] will flourish in the courts of our God, still bearing fruit in old age, still remaining fresh and green, to proclaim that Yahweh is righteous . . ." (Ps 92:13–15). We all are familiar with individuals who in their later years have retained and even developed the elasticity of youth, maintaining a psychological alertness and a mental openness, while enjoying the fruits of a long life. A Pope John, a Mother Theresa of Calcutta, a Dorothy Day, an Albert Schweitzer, an elderly, creative Michelangelo—all very much alive, and people of light and not of darkness! These and many others show by their lives that there is a great difference between one's psychological age and his chronological or biological age (Deeken, 1972, p. 8). Henri Nouwen suggests that those aged who are filled with light instead of darkness are characterized by hope, humor, and vision (McNeill, 1972). Hope detaches a person from the many small preoccupations and crises of life and opens him to the future; and such detachment is a lifelong process. With the development of hope in his value structure, a person sees his worth not in what he achieves but in who he is. He has a sense of humor which enables him to take himself and the world seriously, but never so seriously that he cannot keep things in perspective. This hope and humor give birth to a broad vision of life which looks beyond the confines of existence in this world to eternal light; and aging becomes a growing into the vision of the Light which is Christ.

Whether aging for a given individual is a way to darkness or a way to light depends very much on the value structure of the individual who is aging. And what happens to our older people at large will depend on the values which we seek to promote in society; these in turn will be responsible for the changes or the lack of change in society's attitude toward aging and the aged.

Rabbi Heschel speaks of the years of old age as a time when man may be able finally to attain the high values he failed to develop, the insights he has missed, the wisdom he ignored. The years of old age "are indeed formative years, rich in possibilities to unlearn the failures of a lifetime, to see through inbred self-deceptions, to deepen understanding and compassion, to widen the horizon of honesty, to refine the sense of fairness" (Heschel, 1966, p. 78). In short, old age provides opportunities for inner growth, and man's potential for growth in this period of his life is far greater than many are willing to admit. It will be actualized, however, only if the whole life-development has been one of growth and of openness to discovering new dimensions of life. For of themselves advanced years are no guarantee of the development of wisdom.

It is rather overpowering and frustrating to consider what areas religion must face to bring about an overall re-education of values in society to meet the challenge of aging and to provide formation for aging for people at all age levels. Education for aging must take place all through life, and positive steps must be taken with the very young; we cannot wait until middle age and expect people then to learn to cope with a process which has been going on for some time.

REVERENCE FOR LIFE ITSELF

First and foremost, religion must concern itself with respect and reverence for the gift of life itself. We may think of the appreciation of life in terms of the current abortion and euthanasia issues, but the vision of the greatness of life must go beyond this to the development of a personal awareness of the gift of one's own life in itself and the richness of the experience of one's life in relationship to God, one's fellow-men, and the universe—even if there have been hardships. Perhaps an old Taoist parable will illustrate the point:

A carpenter and his apprentice saw a very large and very old oak tree which happened to be quite gnarled. The carpenter said to his apprentice: "Do you know why this tree is so big and so old?"

The apprentice said: "No. Why?"
Then the carpenter answered: "Because it is useless. If it were useful, it would have been cut down, sawed up, and used for beds and tables and chairs. But because it is useless, it has been allowed to grow. That is why it is now so great that you can rest in its shadow."

Because the tree had not been viewed in terms of utility, it became a full tree, and its value became the tree itself.

When man views life only in terms of utility and function, its greatness escapes him, and the development and growth which could and should occur do not take place. Only when the value of life is life itself in all its ramifications is life free to grow to maturity. Man misses so much of his own meaning and worth when he fails to grasp a sense of the life which he has taken for granted. There is such a rapid tempo to life today that people go running through life so fast that they escape its meaning.

THE VALUE OF LEISURE

There is need for a reawakening of the human and Christian value of leisure which enables man to reflect and ponder on reality; a leisure mentality gives birth to wonder, the ability to be surprised at the extraordinary dimensions of the ordinary. We are not talking here of "free time," for leisure is not a matter of time—it is an abiding attitude which creates an outlook. If man needs some periods of free time in order to gather together his strength and to reassess his perspective, it is in order that this may carry over into his whole life and enrich his vision. Life is not to be dichotomized into periods of work time and free time; this is happening widely, since much of the literature on leisure simply identifies leisure with free time without facing the deeper concept of leisure itself. With growth in a spirit of wonder through true leisure, man becomes more aware of the meaning of life itself—his life—his relationship to his Lord, his brothers, his world—all of which enter into his own experience of life.

Religion must assist man today to stand up against the currents of the times which would impel him to a faster pace of living and would even dictate to him through various media pressures the way in which he should find his leisure, relaxation, and enjoyment. The trends of today consciously or unconsciously are impelling men to escape from themselves and to avoid facing the issues of life and assessing basic values. A return to simplicity of life and a development of leisure are a must from the time of a person's youth; the Church must lead the way. This, of course, requires a continual battle against materialistic forces, and though such a battle may seem overwhelming, still religion must raise its voice to awaken men gradually, if the gift and dignity of life and being are to be more widely appreciated and if we are to be liberated from the "having and functional" syndrome.

Without this awakening, the wisdom of living will never be developed, and we will not learn the lesson that "it takes three things to attain a sense of significant being; God, a soul and a moment. And the three are always here. Just to be is a blessing. Just to live is holy" (Heschel, 1966, p. 84).

SCRIPTURAL AIDS TO PROBLEMS OF AGING

The teaching and preaching message of the Church has to go much farther than it has heretofore; it must advance beyond mere moralizing. Those who constantly teach and preach about moral issues and questions are not entirely faithful to the Word of God in its totality. The Word of God is a gift, a promise, and a hope: God's gift to man is the good news of life, salvation, and freedom; the promise of God's abiding goodness; and the hope of the fullness of life in the resurrection. This Word speaks of wisdom and appreciation of the gift of life now in preparation for the life to come. This dimension of the Word needs to be preached as much as, if not more than, particular moral questions; for it lies at the root of many substantial issues. Positive preaching and teaching of the whole of God's Word would greatly help toward fostering this esteem of the gift of life and being.

The scriptures offer a wealth of spiritual insights helpful to the problems of aging, but they are not sufficiently perceived in this light. One of the most fundamental is the joyful character of the Christian life, for joy is declared to be a fruit of the Holy Spirit. "Rejoice in the Lord always; again I say, rejoice" (Ph 4:4). A true believer cannot live with a mentality of desolation or despondency; such an attitude would betray a lack of faith in the Lord. If the spirituality of past ages has emphasized a somber Christ and Christian life, it is now time that the joy of Christ be sung loudly and clearly. In no way will this compromise the seriousness of believing; rather it should make it evident that seriousness and joylessness are not synonymous and that Christ teaches the need for a deep sense of the joy of being alive.

A deeper appreciation of the doctrine of the Trinity might very well open a person to a greater insight into life, growth, and personal development. When man grasps that God is not a lonely, isolated individual but exists in the loving exchange of three Persons (a profound loving community), then he may realize that relations with others constitute a great part of his being, and that he can become fully human only through a relationship of love and exchange with others. But the doctrine of the Trinity, great mystery that it is, is rarely preached or even adverted to in pastoral practice. In times of individualism and alienation, religion through the doctrine of the Trinity might serve to enable man to perceive in his own life the significance of the strong community thrust in society. And it goes without saying that the whole issue of loneliness can take on a positive significance when there is realization that only God can fully answer man's yearnings, as reflection on the Word of God makes clear. The positive concept of developing an unquenchable thirst for God might well be promoted through better presentation of the scriptures.

THE BLESSING OF HUMAN WEAKNESS

Another dimension which could be of assistance in the growth of a life vision is a deeper sense of the blessing of human weakness. Our society is a strength-oriented one which finds no place for weakness and imperfection; all-out efforts are made in every sphere to stamp out weaknesses. A purely negative approach to debility results in a sense of inferiority and rejection in the face of weaknesses and declining powers. Yet St. Paul, in his Second Letter to the Corinthians, would give a positive picture to weakness: "When I am weak, then am I strong" (2 Co 12:10); "The Lord said to me, 'My grace is sufficient for you, for my power is made perfect in weakness'" (2 Co 12:4). In these words the Spirit teaches us that man has to come to grips with his true self, his limitations, to be in touch with the inner core of his person; and when he has a profound sense of his creatureliness, then he can come to a conviction of the Lord as his source of strength and power. This message would have man realize the great blessing which weakness can serve in assisting him to a healthy, realistic sense of joyous dependence on the Lord, and thus attain to a clearer picture of himself in his humanity. A self-image which would deny the role of God and exclude openness to the divine healing and strengthening power would be a false one and one which may well be at the root of many of the difficulties of aging. This message is so contradictory to an age of excessive self-reliance that every effort should be made to bring it constantly into teaching and preaching.

POSITIVE ATTITUDES TOWARD DYING

And then there is the whole question of a positive approach to dying as a fulfillment of living. Taking cognizance of the many complications of the whole issue of death, the personal dimensions, and the pressures and influence of society's standards, religion, it would seem, should place a greater emphasis on a positive view of death. Rarely, apart from funerals, does one hear about death as the culmination of life. In earlier times sermons on death attempted to increase the fear and dread of dying; now, to counteract this, they make little reference at all to death.

One could go on to cite different aspects of the Christian message which deserve re-emphasis in a positive light and which would assist in the development of the value of being and of life itself. Persons discover different insights into the Christian faith at different stages in their lives, and this is understandable since we are not ready for the full import of many teachings at any one phase of our lives. As the whole person develops, new significances occur, and many teachings which had simply been words become more meaningful—a good reason why much more positive content should be given to preaching and other vehicles of Christian instruction. The Word of God has so much to offer to accompany the insights of psychology in the issue of aging.

THE CHURCH'S MINISTRY TO THE AGING

Ideally, if all people could grasp in their lives the values of being and of living as such, there would be little reason for a special ministry to the aged, except perhaps in terms of the alleviation of material needs. But we can be reasonably sure that not all men will grasp these values and that there will always be need of such pastoral ministry. Henri Nouwen (McNeill, 1972) wisely points out that ministry to the aging should not be special in the sense of societal segregation; for if we allow people to be divided into young, middle-aged, and elderly, then we prevent the young, middle-aged, and elderly from ministering to each other. The minister should serve only as a catalyst to promote this interaction among the generations; for this interaction involves mutual acceptance at all stages of the life process and mutual confrontation and challenging of possible illusions to true growth.

Along with long-term efforts at facing the challenge of aging by effecting a change in values among men, religion must be concerned today with certain programs to meet the present needs of the elderly. Churches and religious communities must devote personnel and energy to facilities and educational programs for the aged, and make efforts to provide such needed social services as counseling, insofar as is possible. In the long-overlooked thrust of efforts for social justice, the Church must continue to concern herself intensely with the issues of housing and financial security for those aged who have been neglected; and she must encourage and support plans for additional federal and state aid to assist the elderly and to bring about a climate of concern for them.

Efforts must be made to tap the potential and wisdom of senior citizens and thus break down any prevailing sense of rejection or uselessness on the part of the aged, and to help society benefit from the many insights of age. There is an old Balinese legend which might well depict the situation of our day.

Once upon a time the people of a remote mountain village in Bali used to sacrifice their old men. A day came when there was not a single old man left, and the traditions were lost. They wanted to build a great house for the meetings of the assembly, but when they came to look at the tree-trunks that had been cut for that purpose, no one could tell the top from the bottom; if the timber was placed the wrong way up, it would set off a series of disasters. But then a young man entered the circle and said: "If you promise never to sacrifice the old men any more, I will be able to find a solution." They promised. He brought forth his grandfather whom he had concealed and the old man taught the community to tell top from bottom [de Beauvoir, 1972, p. 77].

There are undoubtedly countless ways in which many elderly people could assist us to tell top from bottom in some of our current problems.

Finally, religion today must place a stronger thrust on pastoral counseling for the dying and prepare ministers in their professional formation to assist people with the issues of death and dying. But the real challenge for religion is to assist man to a recognition of the value of life—all of life—so that life is fully lived until death: the beginning of the fulfillment of life.

REFERENCES

de Beauvoir, S. *The coming of age.* New York: Putnam, 1972.
Brown, J. P. *Counselling with senior citizens.* Englewood Cliffs, N.J.: Prentice-Hall, 1964.
Deeken, A. (s.j.) *Growing old and how to cope with it.* New York: Paulist, 1972.
Heschel, A. J. *The insecurity of freedom.* New York: Farrar, Straus & Giroux, 1966.
Kent, D. P. The attitudes toward aging in a youth culture. Address given at the Mental Health Workshop, College Misericordia, Dallas, Pa., October 9, 1968.
McNeill, D. (Chm.) Ministry to the aging and dying conference. Pastoral Theology Program, University of Notre Dame, October 23–26, 1972.
Townsend, C. *Old age: The last segregation.* New York: Bantam, 1971.

II
THE BASIC SCIENTIFIC
DIMENSIONS

The Demography of Aging

Leon F. Bouvier

Leon Francis Bouvier received his preparatory education in Massachusetts and a B.S. degree from Spring Hill College, Mobile, Alabama. His M.A. and his Ph.D. degrees were earned at Brown University. Dr. Bouvier has held a number of academic and professional positions, among them Chairman of the Sociology Department at Siena College; Assistant Professor at the University of Scranton; Consultant, Center for Population Research, Georgetown University; and Research Associate, Research Institute for Cuba and the Caribbean, University of Miami. For the academic year 1972–1973, he was Professorial Lecturer at the Joseph and Rose Kennedy Institute for the Study of Human Reproduction and Bioethics at Georgetown University. Currently, he is Associate Professor of Sociology at the University of Rhode Island. Dr. Bouvier is a member of the American Sociological Association, the Population Association of America, and the International Union for the Scientific Study of Population.

We must first consider what is meant by aging and, as related to that concept, what is demography? Aging—or "getting older"—begins at birth and continues without interruption throughout life until death. But aging is often interpreted as the process of approaching that time in life when one is aged or elderly. One might refer to the period then as adult aging, thereby differentiating it from adolescent aging. The former term refers to the down-

37

ward path from the so-called prime of life; the latter, the upward path from childhood to the prime of life—whenever that may be.

Demography deals with aggregates and not with individuals. To a considerable extent, it is concerned with numbers of people, changes in those numbers over time, and changes in the characteristics of specific populations, again over time. The demography of aging, therefore, studies the numerical relationship between the aged group (conventionally defined as those 65 years of age and over) and the overall society, and variations in that relationship over time. This can be conceptualized as the "aging" or "younging" of the society itself. The demography of aging also examines changes in the characteristics of the elderly population and variations in these characteristics over time.

The changing characteristics of the elderly population will be discussed briefly. Emphasis will center on the relationship between the older group and the overall society. Other issues concerned with the aged will be left for the sociologists, the psychologists, and the gerontologists to discuss.

In recent years it has become apparent that fertility is declining, and thus the burden of supporting large numbers of dependent children may soon be alleviated. However, the ever-increasing number of elderly persons and the attendant gerontological problems are becoming a source of concern, and prominent space is allocated by the media to the "problems of the elderly." Unfortunately, demographic data are far too often misinterpreted in the press. Contrary to some reports, the United States is in no danger of being engulfed in a sea of radical, activist senior citizens. Yet such predictions are sometimes made by misinformed writers. The following is but one example, taken from a recent syndicated article, entitled: Your money's worth:

> Within less than a generation, more than 50 percent of the people in our country will be over the age of 50! Before the year 2000—only 27 years from now—one in three Americans will be 65 or older [Porter, 1973, p. 6].

When it is realized that in 1970, only about 10% of the population were 65 years of age or over, this would amount to an incredible increase—and in less than three decades. One purpose of this paper is to illustrate the absurdity of some of these predictions and to alert the non-demographers to their frequent appearance in the press. Another purpose is to discuss the approach of the discipline of demography to the study of aging, and the insights which emerge from such a frame of reference.

THE BASIC DEMOGRAPHIC PROCESSES

Without some knowledge of basic demographic concepts, one cannot thoroughly grasp the meaning of changes in the aged population. Any society loses or gains population in three, and only three, ways. People are born into the society; people move in or out of the society; people living there eventually die. These are the basic demographic processes upon which all numerical calculations are based. Still another term should be introduced: *cohort*. A birth cohort, for example, would include all the people born, for example, between 1900 and 1910. Such a group of people (that is, a birth cohort) could be followed throughout its various stages in the life cycle, literally, until it passes out of existence, perhaps a century later. An understanding of the dynamics of fertility, mortality, and migration, and an understanding of the cohort approach, are necessary if one is to appreciate better the many dimensions which contribute to the changes in the size of the elderly population. Thus, the cohort of infants born between 1910 and 1920 will become the cohort of people aged 65–75 in 1975–1985. Similarly, the immigrants of a particular period become members of certain age-cohorts depending upon their age at arrival in this country.

For now, suffice it to say that all three of the above-mentioned processes play a part in determining the number of persons aged 65 and over in the United States—now and in the future. All three contribute to the determination of the proportion of such people in the United States—today and at the turn of the century—and the cohort approach is the best means to interpret the changes which take place in that population.

THE NUMBER OF ELDERLY

In 1900 there were about 3 million elderly people in the United States. By 1940 the number had trebled to 9 million, and at the most recent census in 1970, 20 million persons aged 65 and over were enumerated. It is expected that this number will reach 29 million by the year 2000, and 20 years later, there well might be over 40 million elderly in this country.

In one century, from 1900 to 2000, the elderly population will have increased from 3 million to 29 million—an almost tenfold growth. During the same century, the nation's population will increase at the very most four-fold. Similarly, decennial growth rates have consistently been much higher for this group than for the nation. For example, since 1960 the number of people 65 and over increased by 21% while the nation's growth was a mere 13%.

This surprisingly large increase demands an explanation. Some have suggested that advances in medical knowledge and facilities have been a major cause of this tremendous gain, implying that more and more older residents have remained alive, with the result a disproportionate numerical increase. Unfortunately, medical progress is not the principal cause of this growth. Indeed, it has played but an inconsequential role. Rather, the larger-than-average increases in the elderly population are the result of the fertility behavior of 65 and 75 years ago. The birth cohorts of the last quarter of the nineteenth century and the first decades of this century were very large and, despite losses through mortality, remain relatively large when they attain age 65.

The 1920s and 1930s were marked by sharp declines in fertility, and this decline will be reflected after 1990 when the decennial rate of growth will drop to about 5% among the elderly population. We are all familiar with the "baby boom"—that period of high fertility between 1946 and 1957. That particular birth cohort will enter its elderly stage of life between 2010 and 2020. Therefore, in that decade, there will be a marked increase in the aged population—perhaps a 30% ten-year growth rate—culminating in a total of 40 million persons 65 and over in the population of the United States in the year 2020.

Mortality and migration also contribute to the fluctuations in the number of aged in the population. Immigration from Europe—heavy around the turn of the twentieth century—almost came to a halt in the 1920s and 1930s. But this earlier immigration has contributed to increasing the number of persons aged 65 and over in the present population. It will not, however, seriously affect future growth. Mortality decline is also a factor, but, in this instance, improvements among the young affect the eventual aged population much more than do improvements among the aged. Since 1900, crude death rates have declined from about 17 per 1000 to about 9 per 1000, but much of this improvement has occurred among infants and the very young. As a result, this progress had the same effect as increased birth rates. That is to say, more infants and young children were kept alive and thus remained within their birth cohort to contribute to the large numbers in the same cohort 60 to 65 years later. To be sure, there have been improvements in mortality rates among the old. But it must be borne in mind that (1) these improvements have been relatively small; and (2) the number of people affected is slight in comparison with the number of people in the population. Thus, such gains are not as statistically important as gains in the younger population.

DEMOGRAPHIC PROJECTIONS

We have discussed past and present changes in the number of elderly, and some reference has been made to projections into the next century. A word about demographic projections is appropriate at this point. In making any population projections for the total society, all three demographic processes must be considered. However, when the projections are limited to the next 50 years, and we are only concerned with the number of persons aged 65 and over, future fertility is not a contributing variable. Even for the year 2035, the members of that elderly group are already born. As Siegel and O'Leary have recently pointed out:

The projected numbers of older persons cited here should be close to the mark because they are unaffected by future fertility. The people who will be over 55, 65, and 75 in the year 2000 or even the year 2020 are now living. The fact that projected fertility is not involved is fortunate; fertility is a component that cannot be predicted closely because it tends to fluctuate widely [U. S. Bureau of the Census, 1973, p. 3].

International migration remains a contributory factor, but it is not of overwhelming importance. Currently, about 400,000 persons migrate legally to the United States every year, and there is no reason to assume that this number will increase in the foreseeable future. Bureau of the Census projections take into consideration not only this migration but its age and sex distribution as well. Projections thus assume that the future will see a continuation of the present level of migration, numerically and in age and sex distribution. Of course, in a consideration of only the aged population, much of future migration is not relevant to the projection. Of the 400,000 entering the United States in 1980, only those 45 years of age or over will be elderly in the year 2000. Projections which do not include any immigration from this moment on suggest that the resulting difference in the year 2000 will be less than one million.

Improvements in mortality among the aged could, of course, contribute to increasing their future numbers, but we must be careful not to overstate this dimension. Nevertheless the repeated popular assertions dealing with imminent cures for dreaded diseases warrant a brief discussion of possible improvements in mortality insofar as they affect the elderly. Continued progress among the young and middle-aged would, of course, contribute to larger numbers of the aged in later years. But in actual fact it is difficult to foresee any significant improvements in these age groups whose death rates are already very low. Some further progress in lowering infant mortality is possible, but much of these gains have already occurred. Furthermore, they would not affect the elderly population until 2040.

Life expectancy at birth has risen from 49 years in 1900 to 70 years in 1955 and 70.5 years in 1970. Note that since 1955 life expectancy at birth has barely improved. But life expectancy at birth does not tell us at what ages any improvements do occur. It would be better to distinguish progress in "life expectation" for those under 65 and those 65 and over. In 1900, 39% of the newborn babies would reach age 65. In 1970, about 72% would —a gain of 33 persons aged 65 per 100 babies. The proportion of persons surviving from age 65 to 80 was 33% in 1900 and 49% in 1970—a gain of 16 per 100. Incidentally, the corresponding survival rates in 1955 were only a little lower than those in 1970. Siegel and O'Leary comment on this point:

Once again, expectation values increased relatively little between 1955 and 1969, both for ages under 65 and over 65. Nearly all of the progress in life expectation recorded in the period 1900–02 to 1969 occurred by 1955 and at the younger ages, therefore, although there were some notable gains at the older ages in the earlier period [U. S. Bureau of the Census, 1973, p. 15].

But what about the future? Most projections assume either that mortality rates will remain the same or that some slight improvement will occur. The projections used here assume that minor improvements will take place in the future but that no dramatic breakthrough will emerge in the next 50 years. On this point, it is interesting to note that even if both heart disease and cancer were completely eliminated as causes of death, the gain in life expectancy at age 65 would be less than 15 years. This, of course, does not take into consideration the likelihood that such persons would merely become "eligible" to die from other causes.

The demographically calculated projections to 2000, and even to 2020, are quite realistic assuming as they do no change in migration and some minor improvements in mortality. That fertility will not be a factor for the next 50 years makes these projections more likely to prove accurate: that is, about 29 million aged in 2000 and 40 million in 2020.

THE AGED POPULATION AS A PROPORTION OF THE TOTAL POPULATION

Today, 10% of the American population are 65 years of age or over. In 1900, only 4.1% were in that age category. There has been a gradual increase in the proportion of those age 65 and over in this century. What about the future? Proportions are not so simple to project as the actual numbers of the elderly, for proportions must, of necessity, take into account all segments of society—the young, the adolescents, and the middle-aged, as well as the elderly. While we may be quite confident of our numerical projections to 2000 or even 2020, we cannot be so assured that our projections on the *proportions* of aged in the general population will come as close to the mark because it is not possible to predict accurately the future course of fertility. If fertility continues its recent decline and women average about two children, then the proportion of persons 65 and over will increase somewhat and by 1990 will represent about 11% of the population. It will then decline slightly because of the small number of elderly entering that category between 1990 and 2000. Should fertility take an expected turn upward to the three-child average, then the proportion of persons 65 and over in 2000 will be smaller—about 9%. Projections beyond 2000 are quite tenuous, depending as they do on future fertility behavior. The proportion of aged will, of course, increase between 2010 and 2020 as the "baby boom" cohort becomes a senior citizen cohort.

Strictly for illustrative purposes, let us assume that the present very low fertility continues indefinitely. Let us further assume that immigration comes to an immediate halt, and that mortality continues at about today's rate moving toward a period of real "zero population growth," where births and deaths equal each other. In demographic terms, this is a stationary population. Such a model would be attained in 70 or 80 years. In such a population, about 16% of the people would be 65 and over.

THE AGING OF SOCIETIES

How does a society go through the "aging" or "younging" process? The age of a society can be operationally defined as its median age (that is, that point where half the population is younger and half is older). Other measures could be the proportion 65 and over or the ratio of persons 65 and over to children under 15. In fact, a population could be aging and younging at the same time if the proportion of both the under-15 and the over-65 were simultaneously gaining—a situation which occurred during some years of the "baby boom."

The principal ingredient contributing to the aging of a society is not declining mortality but declining fertility. Hermalin (1966) has clearly demonstrated that it was the decline in fertility which contributed to the increase in the proportion of persons 65 and over in this century. Furthermore, and perhaps a little surprisingly, declines in mortality do not contribute to a rise in the proportion of the elderly unless these declines are overwhelmingly concentrated in the older ages. Coale has demonstrated this fact in his well-known article: How a population ages or grows younger. He concludes:

> Had the risks of death prevailing in 1900 continued unchanged, and the other variables—rates of immigration and rates of childbearing per mother— followed the course they actually did, the average age of the population today would be greater than it is [Coale, 1964, pp. 49–50].

The reason for this conclusion is, as we stated earlier, that most reductions in mortality have occurred at younger ages and thus have contributed to a younger population. Immigration is also a factor in the aging or younging of a population, but it has led to a younging of the population in the first 60 years of this century (Hermalin, 1966). It should continue doing so unless it becomes concentrated in the older group—an unlikely possibility.

Turning again to mortality: once death rates among people under age 50 reach a point which is so low that any further progress is hardly possible, then any additional reduction in mortality would occur among the older population—a current problem in some of the extremely developed (demographically) nations (Sweden would be an example). Such a situation leads to a slight aging of the society, but its contribution should not be exaggerated since only a relatively small proportion of the population could benefit from such improvements. Siegel and O'Leary have calculated that the proportion of persons 65 and over in 1990 will be 10.3 with constant mortality, 10.5 with slightly declining mortality, and 11.0 with "rapidly" declining mortality. They continue:

So far in this century fertility levels have been the principal determinant of the age composition of the U. S. population and, with already low levels of mortality and immigration, they will become even more determinative [U. S. Bureau of the Census, 1973, p. 6].

What will the actual proportion of the United States population 65 and over be in the year 2000, or in 2020? It is difficult to make confident projections. To an overwhelming extent, this figure depends upon future fertility patterns. It should not fall below 8% or 9%; nor should it attain levels as high as 15%—much less 33.3%—at least not in the next 50 years.

On this point let us return to the newspaper article referred to earlier. In correspondence with the political scientist upon whose research the article was based, I learned that the projection that one-third of the population in 2000 would be 65 or over was based on the possibility of a much longer life span. "We were obliged to give credence to those molecular biologists who estimate longevity extension within twenty years," he said.* A closer examination of this claim is interesting. There are currently 72 million people in this country between the ages of 35 and 70. If each and everyone of them remained alive until the year 2000, when they would be between 65 and 100 years old, that 72 million would represent but one-third of *today's* population—much less the population of the year 2000.

DIFFERENCES WITHIN THE ELDERLY GROUP

The elderly population as a separate entity should also be discussed to note age changes within that group. As the elderly population has grown in substantial numbers since 1900, so too has the 75-and-over group increased even more so. The reasons for the changing distribution discussed above apply *a fortiori* to this oldest group. From 900,000 in 1900, this group increased to over 7½ million in 1970, and will reach 12½ million in 2000, perhaps 14 million in 2020. Thus the elderly population itself is aging and will continue to do so. The proportion 65–69 is getting smaller while the proportion 75 and over is getting larger, and this trend should continue into the next century. In 1900, 29% of the elderly population was over 75; by 1970 it was 38%. In 23 years, perhaps as many as 43% of the elderly population will fall in the 75-and-over age category. This is a not insig-

* Personal correspondence with Dr. Harvey Wheeler, Center for the Study of Democratic Institutions, Santa Barbara, California.

nificant factor to consider in developing programs for the elderly in the year 2000.

Thus far we have demonstrated the importance of fertility, mortality, and migration in understanding the way in which the elderly population has grown both numerically and proportionately. Sex differentials, especially in mortality, are also significant since they determine the sex ratio of the elderly group. In the overall population, there are now 96 males for every 100 females. At birth, however, the sex ratio is about 105 males to 100 females. Throughout life, males are more susceptible to death, especially so in the upper ages. The age-specific death rate for males 65–74 is 50.3; for females it is 27.1. As a result, the number of males is proportionately quite small among the elderly: 72 per 100 females.

Even more significant is the long secular decline in the sex ratio of the elderly. Until 1930 there were slightly more males 65 and over than there were females, in large part the result of the immigration to the United States of many more men than women. By 1960, however, the sex ratio was down to 82.6, and the decline of 10 percentage points in one decade, to 72 in 1970, is extraordinary. If mortality patterns continue as they have, there will be about 65 men per 100 women 65 and over in the year 2000.

The declining sex ratio was first attributable to the drop in immigration, but this massive movement came to an end with the First World War. The present 400,000 legal immigrants per year is a far cry from the 1¼ million noted annually in the final decade of the nineteenth century. Today, sex differentials in mortality are much more important in explaining the continuing decline in the sex ratio. Not only do females have lower death rates, but the difference itself is becoming larger and larger. Women apparently benefit more from the progress in controlling the typically chronic diseases generally associated with the elderly. Take cancer as an example: from 1930 to 1960 the death rate from malignant neoplasms rose sharply for males. For females, the trend was downward. In fact what was once a disease associated with women has now become more prevalent, as a cause of death, among men. Because of these factors, it can be realistically expected that there will be ever more widows in the population as we approach the turn of the century.

CONCLUSION

This paper has deliberately focused on the demographic approach to aging. In this way it can perhaps serve as a background for other reports concerned with the physiological, the sociological, and the psychological aspects of aging. If there are problems in serving the elderly population today, these problems will no doubt be exacerbated in the not-too-distant future.

The fertility of 50 to 70 years ago guarantees a continuation of the large elderly increases in the population: the 20 million of today will be followed by the 29 million of the year 2000 and the 42 million of 2020. This last growth will be directly attributable to our own fertility behavior of just 20 years ago during the "baby boom." Perhaps the most important conclusion is that there is a built-in momentum in population change. The demographic behavior—be it fertility, mortality, or migration—of a given decade has repercussions for the society throughout its life span. In a sense this is fortunate. We can, if we so desire, prepare for future changes in the age structure of the population and be ready when these changes in fact take place. In this instance, we should now be making policy decisions in the field of gerontology, knowing, as indeed we do, that the problems of the aged will not go away—they are just beginning to be felt.

REFERENCES

Coale, A. J. How a population ages or grows younger. In R. Freedman (Ed.) *Population: The vital revolution.* Garden City, N.Y.: Doubleday Anchor, 1964. Pp. 47–58.

Hermalin, A. I. The effect of changes in mortality rates on population growth and age distribution in the United States. *Milbank Memorial Fund Quarterly,* 1966, *44,* 451–469.

Porter, S. Your money's worth. *Washington Star-News,* April 9, 1973.

U. S. Bureau of the Census. Some demographic aspects of aging in the United States. *Current Population Reports.* (Series P-23, No. 43) Washington, D.C.: Government Printing Office, 1973.

Physiology of Aging

NATHAN W. SHOCK

Nathan W. Shock received his B.S. degree in chemistry from Purdue University in 1926, his M.S. degree in organic chemistry from the same university in 1927, and his Ph.D. in physiological psychology from the University of Chicago in 1930. After research and teaching positions at the University of Chicago and the University of California, Dr. Shock became, in 1941, Chief of the Gerontology Research Center, Baltimore City Hospitals, a post which he has retained up to the present, obtaining in 1965 the additional title of Chief, Gerontology Research Center, National Institute of Child Health and Human Development, NIH. He is the author of Trends in Gerontology *and a very large number of articles in the area of gerontology. Dr. Shock has been the recipient of a number of awards, among them the Distinguished Research Award of the Gerontological Society (1965), the Willard O. Thompson Research Award of the American Geriatrics Society (1965), and a Citation for Service, American Association of Retired Persons (1967). He served as president of the International Association of Gerontology from 1969 to 1972.*

It would appear that the major focus of attention in this book will be on the behavioral and social aspects of aging. Because of the traditional association of brain, nervous system, and sense organs with behavior, it might be assumed that my role is to indicate the changes in these organ systems with age. However, all the organ systems of the body play a part in main-

47

taining adequate functioning of the brain and the nervous system. The performance of the heart and blood vessels in maintaining an adequate blood supply to the brain, and the effectiveness of the kidneys in removing waste products from the body, play an important role. Effective oxygenation of the blood requires a respiratory system capable of providing adequate supplies of oxygen and of removing carbon dioxide from the blood. Overall feelings of health and well-being play an important role in behavior. You all have seen the anxiety which frequently develops in elderly people because they fear catastrophic illness and disability. It is, therefore, apparent to me that my role should be to present to you the broad aspects of physiological changes which occur with aging to give you a general picture of what constitutes normal aging. Those who need to deal with aging and the aged and to offer solutions for their problems should know something about both the limitations and the potentials for performance in the aged. Furthermore, the aged themselves would, I believe, gain strength from knowledge about themselves and the changes which are apt to occur with the passage of time.

Aging is a process which takes place over the entire adult life span. Aging represents the progressive, irreversible changes which occur in a cell, an organ, or the total organism with the passage of time. It is as much a part of living as is infancy, childhood, and adolescence. The central biological fact of aging is that the probability of death increases logarithmically with age. For American white males, mortality increases at an accelerating rate with age from a level of about 3.3 deaths per year per thousand population at age 35–44 to 98.3 deaths per year per thousand at age 75–84 (U. S. Department of Health, Education & Welfare, 1972). In fact, the probability of death doubles every 8½ years (Jones, 1959). Since humans die of diseases and not of old age itself, it is clear that aging represents the underlying processes which increase vulnerability to disease. Aging and disease are not synonymous, although aged people with disease represent the most visible group of aged in our population as seen by physicians, social workers, and others who must render services. However, only 5% of the population aged 65 and over are confined to institutions (U. S. Department of Health, Education & Welfare, National Center for Health Statistics, 1972, p. 329); the other 95% of the aged population are living in the community and, although they may suffer from certain disabilities, they are not incapacitated. In fact, many elderly people regard their health status as good to excellent (Shanas, 1962).

CROSS-SECTIONAL AND LONGITUDINAL STUDIES OF AGING

Although gerontology (or the scientific study of aging) is still in its infancy, a great deal has been learned over the past 25 years. Much knowledge has been derived from studies on animal models, but I shall limit my discussion to some of the things we have learned about aging in humans. Most studies of aging have utilized the cross-sectional method: that is, measurements have been made on different individuals of varying ages, and the trend of average values has been used as an index of aging. However, since the old individuals in such a study have already been selected for long life and have experienced widely different environmental conditions, such studies can give evidence only of age differences. In order to evaluate age changes, it is necessary to make repeated observations on the same individual as he passes through life (Birren, 1959). Such longitudinal studies are obviously very difficult to organize and carry out, and very few such studies have been made: at the Boston Veterans Administration Hospital (Bell, Rose, & Damon, 1972); Duke University (Palmore, 1970); Framingham, Massachusetts (Kannel, 1970); Tecumseh, Michigan (Francis, 1961); and the Gerontology Research Center in Baltimore. Most of these studies, including our own, which is based on 650 male volunteer subjects, are still in progress so that most of the data which I shall present are based on cross-sectional studies. However, preliminary analysis of our own longitudinal data indicates that results from cross-sectional studies usually give valid estimates of the average effects of age on many physiological functions.

PHYSIOLOGICAL CHANGES WITH AGE

Not all physiological functions show decrements with age. For example, fasting blood-sugar levels (Smith & Shock, 1949), the acidity of the blood (Shock & Yiengst, 1950), its electrolyte content, osmotic pressure and total volume (Cohn & Shock, 1949) remain unchanged even into advanced old age. These characteristics maintain a uniform composition of the fluids which constitute the environment of the individual cells of the body. Thus the internal environment is closely regulated, at least under basal or resting conditions, into advanced old age.

However, many physiological functions show gradual decrements beginning at age 25 to 30 and extending to age 80 or 90 (Shock, 1962). No functions show any evidence of a sudden decrement at any given chronological age. It must be remembered that these age curves are based on averages and that it is still possible that the rate of decrement may increase at advanced ages in some individuals.

Cardiac Output

Resting cardiac output, or the amount of blood pumped by the heart per minute, falls from an average of 3.54 $L/M^2/min.$ at age 30 to an average of 2.56 at age 80 (Brandfonbrener, Landowne, & Shock, 1955) [Fig. 1]. Examination of Figure 1 in which each point represents determinations on a given subject shows that there are wide individual differences in the effects

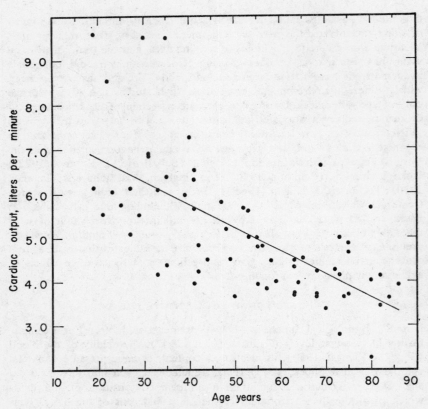

FIG. 1. The Relation Between Resting Cardiac Output and Age in 67 Males Without Circulatory Disorders. The line represents the linear regression on age. [From: Brandfonbrener, Landowne, & Shock, 1955; reprinted by permission.]

of age. Some individuals in their 70s have a cardiac output as good as the average value for 40-year-olds. This wide range in individual differences is characteristic of all the physiological functions we have measured. The important point to note is that aging is a highly individualistic affair, and chronological age alone is not a very good predictor of performance capacity.

Kidney Functioning

Kidney functions also show a gradual loss of approximately 50% over the age span from 30 to 80 years (Shock, 1952). Detailed physiological tests show that part of this reduction in kidney function is the result of a progressive loss of specific structures in the kidney (nephrons) which participate in the process of urine formation and the excretion of waste products (Oliver, 1952). Furthermore, the sensitivity of a kidney to respond to the hormonal signals which regulate the amount of urine excreted is diminished (Miller & Shock, 1953). In other words, more of the hormone signal must reach the kidney in the old animal than in the young in order to change the characteristics of the urine which is excreted. Thus, aging in the kidney is characterized in part by loss of the number of functioning units and by a reduction in their sensitivity to control mechanisms. These characteristics represent general physiological aspects of aging which are also seen in other organ systems.

Pulmonary Functioning

Pulmonary functions also show progressive decrements with age. Vital capacity, or the maximum amount of air which can be expired in a single breath, diminishes from 4.5 L to 2.36 L between the ages of 30 and 80 years (Norris, Shock, Landowne, & Falzone, 1956). Total lung volume undergoes a similar decrement (5.82 L to 4.66 L), but the residual lung volume—that is, the amount of air in the lung which cannot be expired voluntarily—increases by approximately 20% (1.33 L to 2.30 L). The greatest decrement in pulmonary function is found in the maximum breathing capacity—that is, the amount of air which can be voluntarily moved in and out of the lungs in 15 seconds. The average maximum breathing capacity falls from 131 L/min. in 30-year-olds to 50 L/min. in 80-year-olds. This test is of special significance since it involves coordinated movements of voluntary breathing as rapidly as possible. It was found that the age decrement is primarily due to the inability of the older subjects to produce as many breaths in the time allowed as do the young. This illustrates a third general principle of aging: that is, that older subjects show impairments in voluntary control mechanisms and are unable to perform as quickly as can the young.

Basal Metabolism

Basal metabolism, or the amount of oxygen consumed by an individual at rest, shows a gradual decrement between the ages of 30 and 90 (Shock, Watkin, Yiengst, Norris, Gaffney, Gregerman, & Falzone, 1963). Since large individuals will obviously require more oxygen than will small, these measurements are usually adjusted for size by dividing by the surface area of the individual. However, surface area is calculated by a formula based on height and weight. Many adults increase in weight by accumulation of fat. But fat does not require oxygen for its maintenance as does muscle or other functioning tissues so that the calculated surface area is no longer related to the amount of functioning tissue in the individual. Consequently, the basal metabolism per unit of surface area may fall with increasing age simply because body weight increases. When a more physiological estimate of functioning tissue in the body is used as a correction factor (as, for example, the intracellular water content), the age decrement in basal metabolism disappears. The apparent decrement in basal metabolism with age is an artifact and does not indicate that the rate of metabolism of individual cells in the body is slowing down.

Aging in the Endocrine System

The endocrine glands play an important role in the regulation of many physiological processes. The pituitary gland is often characterized as the master organ of the body since it secretes hormones which serve as messengers to other glands of the body—such as the thyroid, the adrenal, and the gonads—and regulates their activity (Freeman, 1967; McGavack, 1967). Some hormones are directly related to behavioral characteristics as well. For example, extreme hypothyroidism results in cretinism, with its attendant impairment of development of mental functions. There is, however, no evidence that aging impairs the ability of the thyroid gland to produce thyroxine (Gregerman, 1967).

Although the sex hormones influence the development of sexual behavior in humans, it is now clear that sexual behavior in mature adults is more closely related to the pattern of sexual behavior developed early in life than it is to the level of sex hormones in the blood (Pfeiffer & Davis, 1972). Interestingly, many of the attempts to increase life span and to improve health status in the later years have focused their attention on the sex glands (McGrady, 1968). Thus the early attempts at rejuvenation in males by the injection of testicular extracts and, later, by the transplantation of testicular tissue were forms of therapy which were seriously pursued in the early part of the century. Time has shown that none of these procedures had any long-term effect on physical vigor or on longevity. It is now recognized that estimates of the amount of a hormone in the circulating blood is a poor index of the level of activity of the gland itself and gives little information about the amount of hormone which is available for physiologic utilization (Gregerman & Bierman, 1974). For the amount of hormone in the blood at any time depends not only on the amount being produced by the gland but also the amount which is being removed by other organs. Furthermore, it is now known that many of the hormones are bound to proteins in the blood and are physiologically inactive. Thus an estimate of the functional activity of any gland requires very complicated experiments which cannot be applied to human subjects. In recent years new methods have been developed which, it is hoped, can resolve many of these questions. In the case of testosterone, blood levels in 80- to 90-year-old subjects is only 40% of that found in 30-year-olds (Vermeulen, Rubens, & Verdonck, 1972). However, individual differences are extremely large, and no experiments have yet been conducted to relate sexual activity with testosterone blood-levels in individual subjects.

The ovary undergoes age changes which result in a progressive reduction of the rate of egg production. In the human female, ovarian senescence is expressed by the menopause, when egg production ceases and production of female sex hormones falls precipitously. After the age of 40 there is a decrease in estrogen excretion (Pincus, Romanoff, & Carlo, 1954), and by the age of 60 blood levels of estradiol in human females falls to 10% of the levels observed in young menstruating females (Longcope, 1971). The full physiological significance of the reduction in the production of female sex hormones is not understood, but it may play a role in the increased vulnerability of post-menopausal females to diseases, such as heart disease (Furman, 1973) and osteoporosis (Heaney, 1973).

Time will not permit a detailed review of age changes in individual endocrine glands. However, the results of many studies may be summarized generally with the statement that impaired ability to produce its specific hormone has not been observed in the pituitary, adrenal, pancreas, or parathyroid gland. However, a number of specific glands (the pituitary and the pancreas, for example) show a reduced sensitivity to the physiological stimulus which ordinarily induces the release of hormone (Andres, 1972; Andres, Pozefsky, Swerdloff, & Tobin, 1970). For example, the release of insulin by the pancreas is stimulated by a rise in the blood-sugar level. With increasing age a significantly greater increase in the blood-sugar level is required to stimulate the release of insulin into the blood from the gland. Similarly, the pituitary shows a decreased sensitivity to releasing hormones of the hypothalamus with an increase in age (Pecile, Müller, Falconi, & Martini, 1965). Thus aging in the endocrine system is, to a large extent, a reflection of the breakdown of control mechanisms which is primarily related to a reduction in sensitivity of the gland to regulatory stimuli.

Muscle Strength

Muscle strength rises to a peak at about 35 years of age and then undergoes a gradual reduction over the remaining life span so that at age 80 average muscle strength in males is approximately the same as that of 12-year-old boys (Birren, 1959). Biochemical studies on muscles show that the changes with age are very similar to those which occur over a short period of time when specific muscles in young animals are immobilized (Yiengst, Barrows,

& Shock, 1959). Histological studies also show a loss of functioning muscle fibers with advancing age (Andrew, Shock, Barrows, & Yiengst, 1959). Thus it appears that part of this loss in muscle strength is in reality an atrophy from disuse.

Exercise

The performance of physical work or exercise requires the integrated activity of the circulatory, respiratory, endocrine, and neuro-muscular systems of the body. The overall effects of aging on the capacity to perform muscular work are, first of all, a reduction in the maximum rate at which work can be performed and, secondly, an increase in the time required to readjust physiological characteristics to the pre-work levels. The maximum rate of work, as well as the maximum amount of oxygen which can be delivered to working muscles, fall by about 60% over the age span of 20 to 80 years (Norris & Shock, 1960). Young adult males can, under conditions of maximum work-output, increase their heart rate from resting values of 60–70 beats per minute to as much as 180–200 beats per minute (Robinson, 1938). In contrast, males over the age of 70 can achieve maximum heart rates of only 150–160. The same amount of sub-maximal exercise induces a greater increment in heart rate and blood pressure in old subjects than in young (Norris, Shock, & Yiengst, 1953). Furthermore, more time is required in the old subjects than in the young for the return of heart rate and blood pressure to resting values after displacement by exercise. Thus the overall effect of aging is a diminished capacity for work, which probably is a reflection of impaired control mechanisms as well as a reduction in muscle elements. From the standpoint of behavior, these limitations in work capacity are of considerable importance since the subject himself may become increasingly aware of his limitations.

Loss of Sensory Functions

The loss of sensory functions with increasing age plays an important role in behavioral characteristics of the elderly. Visual acuity diminishes, and the range of accommodation of the eye is reduced. The incidence of glaucoma and cataract, both diseases of the eye, increases progressively with age. Some loss of hearing occurs, especially for tones of frequency over 4,000–5,000 cycles per second (McFarland, 1968; Weiss, 1959). This loss of perception of higher frequencies is of special significance in the understanding and comprehension of the spoken word. Although deficits in both vision and hearing are associated with advancing age, it should be emphasized that the effects of these deficits can be minimized by the appropriate use of glasses and hearing aids.

Role of the Central Nervous System

The pivotal role of the nervous system in determining and modulating behavior leads to the presumption that it is here that age changes can best be identified. But this is an extremely difficult assignment since neither physiologists nor biochemists have as yet been able to identify the physiological basis of important behavioral mechanisms such as learning, memory, motivation, etc. Studies on the biochemical characteristics of brain tissue are not very informative since the results are based on an unknown mixture of neuronal and glial, or supporting, cells in the brain tissue (Perez & Moore, 1970). Physiological studies have shown a small decrement in the speed of conduction in peripheral nerves, but the fall is not great enough to explain the reduction in speed of response which is seen with advancing age (Norris, Shock, & Wagman, 1953). Choice reaction time is lengthened in the elderly more than is simple reaction time (Welford, 1959). Such results lead to the presumption that slowing of response time in the elderly is related more to interconnecting events which occur within the central nervous system than to simple conduction time or even synaptic delays. It is true that the frequency of the alpha rhythm of the electroencephalogram slows with advancing age, but the relationship of this phenomenon to behavioral characteristics is not clear (Obrist, 1965; Shmavonian, Yarmat, & Cohen, 1965). It is often presumed that impairments of mental function represent a reduction in cerebral blood flow, with a resultant anoxia or impairment of the delivery of substrates necessary for neural function (McFarland, 1968). Measurements of cerebral blood flow show a slight reduction with advancing age, but there is very little difference between the cerebral blood flow of 60-year-olds and 80-year-olds (Kety, 1960). There is also histological evidence for the loss of neurons with advancing age, but here again the loss is gradual over the entire life span and does not seem to be large enough to explain the changes seen in the behavioral characteristics (Brody, 1970).

Differential Effect of Aging on Different Organ Systems

From this brief and somewhat superficial review of age changes in various organ systems, it is clear that aging does not affect all systems in a comparable fashion [Fig. 2]. The amount of decrement over the age span of 30–80 years ranges from zero for certain blood characteristics such as fasting blood-sugar, 10% or 15% for nerve-conduction velocity, 15%–20% for basal metabolic rate based on surface area, to 40%–50% for cardiac output and 50%–60% for more complex performances such as maximum breathing capacity and physical exercise (Shock & Solomon, 1972).

These differences between organ systems raise the question as to whether there is a general aging phenomenon. It is the belief of some gerontologists

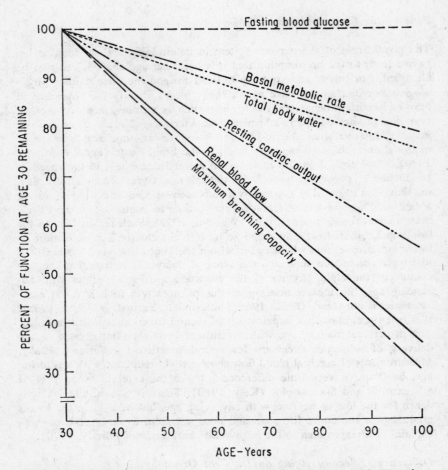

FIG. 2. Estimated Linear Age Decrements for Different Physiologic Functions; fasting blood glucose (data from Smith & Shock, 1949), basal metabolic rate (data from Shock, Watkin, Yiengst, Norris, Gaffney, Gregerman, & Falzone, 1963), total body water (data from Brandfonbrener, Landowne, & Shock, 1955), renal blood flow (data from Shock, 1952), maximum breathing capacity (data from Norris, Shock, Landowne, & Falzone, 1956). The average value for 30-year-old subjects is taken as 100% for each function and linear decrements with increasing age are plotted as percent of the mean value at age 30. [Figure from Shock & Solomon, 1972; reprinted by permission.]

that there is perhaps a single key process, presumably at the cellular level, which represents an underlying cause of aging (Strehler, 1962). At present we simply do not know whether or not this is true. But it seems more probable that aging, as we know it in the human at least, is the net result of a number of processes which may be going on at different rates within the same individual.

Since length of life is, at least to some extent, genetically determined, a key question is the extent to which life span can be altered by environmental factors. At the present time, few individuals attain their full genetic potential life span because of the effects of diseases. Consequently, any changes in regime which will delay or prevent the occurrence of diseases, such as cardiovascular diseases and cancer, will have an impact. Yet there is no evidence that a drug, such as procaine, or treatments with cellular extracts, or the administration of hormones, will significantly improve life span (McGrady, 1968). On the other hand, we know that there are certain environmental factors which will increase the probability of death (Kannel, 1970). Some of these risk factors are the following: (1) The presence of obesity. With increasing degrees of overweight, the probability of developing a number of diseases—such as arteriosclerosis, hypertension, diabetes, and joint disease—increases significantly. (2) Cigarette smoking is also a risk factor which increases the probability of developing not only lung cancer but also cardiovascular disease. (3) The consumption of excessive amounts of fat in the diet increases the risk of developing atherosclerosis. As more and more is learned about the basic mechanisms of aging, we will undoubtedly be able to add other environmental factors to this list.

SUMMARY

I have tried to make the following points:

1. Aging is a normal phenomenon, part of the total developmental sequence in the total life cycle.

2. From a physiological standpoint, some functions, such as the characteristics of the blood, are well maintained even into advanced old age.

3. In the physiological systems which do show decrements, the reduction in function takes place gradually over the entire age span. At present, there is no evidence that the rate of change in physiological characteristics increases markedly at any specific chronological age.

4. There are marked individual differences in the effects of age.

5. Age affects different organ systems differently.

6. Aging is characterized by a reduction in reserve capacities. A part of this reduction in reserve can be attributed to the loss of cells and functioning units in different organs of the body.

7. Age changes in cellular enzymes are minimal.

8. With increasing age, physiological responses and adjustments to stresses are slower. Although the aged subject may be able to carry out the appropriate adjustment to a stress, he requires more time to do so than does a young individual.

9. Sensory inputs are diminished in quantity and quality in the aged.

10. Aging is a reflection of impairments in the sensitivity and adequacy of many physiological control mechanisms.

11. Environmental factors can influence the basic genetic pattern of aging.

12. There is a need for more information on the physiological and biological mechanisms of aging.

REFERENCES

Andres, R. Aging and carbohydrate metabolism. In L. A. Carlson (Ed.) *Nutrition in old age.* Uppsala: Almquist & Wiksell, 1972. Pp. 24–29.

Andres, R., Pozefsky, T., Swerdloff, R. S., & Tobin, J. D. Effects of aging on carbohydrate metabolism. In R. A. Camerini-Davalos & H. S. Cole (Eds.) *Early diabetes.* New York: Academic, 1970. Pp. 349–355.

Andrew, W., Shock, N. W., Barrows, C. H., Jr., & Yiengst, M. J. Correlation of age changes in histological and chemical characteristics in some tissues of the rat. *Journal of Gerontology,* 1959, *14,* 405–414.

Bell, B., Rose, C. L., & Damon, A. The Normative Aging Study: An interdisciplinary and longitudinal study of health and aging. *Aging & Human Development,* 1972, *3,* 5–18.

Birren, J. E. Principles of research on aging. In J. E. Birren (Ed.) *Handbook of aging and the individual: Psychological and biological aspects.* Chicago: University of Chicago Press, 1959. Pp. 3–42.

Brandfonbrener, M., Landowne, M., & Shock, N. W. Changes in cardiac output with age. *Circulation,* 1955, *12,* 557–566.

Brody, H. Structural changes in the aging nervous system. In H. T. Blumenthal (Ed.) *Interdisciplinary topics in gerontology.* Vol. 7. *The regulatory role of the nervous system in aging.* Basel: Karger, 1970. Pp. 9–21.

Cohn, J. E., & Shock, N. W. Blood volume studies in middle-aged and elderly males. *American Journal of Medical Sciences,* 1949, *217,* 388–391.

Francis, T., Jr. Aspects of the Tecumseh study. *Public Health Reports,* 1961, *76,* 963–965.

Freeman, J. T. Endocrinology in geriatrics; historical background. In L. Gitman (Ed.) *Endocrines and aging.* Springfield, Ill.: Thomas, 1967. Pp. 3–35.

Furman, R. H. Coronary heart disease and the menopause. In K. J. Ryan & D. C. Gibson (Eds.) *Menopause and aging.* (DHEW Publ. [NIH] 73–319.) Washington, D.C.: Government Printing Office, 1973. Pp. 39–55.

Gregerman, R. I. The age-related alteration of thyroid function and thyroid hormone metabolism in man. In L. Gitman (Ed.) *Endocrines and aging.* Springfield, Ill.: Thomas, 1967. Pp. 161–173.

Gregerman, R. I., & Bierman, E. L. Aging and hormones. In R. H. Williams (Ed.) *Textbook of endocrinology.* (5th ed.) Philadelphia: Saunders, 1974. Pp. 1059–1070.

Heaney, R. P. Menopausal effects on calcium homeostasis and skeletal metabolism.

In K. J. Ryan & D. C. Gibson (Eds.) *Menopause and aging.* (DHEW Publ. [NIH] 73–319.) Washington, D.C.: Government Printing Office, 1973. Pp. 59–67.

Jones, H. B. The relation of human health to age, place, and time. In J. E. Birren (Ed.) *Handbook of aging and the individual: Psychological and biological aspects.* Chicago: University of Chicago Press, 1959. Pp. 336–360.

Kannel, W. B. The Framingham Study and chronic disease prevention. *Hospital Practice,* 1970, *5,* 78–81; 85–87; 92–94.

Kety, S. S. The cerebral circulation. In J. Field, H. W. Mangoun, & V. E. Hall (Eds.) *Handbook of physiology,* Section 1: *Neurophysiology.* Vol. III. Washington, D.C.: American Physiological Society, 1960. Pp. 1751–1760.

Longcope, C. Metabolic clearance and blood production rates of estrogens in post-menopausal women. *American Journal of Obstetrics and Gynecology,* 1971, *111,* 778–781.

McFarland, R. A. The sensory and perceptual processes in aging. In K. W. Schaie (Ed.) *Theory and methods of research on aging.* Morgantown: West Virginia University Press, 1968. Pp. 9–52.

McGavack, T. H. Endocrine ichnography of aging. In L. Gitman (Ed.) *Endocrines and aging.* Springfield, Ill.: Thomas, 1967. Pp. 36–50.

McGrady, P. M., Jr. *The youth doctors.* New York: Coward-McCann, 1968.

Miller, J. H., & Shock, N. W. Age differences in the renal tubular response to antidiuretic hormone. *Journal of Gerontology,* 1953, *8,* 446–450.

Norris, A. H., & Shock, N. W. Exercise in the adult years—with special reference to the advanced years. In W. R. Johnson (Ed.), *Science and medicine of exercise and sports.* New York: Harper, 1960. Pp. 466–490.

Norris, A. H., Shock, N. W., Landowne, M., & Falzone, J. A., Jr. Pulmonary function studies; age differences in lung volumes and bellows function. *Journal of Gerontology,* 1956, *11,* 379–387.

Norris, A. H., Shock, N. W., & Wagman, I. H. Age changes in the maximum conduction velocity of motor fibers of human ulnar nerves. *Journal of Applied Physiology,* 1953, *5,* 589–593.

Norris, A. H., Shock, N. W., & Yiengst, M. J. Age changes in heart rate and blood pressure responses to tilting and standardized exercise. *Circulation,* 1953, *8,* 521–526.

Obrist, W. D. Electroencephalographic approach to age changes in response speed. In A. T. Welford & J. E. Birren (Eds.) *Behavior, aging, and the nervous system.* Springfield, Ill.: Thomas, 1965. Pp. 259–271.

Oliver, J. R. Urinary system. In A. I. Lansing (Ed.) *Cowdry's problems of ageing.* (3rd. ed.) Baltimore: Williams & Wilkins, 1952. Pp. 631–650.

Palmore, E. (Ed.) *Normal Aging.* Durham, N.C.: Duke University Press, 1970.

Pecile, A., Müller, E., Falconi, G., & Martini, L. Growth hormone-releasing activity of hypothalamic extracts at different ages. *Endocrinology,* 1965, *77,* 241–246.

Perez, V. J., & Moore, B. W. Biochemistry of the nervous system in aging. In H. T. Blumenthal (Ed.) *Interdisciplinary topics in gerontology.* Vol. 7. *The regulatory role of the nervous system in aging.* Basel: Karger, 1970. Pp. 22–45.

Pfeiffer, E., & Davis, G. C. Determinants of sexual behavior in middle and old age. *Journal of the American Geriatrics Society,* 1972, *20,* 151–158.

Pincus, G., Romanoff, L. P., & Carlo, J. Excretion of urinary steroids by men and women of various ages. *Journal of Gerontology,* 1954, *9,* 113–132.

Robinson, S. Experimental studies of physical fitness in relation to age. *Arbeitsphysiologie,* 1938, *10,* 251–323.

Shanas, E. *The health of older people: A social survey.* Cambridge: Harvard University Press, 1962.

Shmavonian, B. M., Yarmat, A. J., & Cohen, S. I. Relationships between the autonomic nervous system and central nervous system in age differences in behavior. In A. T. Welford & J. E. Birren (Eds.) *Behavior, aging, and the nervous system.* Springfield, Ill.: Thomas, 1965. Pp. 235–258.

Shock, N. W. Age changes in renal function. In A. I. Lansing (Ed.) *Cowdry's problems of ageing.* (3rd ed.) Baltimore: Williams & Wilkins, 1952. Pp. 614–630.

Shock, N. W. The physiology of aging. *Scientific American*, 1962, *206*, 100–110.

Shock, N. W., & Solomon, N. Physiology of aging. In A. Davidoff, S. Winkler, & M. H. M. Lee (Eds.) *Dentistry for the special patient: The aged, chronically ill and handicapped.* Philadelphia: Saunders, 1972. Pp. 13–24.

Shock, N. W., Watkin, D. M., Yiengst, M. J., Norris, A. H., Gaffney, G. W., Gregerman, R. I., & Falzone, J. A. Age differences in the water content of the body as related to basal oxygen consumption in males. *Journal of Gerontology,* 1963, *18,* 1–8.

Shock, N. W., & Yiengst, M. J. Age changes in acid-base equilibrium of the blood of males. *Journal of Gerontology,* 1950, *5,* 1–4.

Smith, L. E., & Shock, N. W. Intravenous glucose tolerance tests in aged males. *Journal of Gerontology,* 1949, *4,* 27–33.

Strehler, B. L. *Time, cells, and aging.* New York: Academic, 1962.

U. S. Department of Health, Education & Welfare. Annual summary for the United States, 1971; births, deaths, marriages, and divorces. *Monthly Vital Statistics Report,* Aug. 30, 1972, *20,* 17.

U. S. Department of Health, Education & Welfare, National Center for Health Statistics. *Health resources statistics: Health manpower and health facilities, 1971.* (DHEW Publ. [HSM] 72–1509.) Washington, D.C.: Government Printing Office, 1972.

Vermeulen, A., Rubens, R., & Verdonck, L. Testosterone secretion and metabolism in male senescence. *Journal of Clinical Endocrinology and Metabolism,* 1972, *34,* 730–735.

Weiss, A. D. Sensory functions. In J. E. Birren (Ed.) *Handbook of aging and the individual: Psychological and biological aspects.* Chicago: University of Chicago Press, 1959. Pp. 503–542.

Welford, A. T. Psychomotor performance. In J. E. Birren (Ed.) *Handbook of aging and the individual: Psychological and biological aspects.* Chicago: University of Chicago Press, 1959. Pp. 562–613.

Yiengst, M. J., Barrows, C. H., Jr., & Shock, N. W. Age changes in the chemical composition of muscle and liver in the rat. *Journal of Gerontology,* 1959, *14,* 400–404.

Sociology of Aging

HOWARD A. ROSENCRANZ

Howard A. Rosencranz was born and educated in the Midwest. His undergraduate degree is from Winona State College, Minnesota, and his graduate degrees from Michigan State University. After a period at the University of Missouri, he came to the University of Connecticut in 1969. In his professional career, Dr. Rosencranz has long been identified with the field of gerontology. He has been a member of the State of Missouri Mental Health Committee for the Aged, 1964–1965; a member of the Committee on Research and Special Projects of the Psychological and Social Science Section of the Gerontological Society, 1967–1968; Vice Chairman of the Midwest Council for Social Research on Aging, 1966–1967; and Vice President of the Connecticut Society of Gerontology, 1971–1972. His professional publications reflect this same abiding interest. Currently, Dr. Rosencranz is Professor at the University of Connecticut and Director of the University Program of Gerontology.

Regardless of the particular substantive discipline, the observation is often made that aging is a statement of change. To this the sociologist would add—not only individual, but group change. In one sense, the sociologist's contribution to understanding the aging process lies in the examination of the relationships between aging persons and their changing social context.

From the biologist and psychologist we learn about the modalities of decrement which aging organisms experience as longevity increases. From the ethnographer we become aware of the regularized patterns which different societies consciously or unconsciously establish for and toward their elderly. From the data of the demographer, age-composition analyses suggest effects of changing numbers of young and old in given human populations, factors which establish the foundations of socio-economic-political systems at given points in time.

It is most important to realize that these multidisciplinary components are not separable phenomena and that it is the interaction between societal structures and individual adaptations which are responsible for the changing role and status of older people.

Remedial policies, rationally planned to solve problems, themselves become forces—structures if you please—which create new adaptive behavior patterns. For example, the Social Security System, originally devised as an income-maintenance program, has served 1) to define old age at year 65 (a definition persistently used even though it ignores more appropriate biological, behavioral, and social considerations) and 2) to delineate the "expected" age of male retirement in our society. Thus we see that aspects of interrelatedness, causes and effects, overlap and transcend traditional areas of inquiry. Suddenly the sociologist discovers that "state of health" becomes a critical social variable, just as more and more he finds himself examining such social-psychological variables as self-concept and morale.

If the sociologist traditionally examines the fabric of society by utilizing such constructs as social institution and social roles, and by describing the salient social structures which affect and are affected by participants within the structures, then in studying aging, one of the major questions becomes, "What is happening to older people today and in what ways are they contributing to the changes which affect all of us?"

IMPACT OF AGING ON FAMILY RELATIONSHIPS

Let us begin with the family and consider in turn more recent findings for other social institutions. Our first consideration, then, will be family relationships.

The impact of aging on the family appears to be changes of quality and intensity rather than of kind. Periodically—about every two decades—a few observers of social process become quite convinced that the American family is "going to pot" (no pun intended). But it is predicted that the young, the old, technology, divorce rates, or women's "lib" will "seal the doom" of this primary social unit. And yet on the functional level the family persists. In gerontological literature one very popular topic of discussion some time ago centered upon the demise of the extended family, particularly in reference to the consequences for older people. The idealized large-sized, multigenerational family living under one roof, characteristically and romantically associated with "better times," probably never was a common pattern in this country. (An exception might be found in some rural areas and among certain ethnic groups.) Early census data suggest that in colonial America four persons constituted a more common household size; few families consisted of three generations. Median household size was fewer than six in 1790 and in 1850. Similarly, Eugene Friedman points out that "mobility" is not a recent occurrence in American life nor should it be attributed only to urbanization. "The frontier" provided aspiration as well as opportunity for sons to leave parental households (Friedman, 1960).

Yet we all know that certain changes have taken place. It seems that the usual functions and events within the family are occurring at different times in the life cycle. Marriage occurs earlier; birth of the first child and marriage of the last child occur earlier; with increased life expectancy, death for both spouses occurs later. These changes indirectly affect older people, but to a greater extent they affect parental role by decreasing the duration of the major *adult-role* or middle-age functions. Older people have, of course, been affected by other shifts such as increased geographical separation of nuclear units, increases in independent living arrangements, increased numbers of working married women, and growth of economic structures which perpetuate independence among family members. In peculiar ways these shifts contribute to reduced interaction of older people with middle-aged children. Several studies, based on large-scale samples, suggest that the social isolation experienced by some elderly is less a consequence of family dissolution, or of rejection of older persons by middle-aged children, than it is of new conditions in which the "very" old find themselves.

Take the grandparent role as a case, especially for women. From one point of view it may be said that longer survivorship "uses up" this role. I am suggesting that the traditional concept of "grandparenting" applies to the mutual relationship between an old person and the very young, wherein the older kin provides guidance, care, and early socialization experiences. Is this not a more atypical expectation to be extending to late teen-agers and young adults, who are full-fledged citizens at age 18?

Today, longer life has provided a greater generational overlap. The kinship pattern is still there, but the former content of the extended role no longer applies. At least four additional social factors contribute to the demise of the classical concept of the older person's role in the family: (1) the present generation of elderly are essentially homeowners and are reluctant to give up their homes; (2) money from children and relatives is almost the smallest source of income for the elderly, but the elderly do not want much help from children; (3) the category of elderly who could benefit most from economic and emotional support are persons who have never married or who are without relatives; (4) increased widowhood and second marriages do change the relationship between middle-aged children and older parents.

SECOND MARRIAGES FOR THE ELDERLY

Let us speak for a moment about widowhood since the gap between death rates for males and females has been steadily increasing. Projections indicate that by 1990 there will be 170 women aged 75 and over for every 100 men over age 75. Today for this same age bracket, 6 of every 10 persons are women. The large number of widows determines other social and family characteristics, especially *living arrangements* and *income*. Income among elderly living alone, or not in family contexts, is less than one-half of that of elderly with spouses and family. Increasingly, second marriage for older people is a pattern which helps alleviate low income and loneliness, and perpetuate independence from children. Yet while most second marriages are successful, and provide continued economic and social autonomy for the older couple, remarriage is sometimes dimly viewed by middle-aged children who seemingly question the capabilities of their older parents for making proper choices (McKain, 1969).

Harold Brotman estimates that in an average year there will be "almost 2,000 blushing 75+ brides and more than 6,000 nervous 75+ grooms going to the altar and moving out of widowhood" (Brotman, 1968, p. 6). And notice that these were figures for people age 75 and over. If those between 65 and 74 years of age are included, second marriages of older people become a significant new social pattern.

While additional family changes could be enumerated, it might be said in summary that patterns for contemporary older persons in the United States, when compared to those in earlier periods, suggest less "role-loss" than existence for a longer period with fewer defined behavioral expectations, and with newer roles still in the process of being regularized. Certainly, it is evident that most healthy and economically able older people have options for continued family participation with their children, and with their children's children, and, within the context of possible second marriages after the death of a spouse, for new conjugal relationships. It is also clear that these options are not always chosen.

MALE PARTICIPATION IN THE LABOR FORCE

Closely tied to family organization is male participation in the labor force. The meaning of work as a major life role for males in our society is quite well understood insofar as it is a determinant of status, lifestyle, free time, and daily routine, as well as of economic return. Similarly, we are in a better position to understand the importance and social and psychological effects of the loss of this role today. Less well understood is the differential reaction to the loss of work. Since retirement is a critical stage of transformation in the life cycle, the trends of earlier retirement should be mentioned.

In industrial societies throughout the world, the proportion of men age 65 and over still in the labor force has been declining for a number of years. Though some interruptions occur, this decline is attributable partly to shifts in occupational and industrial structures, to rising income levels, to social security programs, and to such factors as the age-composition of a population which yields the numbers of people available for productivity. In this country in 1900, two-thirds of all males over age 65 were still working. By 1970 this percentage dwindled to 25%. Both "voluntary" retirement and compulsory retirement are increasing (Palmore, 1964).

Generally, when workers have the choice of continued work, economic deprivation and health status appear to loom large as factors taken into consideration. But other variables also affect the retirement decision. For example, until at least the recent past, as one ascended the occupational hierarchy from unskilled to professional and managerial jobs, the more likely it would be that one would be in a position to have options available, including choice of retirement age. Of course, as the bureaucratization of the work organization increases, elements of autonomy are declining, and for the professional as well, including lawyers and doctors. But self-employed persons still have such prerogatives. What is interesting, as Strieb and Schneider and other researchers have discovered, is that those who, by virtue of income and lifestyle, have the potential for enjoying retirement most are also those who have the option for continued work, and frequently choose it (Streib & Schneider, 1971). So commitment to work, enjoyment of it, and attitudes toward retirement must be added to the factors mentioned first, income and health. If dissatisfaction with work continues at the level which is being observed today—in a sense, a kind of dwindling work ethic—if leisure-time experiences (such as industrial sabbaticals) become more common during the middle years, and if the security of adequate retirement income continues to be a governmental responsibility, then retirement may be less problematic. Repeated amendments to the original Social Security system have increased retirement incomes, and, more recently, governmental monitoring of private and corporate pension plans bespeak the likelihood of future income maintenance for older people in our society.

LEISURE ACTIVITIES

Leisure represents the opposite side of the coin of work. The "elusive" aspects of leisure reside in the realm of satisfaction which the leisure activities provide. While it is no profound task to tabulate activities people engage in—we all have seen reports on hours spent watching television, fishing, gardening, etc.—it is more difficult to categorize the gratifications these activities provide. Dollars spent on leisure activities or leisure-time equipment are also periodically reported. Both these types of "leisure-reckoning" dramatically underscore leisure gains as far as people in this country are concerned. Students of leisure, such as Max Kaplan, point out that the worker of the Western world, but especially the retiree, has increased amounts of "block or lump" time (i.e., more periods of continuous free time) at his disposal (Kaplan, 1960). Juanita Kreps finds a reduction in both total years of work and total hours per week (Kreps, 1963).

The paradox which remains with respect to leisure, even at the definition level, is the realization that work activities for one person represent leisure activities for another. Carpentry would be an example. And beyond this, a feature which disturbs many gerontologists is that, although idleness and meditation may be acceptable for St. Thomas and for the gurus of teenagers today, American activity-oriented middle-agers become distraught when grandpa sits on the porch in his rocking chair for undue lengths of time. While there is some evidence, based on life-satisfaction scales and morale measures, that older people who participate in social groups and in a variety of activities are happier and more satisfied with life than those who do not, there is the increasing recognition that it is an error to make middle-age activity standards a criterion for good adjustment in later life.

SOCIAL PARTICIPATION PATTERNS

Turning last to social participation patterns of older people: these, as we might expect, do decrease with age, especially for the "very old." This decrease in both formal organizations and informal group membership is less evident immediately after retirement for both the worker and his spouse. Political participation, at least at the voting level, is high for the "young" old; only middle-agers turn out for the polls with more regularity. On the other hand, the latent "Senior Power," which the large numbers of elderly potentially represent, has never quite materialized. Advocacy by middle-agers rather than by older people themselves was responsible for most of the service programs which developed for the elderly during the 1960s. Fred Cottrell outlines why a "bloc" vote of elderly has been slow in coming (Cottrell, 1960; Binstock, 1972). As they move up into later life, the newer generations of the elderly are likely to be more politically aggressive.

The participation of older persons in formal religion remains to be more thoroughly studied. It is known that, of all types of formal memberships, church membership is retained longest by older people (Rosencranz, Pihlblad, & McNevin, 1968). For the very old with health and mobility restrictions, active religious participation is often impossible. Religiosity, on the other hand, is not exclusively measured by church attendance, and the same difficulty in measuring religiosity pertains to older people as for any other age group. Social class, sex, education, and ethnicity variables may well account for differences in religiosity as they do for the different patterns seen among older people in all formal organizational participation.

However, there are newer patterns of secondary social participation emerging for elderly in the United States. Increasing "age-homogeneous" relationships are a consequence of the growth of retirement communities, of "age-segregated" residential housing, of the formation of senior citizen centers, golden-age clubs, and leisure activities in which older people associate primarily with other elderly. Furthermore, Medicare has facilitated the growth of extended-care and nursing homes for the aged (now numbering some 23,000), and such centers provide age-graded health care. This is a bothersome condition, for social planners are often convinced that older people should interact in an age-grade mix—the age-distribution one would find in a natural neighborhood. It may be a contradiction, in fact, of what older people—when the question is put to them—say they prefer. As shown in many surveys, *at the verbal level*—perhaps because they think it is expected of them—older people say they prefer to be around people of all ages. But *behaviorally* they seek out age-peers to interact with, and when choosing new housing and social activities, they frequently choose others of their own age bracket. If this seems strange, we should at least realize that other age-cohort groups from childhood on make essentially the same choices. Students of human nature should not be surprised at this predilection of older people.

DISENGAGEMENT THEORY

It would be inappropriate to conclude even a short treatment of the sociology of aging without alluding to one tentatively held theory of social aging—especially since it has received so much attention in gerontological literature. I am referring to the disengagement theory, originally postulated by Elaine Cumming and William Henry in 1961. The tenets of disengagement were an outgrowth of the Kansas City Studies of Adult Life—one of the more sophisticated social-psychological studies which was longitudinal in nature (Cumming & Henry, 1961). Essentially this non-crescive theory suggests that a mutual withdrawal takes place between the individual and his society at the end of the life cycle. Gradual elimination of participation possibilities in society, or successive role elimination, is an indication of societal retraction. It occurs simultaneously with a psychological retraction on the part of the person and is evinced in increased tendencies toward the self and an inner preoccupation. Although it does not happen at the same chronological point for all persons, and though there may be unevenness in the "mutuality" between society and the person, this developmental stage describes well a serious adjustment pattern for many elderly. Other gerontologists reject this conceptualization and not only emphasize the desirability of optimal activity and social participation, but maintain that more successful aging is demonstrated by active persons.

Finally, may I allude to the significance of social attitudes which commonly do a disservice to older people in our society, and to each of us, who will be affected by those negative stereotypes should we be fortunate enough to reach the more mature years. The social psychologist has taught us that our self-concepts are quite related to the attitudes others hold about us. In viewing older people, it is incorrect to regard all elderly as sick, dependent, politically conservative, alienated, or disadvantaged. Ethel Shanas (1962) has shown that middle-aged children tend to view older parents as sicker than they are, poorer than they are, and personally less autonomous than they are. This may be a manifestation of role-reversal or merely evidence of responsible concern. Similarly, research by Cutler (1970) and by Glenn (1972) strongly questions the belief that aging individuals become more conservative in political attitudes and values.

Generally speaking, and difficult as it is to avoid seeking "one-formula" solutions, it is important to realize that with the exception of chronicity, older persons are hardly a homogeneous group. Older persons differ from each other with respect to lifestyles, experiences, values, social class, educational attainment, and ethnicity as well as in health and income status. In fact these social characteristics, differentially found, become the crucial variables inherent in problems associated with aging.

REFERENCES

Binstock, R. H. Interest group liberalism and the politics of aging. *The Gerontologist*, 1972, *12*, 265–280.

Brotman, H. B. Who are the aged: A demographic view. Unpublished memorandum, Administration on Aging, U. S. Department of Health Education and Welfare, Washington, D.C.: 1968.

Cottrell, F. Governmental functions and the politics of age. In C. Tibbitts (Ed.) *Handbook of social gerontology: Societal aspects of aging*. Chicago: University of Chicago Press, 1960. Pp. 624–665.

Cumming, E., & Henry, W. E. *Growing old: The process of disengagement*. New York: Basic Books, 1961.

Cutler, N. E. Generation, maturation, and party affiliation: A cohort analysis. *Public Opinion Quarterly*, 1970, *33*, 583–588.

Friedman, E. A. The impact of aging on the social structure. In C. Tibbitts (Ed.) *Handbook of social gerontology: Societal aspects of aging*. Chicago: University of Chicago Press, 1960. Pp. 120–144.

Glenn, N. D., & Hefner, T. Further evidence on aging and party identification. *Public Opinion Quarterly*, 1972, *36*, 31–47.

Kaplan, M. *Leisure in America.* New York: Wiley, 1960.

Kreps, J. *Employment, income and retirement problems of the aged.* Durham, N.C.: Duke University Press, 1963.

McKain, W. C. *Retirement marriage.* (Monograph 3.) Storrs, Conn.: Agricultural Experiment Station, 1969.

Palmore, E. Retirement patterns among aged men. *Social Security Bulletin,* 1964, *27* (8), 3–10.

Rosencranz, H. A., Pihlblad, C. T., & McNevin, T. E. *Social participation of older people in the small town.* (Research monograph 2.) Columbia: University of Missouri Press, 1968.

Shanas, E. *The health of older people.* Cambridge: Harvard University Press, 1962.

Streib, G. F., & Schneider, C. J. *Retirement in American society.* Ithaca, N.Y.: Cornell University Press, 1971.

III
THE PSYCHOLOGY AND
PSYCHOPATHOLOGY OF AGING

Psychology of Aging

M. POWELL LAWTON

M. Powell Lawton received his A.B. degree from Haverford College in 1947 and his Ph.D. from Columbia University in 1952. After serving at the Veterans Administration Hospital in Providence, and the Norristown State Hospital, he came to the Philadelphia Geriatric Center in 1963, where for the past decade he has been serving as Research Psychologist, and Director of Behavioral Research. Dr. Lawton is an associate editor of Social Gerontology *and of the* Journal of Gerontology, *and co-editor, with C. Eisdorfer, of the recent publication (1973):* The psychology of aging and human development. *He is a member of the American Psychological Association, and, in keeping with his special professional interest, of the Gerontological Society.*

The psychology of aging cannot be discussed without reference to biology on one side and to society on the other. Knowing that specialists from these areas will be speaking in depth about the aging individual, I shall attempt to deal primarily with my assigned topic: The Psychology of Aging. It may be noted that Individual Differences, meaning particularly cognitive development, is another topic which will be given separate treatment in the Institute. Psychopathology and Successful Aging are still other related topics. Thus, it seems that personality—the aspect of the aging individual about which we know the least—is what is left in my hands.

PERSONALITY IN OLD AGE

It is not surprising that personality in old age is the least developed aspect of gerontological psychology. Long ago, Freud decided that the elderly were too rigid to benefit from psychoanalytic treatment, and counseled others to devote their scarce time to those who had a better chance of benefiting from the therapy. My conviction is that this particularly influential example of the "age-ism" (Butler, 1969) which infects our society has a great deal to do with our failure to explore the interior of the aged person as we have in the case of children, adolescents, and non-aged adults. A great deal of our general knowledge about personality structure and dynamics has come either directly from therapists' intensive exposure to the psyche, or from researchers who themselves have been spurred by hypotheses developed by therapists. Recent data from the National Institute of Mental Health (Kramer, Taube, & Redick, 1973) show clearly this lack of exposure. Of all the patients treated in community mental health centers, 4% were 65 and over, and in mental health clinics, only 2%, in spite of the fact that 10% of the population is in this age range. By contrast, older people constitute 22% of the group receiving the least desirable type of therapy: treatment in mental hospitals. This gross neglect of the psychiatrically disturbed older person makes clear the reasons for our lack of knowledge regarding the way in which the personalities of older people develop.

I shall offer some very brief glimpses into research approaches to the aged personality, approaches which represent widely differing methods and concepts. I shall try to portray the great complexity of the person wearing the mask of age and to argue against the idea that biology, psychology, or sociology alone can give us the key to understanding.

Much of the research on personality in the older person has emphasized its developmental aspects, including both the biological substratum and the social context of the process. The term "developmental" carries some connotation of inevitability, or regular progression through a series of stages common to all members of the species. The "growth curve" as portrayed by some developmental psychologists [Fig. 1] construes learning as stopping in early adulthood, staying on a plateau through the majority of a lifetime, and diminishing in old age. I am sure that the paper on Individual Differences will have more to say about this concept of intellect and aging. In a more general sense, I should like to call immediate attention to the limitation of this concept of the human life cycle.

ERIKSON'S DEVELOPMENTAL STAGES

A dynamic view of development sees the individual as involved in a continuous process of growth, loss, and re-stabilization throughout his lifetime.

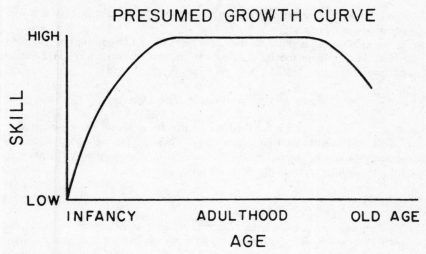

FIG. 1. Growth Curve

Erikson (1968), looking at the entire life span, conceived of personality evolution as a graded series of problem–resolution tasks which are familiar and which will not be reviewed in detail here. Passage to the successively higher developmental stages implies resolution of the conflicts characteristic of the earlier stages, though residues and transformations of these conflicts recur at later stages. For Erikson, the stages are:

1. in early infancy, the development of a sense of basic TRUST *vs.* a sense of distrust;
2. in later infancy, when anal–muscular maturation has occurred, a growing sense of AUTONOMY *vs.* a sense of shame and doubt;
3. in early childhood, the period of greatest locomotor development, a developing sense of INITIATIVE *vs.* a sense of guilt;
4. in the middle years of childhood, a sense of INDUSTRY *vs.* a sense of inferiority;
5. in adolescence, a sense of EGO IDENTITY (certainty of self, and a sense of continuity and belonging regarding career, sex role, and a system of values) *vs.* role confusion;
6. in early adulthood, the development of INTIMACY (mutuality with a loved partner of the opposite sex with whom the individual is able to regulate the cycles of work, procreation, and recreation) *vs.* a sense of ego isolation;
7. in middle adulthood, the development of GENERATIVITY (expansion of

ego interests and a sense of having contributed to the future) *vs.* a sense of ego stagnation; and

8. in late adulthood, a sense of EGO INTEGRITY (a basic acceptance of one's life as having been inevitable, appropriate, and meaningful) *vs.* a sense of despair (fear of death) (Erikson, 1968, p. 85).

PECK'S STAGES FOR THE LATER LIFE SPAN

As one can see, Erikson subsumed all of life from about age 60-on under the single ego-identity *vs.* despair category. These stages were extended into the later part of the life span by Peck (1955), who differentiated several periods of middle age and old age in the following manner:

Middle Age:

1. Valuing wisdom *vs.* valuing physical powers, a substitution consistent with the decline in physical vigor with age—"putting the use of their heads above the use of their hands" (Peck, 1955, p. 45).
2. Socializing *vs.* sexualizing in human relationships—again, consistent with the direction of biological development, and representing growth toward new forms of experience.
3. Cathectic flexibility *vs.* cathectic impoverishment. Since middle age is a time of life when the risk is great of developing rigidity in control of the way in which emotions may be deployed, the maintenance of the capacity to develop new emotional investments in people and objects is of prime importance.
4. Mental flexibility *vs.* mental rigidity—similar to cathectic flexibility, but on a cognitive rather than an emotional level.

Old Age:

1. Ego differentiation *vs.* work-role preoccupation—the attainment of the ability to value oneself for what one *is* rather than for what one *does* in terms of work and other middle-life roles.
2. Body transcendence *vs.* body preoccupation. While health and biology have gross effects on adjustment, some people achieve greater ego autonomy from physical constraints than do others.
3. Ego transcendence *vs.* ego preoccupation—in particular, coming to terms with the idea of one's own death, and a positive appreciation of the heritage one may leave in the world after one's death.

Unfortunately, there has been almost no effort to subject Peck's hypotheses to research verification.

OTHER APPROACHES TO THE STUDY OF THE AGED PERSONALITY

One of the most influential of developmental theories is the social-psychological disengagement theory, which suggests that both the individual and society move toward the breaking of the aging individual's ties with the outer world and its institutions (Cumming & Henry, 1961). While the assumption that the biological changes of aging move both the individual and society toward this disengagement process is implicit in this statement, ample room is left for variations due to both individual and societal differences.

Another theory is that of Neugarten & associates (1964) and Gutmann (1969), which sees parallel but relatively independent processes of internal changes which precede and then run concurrently with socio-adaptational changes. The internal changes show the individual moving from a sense of active mastery in relation to the environment to a more passive, adaptive stance, and to one in which his own physical and psychological experiences are more gratifying than those involving relationships with other people and external situations. But external social conditions appear to explain considerably more of the variation in personal adjustment than does the mere fact of chronological age.

Another approach to the study of the aged personality is in terms of ideal types, where the concurrence of a number of personality traits is empirically verified and examined in terms of traditional psychodynamic mechanisms. One of the best of these efforts (Reichard, Livson, & Peterson, 1962) described physically healthy aged men in terms of five syndromes, which vary in their adaptive success:

The mature constituted the ideally adjusted people who accepted themselves and their past, yet met the present with zest and action.

The rocking-chair type were also characterized by their high degree of acceptance of themselves and their current situation, though their acceptance was passive. They resembled to some extent the high-morale disengaged personality.

The armored were less ideally adapted insofar as very tight personality defenses were required to keep impulses and negative emotions in check. While this tight control suggested potential vulnerability, their armor, generally maintained through a high level of activity, appeared entirely adequate.

The angry were clearly less well-adjusted, having made a way of life of externalizing their difficulties. They were chronically dissatisfied, but adapted to the extent of seeing their problems not inside themselves, but in terms of bad breaks, unfriendly or malicious others, and so on.

The self-haters were equally dissatisfied, but internalized rather than externalized their aggression. Depression seemed endemic to their lifestyles, though they maintained a precarious behavioral adjustment.

While the types of Reichard and her associates were seen at only one point in time, the researchers' view is clearly a developmental one. The mutual interaction of past and present is repeatedly emphasized in their discussions of the typologies.

Naturally, no research-based theory can do justice to the complex system which constitutes personality and accounts for its dynamic nature. The remainder of this paper will be devoted to elaborating the assertion that all of life involves a constant modification of the person by means of exercising old skills, learning new ones, assimilating environmental influences, altering and restabilizing one's concept of oneself, and, through it all, behaving in ways which reflect this varying input of influences.

COMPETENCE AS THE KEY TO BEHAVIOR AND FEELING

For the sake of clarity, let us organize the causative aspects of individual behavior into sets spread along the time line of chronological age. There is a rough correspondence of this time line to the relative stability, or resistance to modification, of the various aspects, as indicated in Figure 2. On the rightmost end is "Now," which is meant to portray the resultant of the multiple influences. I have avoided giving a formal definition of "personality," and shall continue to do so, but our best views of personality are gained from looking at what the person does—behavior—and what he feels —or says or acts as if he feels.

"Competence" is the key to both outer behavior and inner feeling (White, 1959; Lawton, 1972). In this view, learning and growth involve parallel, complementary, and sometimes conflicting processes of (*a*) satisfying needs so as to decrease tension, and (*b*) creating tension and new needs so as to break monotony (Wohlwill, 1966; Lawton & Nahemow, 1973). Need satisfaction and problem solution are accompanied by a feeling of gratification related to the experience of one's own competence thus being demonstrated (Perin, 1970). At any given point, one may theoretically assess the sum of behavioral competencies and incompetencies and the sum of internally experienced competence to arrive at an overall estimate of "adjustment." Thus, an intelligence test measures one aspect of behavioral competence; supporting a family, another; and finding one's way around

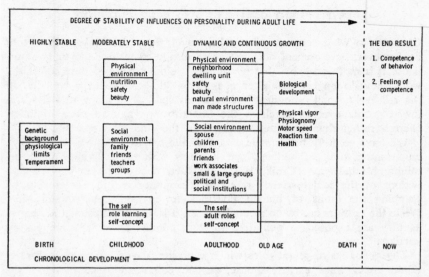

FIG. 2. The Complexity of Personality: Biological, Environmental, Social, and Psychological Influences on Competence.

a strange city, still another. From the inside, intellectual pride, the warmth of loving and being loved, and, on a more concrete level, confidence in seeking an address may be globally experienced as a positive emotion.

The competence and feeling of competence experienced now have been referred to as our most reliable indicators of personality. But they are highly variable, and are really the *result* of the array of varied influences shown in Figure 2. To the far left are the biological givens of the individual: his genetic background sets physiological limits on diverse aspects such as air temperature tolerance, hair color, rate of information processing, and possibly even "temperamental" functions such as emotional expressiveness or sensitivity.

Early learning, in constant interchange with physical maturation, forms some of the most enduring aspects of personality. Environmental factors, such as malnutrition or a deprived sensory world, may contribute to the formation of relatively fixed ways of experiencing the outer world. Similarly, early socialization experiences in the family and with one's age peers are intertwined with the development of roles and the sense of self which will be of lifelong importance in determining how one behaves and what one feels.

DEVELOPMENT CONTINUES INTO LATE ADULTHOOD

Contrary to what some of the earlier psychodynamic thinkers have told us, however, development does not cease at adolescence or at young adulthood. It is more probable that psychologists simply stopped thinking of the work they do on subjects after age 20 as "developmental." Actually, in the relatively small amount of research available to date which has followed people over as much as the first third or half of their lifetimes, change, rather than consistency, has been the rule (Bayley, 1963).

We have recently been made aware of the extent to which the physical environment limits, facilitates, and interacts with the individual in determining his behavior (Craik, 1973). In fact, one of the major preoccupations of the social science research community currently seems to be mapping the limits of human plasticity to environmental modification. While the answers are by no means at hand, it is clear that people do change as they are exposed to pollution, to slum conditions, or to architectural barriers.

The major instrumental roles which a person plays become defined after adolescence: wage earner, spouse, parent, community leader. While the way these roles are formed is strongly conditioned by pre-existing personality dispositions, they are no less affected by the kinds of contemporary social experiences which accompany their definition. And, finally, the experience of learning and performing these roles is central to the maintenance and modification of the self-concept, through the feeling of competence which accompanies this process.

Through the greater part of the adult life span, social, personal, and environmental, rather than biological, factors shape ordinary activity under the usual conditions of living. That is, we quickly learn our physiological limits, and as long as we remain in good health and in a favorable environment, we can behave as if we had no limiting biological apparatus.

As age increases, however, the probability grows that a significant effect of biological factors on behavior and feeling will occur. At this point, the relative balance of other influences on behavior also changes. The interpersonal world changes; old social roles become more difficult to perform; roles which are not necessarily welcomed ("old man", "retiree") are forced upon one; and negative social attitudes impinge increasingly on our experience. The self continues to be modified, and late-life developmental tasks such as those detailed by Peck (1955) must be performed under drastically altered environmental, social, and biological conditions.

This concurrence in time of so many changes may well require a more marked readjustment than many earlier adult life stages have demanded. Disengagement theory has correctly emphasized that *both* the individual and society react to the developmental biology of aging. In a very real sense, the individual has less control over his own destiny. I have suggested (Lawton, 1970) that older people's vulnerability to the environment increases as their personal competence decreases—and here "competence" may be viewed in terms of physical health, mental health, economic independence, or social status. In a very real sense, the individual's "personality" must be defined partly in terms of the context in which it appears. A positive, supporting environment will allow the continuation of competent behavior and the positive inner experience of competence, while the barrier-laden environment will foster a loss of competence. In our assumption that environments should be designed for the healthy adult we are cutting deeply into the heart of the older person's self-concept.

INTERVENTION ON BEHALF OF THE ELDERLY

Thus, I am suggesting that the "personality of old age" has an immense number of complexly related determinants, no one of which can be said to have *the* dominant effect on the individual. I also suggest that competent behavior and the inner feeling of competence are the criteria by which we should judge any of our efforts to intervene on behalf of the elderly.

This emphasis on competence gives us some immediate insight into the importance of doing all that is possible to encourage the continuation of previously learned skills in the aging person. Thus, for many older people the fact that they spend most of the day in humdrum activity such as housework, walking to the store, or personal grooming should not be interpreted necessarily as deprived living. In fact, it is precisely the removal of the opportunity to perform such tasks which may constitute the major negative consequence of institutional life.

It is possible to identify a large number of modifiable conditions in the environment which make it more difficult for a person to exercise his skills and which, therefore, foster feelings of incompetence:

—lack of independent living facilities
—distance from family and friends
—barriers to instrumental activity, such as living in a crime-ridden neighborhood, or having to traverse a long flight of steps to get out of one's dwelling unit
—inadequate transportation
—a dwelling unit too large or too old to maintain properly
—mandatory (rather than optional) retirement programs
—lack of medical or psychological assistance.

Obviously, the list could be extended. Though these barriers are non-psychological, it is my conviction that intervention in these areas is by far the most potentially rewarding route to the betterment of the aging individual's psychological status. Like individuals of any age, older persons in real distress may need expert psychological consultation. Clinically apparent problems are, however, much less frequent than the kind of everyday problem created by the social and physical milieux in which the elderly live. The opportunity for a gain in competence through coping successfully with these problems is very frequent and should have the attention of every person in a position to help the elderly. I have, perhaps, ignored the interior of the older person. However, while I feel that both individual and group psychotherapeutic intervention have a major role to play in psychopathological conditions, I think that most of the "normal" psychological problems of the elderly are related to the social and physical environments we provide for them, and that maximum help can come from planning at a social and institutional level.

REFERENCES

Bayley, N. The life span as a frame of reference in psychological research. *Vita Humana,* 1963, *6,* 125–139.

Butler, R. N. Age-ism: Another form of bigotry. *The Gerontologist,* 1969, *9,* 243–246.

Craik, K. H. Environmental psychology. *Annual Review of Psychology,* 1973, *24,* 403–422.

Cumming, E. & Henry, W. E. *Growing old: The process of disengagement.* New York: Basic Books, 1961.

Erikson, E. H. Generativity and ego integrity. In B. L. Neugarten (Ed.) *Middle age and aging.* Chicago: University of Chicago Press, 1968. Pp. 85–87.

Gutmann, D. *The country of old men.* (Occasional papers in Gerontology No. 5.) Ann Arbor: Institute of Gerontology, University of Michigan, 1969.

Kramer, M., Taube, C. A., & Redick, R. W. Patterns of use of psychiatric facilities by the aged: Past, present, and future. In C. Eisdorfer & M. P. Lawton (Eds.) *The psychology of adult development and aging.* Washington, D.C.: American Psychological Association, 1973. Pp. 428–528.

Lawton, M. P. Ecology and aging. In L. Pastalan & D. H. Carson (Eds.) *The spatial behavior of older people.* Ann Arbor: University of Michigan Press, 1970. Pp. 40–67.

Lawton, M. P. Assessing the competence of older people. In D. Kent, R. Kastenbaum, & S. Sherwood (Eds.) *Research, planning and action for the elderly.* New York: Behavioral Publications, 1972. Pp. 122–143.

Lawton, M. P., & Nahemow, L. Ecology and the aging process. In C. Eisdorfer & M. P. Lawton (Eds.) *The psychology of adult development and aging.* Washington, D.C.: American Psychological Association, 1973. Pp. 619–674.

Neugarten, B. L., & associates. *Personality in middle and late life.* New York: Atherton, 1964.

Peck, R. Psychological developments in the second half of life. In J. E. Anderson (Ed.) *Psychological aspects of aging.* Washington, D.C.: American Psychological Association, 1955. Pp. 42–53.

Perin, C. *With man in mind.* Cambridge: M.I.T. Press, 1970.

Reichard, S., Livson, F., & Peterson, P. G. *Aging and personality*. New York: Wiley, 1962.

White, R. W. Motivation reconsidered: The concept of competence. *Psychological Review*, 1959, *66*, 297–333.

Wohlwill, J. The physical environment: A problem for a psychology of stimulation. *Journal of Social Issues*, 1966, *22*, 29–38.

Individual Differences in Aging

ANNE ANASTASI

Anne Anastasi received her A.B. degree from Barnard College and her Ph.D. from Columbia University. Since 1947 she has been on the faculty of Fordham University, where she is currently professor of psychology. She is the author of more than 130 journal articles, monographs, and contributed papers. Her major publications include: Differential psychology *(1939, 1949, 1958),* Psychological testing *(1954, 1961), and* Fields of applied psychology *(1964). In addition, she has edited two other books:* Individual differences *(1965) and* Testing problems in perspective *(1966). Dr. Anastasi has had a distinguished career in professional and in scholarly circles. She has been president of the Eastern Psychological Association (1946–1947), the American Psychological Foundation (1965–1967), and finally the American Psychological Association (1971–1972).*

In their efforts to understand the aging process, psychologists can choose among several approaches. They can study the behavioral changes observed in later life through experimental, psychophysiological, developmental, or clinical methods; and they can compare aging in widely different cultures or in biologically dissimilar animal forms.* The approach to which I shall address myself is that of differential psychology (see Anastasi, 1958, Ch. 8; 1968, Ch. 11).

Specifically, the differential psychologist investigates the nature and extent

* A good source of information on the various approaches which have been pursued and on the current state of the field is the recently published book: *The psychology of adult development and aging,* edited by Eisdorfer & Lawton (1973).

of individual and group differences in behavioral characteristics through psychological tests or other assessment techniques. A major goal of differential psychology is to relate such behavioral differences to concomitant variables in order to contribute to an understanding of the causes of individual differences. With regard to aging, the differential psychologist asks questions such as the following: To what extent does performance actually change with age beyond maturity? In what specific ways are such changes manifested? How large are individual differences within age groups, as compared to differences between groups? What characteristics of the elderly person's environment and past experience are associated with different performance levels in particular traits?

INSTITUTIONAL SAMPLES

Let us examine some typical results obtained through psychological testing of the elderly. At the outset, we must recognize that, particularly in research on aging, data alone can be highly misleading. It is especially important in this field to ask how the data were obtained and to be alert to possible misinterpretations. For example, the earliest psychological studies on aging were often conducted in institutions for the aged, where groups of elderly persons were readily accessible for investigation and conveniently available at a single location. But the institutionalized elderly constitute a negatively selected sample and are not representative of their respective age levels. Such persons are more likely to show physiological or neurological pathology, severe sensory or motor defects, and the other special handicaps which, in part, led to their institutionalization. From another angle, living in an institution for prolonged periods is itself likely to have a deleterious effect on the individual's intellectual and emotional condition. Thus to find that 70- or 80-year-olds in such institutions perform poorly on aptitude tests or manifest personality disorders tells us little about the characteristics of aging as such. The findings of these studies obviously cannot be generalized to the whole population at the corresponding age levels.

By way of contrast, a group of scientists at the National Institute of Mental Health studied 47 noninstitutionalized healthy men ranging in age from 65 to 92 (Birren, Butler, Greenhouse, Sokoloff, & Yarrow, 1963). The men were volunteers, carefully screened on the basis of optimum health and community residence. The investigators report that the men as a whole were found to be "vigorous, candid, interesting, and deeply involved in everyday living. In marked contradiction to the usual stereotype of 'rigidity' and of 'second childhood,' these individuals generally demonstrated mental flexibility and alertness. They continued to be constructive in their living; they were resourceful and optimistic" (p. 314). As the authors expressed it, when the elderly retain their health with advancing age, they are remarkably "young."

CROSS-SECTIONAL STUDIES

In order to obtain more nearly representative samples than could be found in institutions, several investigators have tested large samples of adults spanning a wide age range. The general procedure was to classify these persons into age levels and to compare the average test scores of the different age groups. In one early study, for example, a standardized intelligence test was administered to about 1200 persons between the ages of 10 and 60, constituting nearly the entire population between those ages in 19 rural New England villages (Jones & Conrad, 1933). In another, a short intelligence test was given to slightly over 800 persons ranging in age from 7 to 94 years (Miles & Miles, 1932). The adult subjects in this study were contacted largely through lodges and social clubs. Still another source of similar data is provided by the standardization samples of the Wechsler intelligence scales, which were specially developed for use with adults (Doppelt & Wallace, 1955; Wechsler, 1944, 1955). To establish the norms, the Wechsler scales were administered to large, nationwide samples; particularly in the later edition of the scales, the samples were chosen so as to be highly representative of their age groups in the general population.

These studies agree fairly closely in showing a peak of performance in the 20- to 30-year level, followed by a gradual decline in mean score, with a sharper decline after 60. In interpreting such age decrements, we must remember that all these studies utilized a cross-sectional rather than a longitudinal method. In other words, age decrement was inferred by comparing the performance of different persons at the various age levels, each person being tested only once. There are serious pitfalls in this procedure. A major difficulty is that the different age samples may not be comparable in such background characteristics as amount and nature of education. It is well known, for example, that the educational level of the American population has been increasing over time. Thus 60-year-olds tested today will on the average have had less schooling than today's 20-year-olds.

A more detailed analysis of some of the cross-sectional data illustrates the role of education in complicating the obtained age differences. Thus in one study (Miles & Miles, 1932), the total sample was subdivided into four groups on the basis of the amount of schooling completed. Although age decrements were found within each of these subgroups, the mean differences between the four educational groups were such as to counterbalance some of the age differences. For instance, 20-year-old elementary or high school graduates averaged lower on the test than did 60-year-old college graduates or 80-year-olds with graduate school training.

The influence of educational difference is demonstrated in another way by the Wechsler standardization data. First, it should be noted that, since a test standardization sample is a *normative sample,* it should reflect existing population characteristics at each age level (Anastasi, 1956). Because of the increasing educational level of the general population, older groups at any one point in time will have received less education on the average than younger groups. The Wechsler standardization samples clearly reveal this educational difference: the maximum years of schooling are found in the 20- to 30-year groups; and amount of education drops consistently in the older groups. Thus the older groups in the standardization sample may have performed more poorly on the test, not because of an age decrement but because they had received less education than the younger groups.

This interpretation is supported by a comparison of the standardization samples of the earlier and later editions of the Wechsler scales, tested approximately 15 years apart. In the more recently tested sample, the drop in score with age is smaller and begins at an older age. The decline in amount of education with age is also less pronounced and sets in later.

Amount of formal education is only one of many variables in which different age groups may vary. Many other cultural changes have occurred in our society during the past half-century which make the experiential background of 20-year-olds and 70-year-olds quite dissimilar. Certainly changes in communication media like radio and television and in transportation have greatly increased the range of information available to the developing individual. Improvements in nutrition and medical care would also indirectly influence behavior development. The basic implication is that cross-sectional studies of adult intelligence are likely to show an apparent age decrement because cultural changes are confounded with the effects of aging.

LONGITUDINAL STUDIES

In recognition of the limitations of cross-sectional studies, investigators have been turning more and more to longitudinal studies. In these studies, the *same* adults have been retested, usually only once, after a lapse of from 5 to 40 years. These studies have quite consistently failed to reveal the age decrement of the cross-sectional studies. In fact, the mean scores often improve with age, even when comparisons extend into the sixties and seventies. Several of these longitudinal investigations have been conducted with intellectually superior groups, such as college graduates or individuals initially chosen because of high IQs (Bayley & Oden, 1955; Burns, 1966; Campbell, 1965; Nisbet, 1957; Owens, 1953, 1966). For this reason, some writers have argued that the findings may be restricted to persons in the higher intellectual or educational levels and do not apply to the general population. However, similar results have been obtained in other longitudinal studies with normals (Charles & James, 1964; Eisdorfer, 1963; Schaie & Strother, 1968; Tuddenham, Blumenkrantz, & Wilkin, 1968) and even with mentally retarded adults outside of institutions (Baller, Charles, & Miller, 1967; Bell & Zubeck, 1960; Charles, 1953).

Neither cross-sectional nor longitudinal studies alone can provide a conclusive interpretation of observed age changes. What is needed in order to tease out the effect of cultural change is a combination of cross-sectional and longitudinal procedures. On the one hand, age differences in educational level may produce a spurious age decrement in test performance in cross-sectional studies. On the other hand, as a person grows older, he is exposed increasingly to cultural changes which may improve his performance on aptitude tests.

A few studies do provide data which permit at least a partial analysis of the contributing factors. Two such investigations involved the retesting of college freshmen after a lapse of 25 years in one case (Campbell, 1965) and 40 years in the other (Owens, 1966). In addition, the investigators tested *present* freshmen attending these colleges, at the same time as they retested the original groups. Thus multiple comparisons could be made between the two groups tested at the same age 30 or 40 years apart, and the performance of a single group tested before and after the same time intervals. In both studies, the initial group improved over its own earlier performance, but performed about on a par with the younger group tested at the same time. Such findings suggest that it is cultural changes and other experiential factors, rather than age per se, which produce both the rises and declines in scores found with the more limited experimental designs.

Another, particularly well-designed study utilizing this combined approach was conducted on a more nearly representative sample of the adult population (Schaie & Strother, 1968). Carefully chosen tests of different abilities were administered to a stratified-random sample of 500 persons. The population base from which this sample was drawn consisted of approximately 18,000 members of a prepaid medical plan, whose membership was fairly representative of the census figures for a large metropolitan area. The sample included 25 men and 25 women at each 5-year interval from 20 to 70 years. Seven years later, all the original subjects who could be located were contacted and 302 of them given the same tests again. This subsample was shown to be closely comparable to the original group in age, sex ratio, and socioeconomic level.

The design of this study permits two types of comparison: (1) a cross-sectional comparison among different age groups from 20 to 70 tested at the same time, and (2) a longitudinal comparison within the same individuals, initially tested at ages ranging from 20 to 70 and retested after 7 years. The results showed either no change or an improvement in performance on the retests of the same persons. The one exception occurred in two highly speeded tests, in which performance was poorer after the 7-year interval. The cross-sectional comparisons, on the other hand, showed significant intergenerational differences on all tests. In other words, those born and reared more recently performed better than those born and reared at an earlier time period. The strong implication of these findings is that the ability decrements attributed to aging are actually the result of progressive cultural changes in our society.

EFFECT OF INTERVENING EXPERIENCES

Thus far we have been focusing upon general group trends and average performance in relation to age. Among persons of any given age, of course, there are wide individual differences in any trait. What is even more relevant to the present topic, however, is that the *changes* which occur with aging vary with the individual. Thus between the ages of 50 and 60, for example, some persons may show a decrease, some no appreciable change, and some an increase in test performance. The amount of change, whether it be a rise or drop, will also vary widely among individuals.

What factors are associated with these individual differences in age changes among normal adults in the general population? There is a growing body of research data pertaining to the influence of intervening experiences upon such age changes. Several longitudinal studies have subdivided their samples on the basis of the amount of education completed between the first and second testing (Campbell, 1965; Husén, 1951; Lorge, 1945; Owens, 1953). For example, a Swedish study compared the test performance of 722 young men examined upon induction into military training with the scores they had obtained ten years earlier in the third grade of primary schools (Husén, 1951). For purposes of analysis, the sample was divided into five groups on the basis of total amount of education, ranging from the compulsory 7 years to 12–13 years. Initial and final IQs over the 10-year period were compared within each of the five educational groups. The results showed an average drop of slightly over 1 point in the group with only 7 years of schooling; the other groups showed average gains of 2, 3, 7, and 11 points, respectively. Thus the longer an individual had continued his education during the 10-year interval, the more gain he tended to show on the retest, relative to the general norms.

This study covered a relatively young age span. But similar results have been obtained with older adults, over the ages when decrements are generally expected. Pertinent data can be found in the two previously cited longitudinal investigations of college freshmen. When these groups were retested several decades later, the changes in score were also analyzed in terms of the amount of intervening education. This ranged from early college dropout to college graduation and subsequent graduate or professional school training. In both studies, larger retest gains were found among those who had continued their education longer.

It should be noted in this connection that the traditional "intelligence test" employed in many of these aging studies measures largely abstract verbal and numerical abilities. These are the abilities most often called into play in the course of school learning. Test constructors have drawn upon the common pool of intellectual experiences represented by organized academic curricula. Hence most intelligence tests can be more accurately designated as tests of scholastic aptitude. They reflect how well the individual has acquired the sort of intellectual skills taught in school. And they can in turn predict how well he is prepared for the next level in the educational hierarchy. As the individual grows older and his formal educational experiences recede farther into the past, this fund of common experience may become increasingly less appropriate to assess his intellectual functioning. Adult occupations are more diversified than childhood schooling. The cumulative experiences of adulthood may thus stimulate the development of different patterns of abilities in different persons.

In the light of these considerations it is not surprising to find that increases or decreases in intelligence test scores among older persons are related to the amount of formal education they received. Similarly, persons whose occupations are more "academic" in content, demanding continued use of verbal or numerical abilities, are likely to maintain their performance level or show improvement in intelligence test scores over the years. Those engaged in occupations emphasizing mechanical activities or interpersonal skills, on the other hand, may show a loss.

MULTITRAIT vs. GLOBAL MEASUREMENT

One of the ways in which current research on aging differs from the earlier studies is in the use of multiple aptitude tests in place of global tests of so-called intelligence. To be sure, intelligence tests such as the Stanford-Binet and the Wechsler scales still serve a useful function in the hands of a properly trained clinical psychologist; such a person can interpret the test scores in the light of additional information obtained through an intensive individual case study. For research purposes, however, as well as for many educational and personnel decisions, the traditional intelligence tests are too limited in scope and are subject to misinterpretations.

The most common misinterpretation stems from the prevalent belief that an Intelligence Quotient (IQ) obtained with a traditional intelligence test measures a stable, unchanging, and even innate characteristic of the individual. In actual fact, no test can measure such a characteristic, and the very concept of innately fixed abilities is scientifically questionable. All tests measure only what the person can do at the time; and such performance reflects not only his hereditary background but the cumulative effects of all relevant past experiences, including, among others, his formal education.

A second common misinterpretation of intelligence test scores represents an overgeneralization of test coverage. Intelligence tests do not sample all human abilities. Nor do different intelligence tests cover the same abilities or in the same proportions. Most are predominantly verbal in content; many also cover numerical aptitudes; a few extend their coverage to spatial and perceptual content and to nonverbal reasoning tasks. In their content, as well as in the way they are validated, most intelligence tests focus on school-related functions. We have already noted that they can be more accurately described as tests of scholastic aptitude.

Research on the nature and organization of abilities has identified several broad intellectual traits. Such findings in turn led to the development of multiple aptitude batteries which provide, not a single global score like an IQ, but a profile of scores in major abilities. With such batteries we can obtain both a fuller and a clearer picture of what the individual can do. Among the abilities most frequently included are verbal comprehension, numerical aptitude, spatial visualization, mechanical comprehension, and perceptual speed and accuracy.

Even in the earlier research on aging, there were indications that age differences were not uniform across all traits. That speed of response tends to decline with age was suggested in some of the earliest studies and has been corroborated by more recent and more sophisticated longitudinal investigations (Schaie & Strother, 1968). Tasks depending upon perceptual discrimination and spatial visualization also show evidence of some age decrement (Schaie & Strother, 1968; Welford *et al.*, 1951). These perceptual difficulties remain when sensory defects are corrected or otherwise ruled out. It has been proposed that part of the perceptual and spatial deficiency may center upon the process of organizing new data and integrating such data with relevant material from past experience (Birren, 1959; Welford *et al.*, 1951).

In motor skills, age decline is less pronounced than is generally supposed. An unusually thorough investigation of age differences in motor skills was conducted by a group of psychologists at Cambridge University (Welford, 1958; Welford *et al.*, 1951). Most of the data were obtained under laboratory conditions, although preliminary studies in industry were also undertaken. A special feature of this research was the analysis of different aspects of the subject's motor performance, in order to explore more fully the nature of age changes. Results indicated that the major impairments occurred in the perceptual rather than in the motor aspects of the activities. Moreover, older persons tended to change their methods of performing tasks and thus to compensate for their deficiencies. The rigidity or flexibility of the given task determines the degree to which such compensatory changes in procedure can be effectively utilized by the subject. When the task permits a variety of approaches and the method is largely under the individual's control, compensatory changes in performance are likely to occur. Such tasks may show no decline or even an improvement with age owing to over-compensation. On the other hand, when performance is narrowly restricted with respect to constituent reactions, compensation is practically impossible.

One also hears a great deal about the inability of older persons to learn new skills, whether motor or cognitive. "You can't teach an old dog new tricks" is a familiar proverb. Adults frequently deplore their inability to learn a new language or a new motor skill as well as they could in their younger days. Closer inquiry usually reveals, however, that in such cases the conditions of learning were far from comparable at the different life periods involved. Time available for learning, distractions, and motivation to learn are often quite dissimilar for child and adult. The learning of new skills is frequently undertaken casually and halfheartedly by the adult; while for the child or adolescent it is the core of his serious responsibilities, other activities being relegated to "extracurricular" status.

When older and younger persons are given learning tasks under more nearly comparable conditions, as in a controlled experiment, the differences in their performance are smaller than anticipated. This is particularly true when the usual age difference in the amount of education is ruled out. It should also be noted that learning is not a general trait: how well one learns depends in part on what is to be learned. Different learning techniques are appropriate to the learning of different types of content or skills. Specific learning tasks, moreover, may be aided or hindered by the individual's previous learning. There is some suggestive evidence that older persons learn relatively well in situations where their prior experience facilitates learning and relatively poorly where prior experience interferes or conflicts with what is to be learned (see Anastasi, 1958, Ch. 8; Birren, 1959, Ch. 19).

On the basis of learning experiments conducted in the previously cited Cambridge research, the investigators related some of the learning deficiencies with the difficulty experienced by the elderly in the perceptual organization of new data. They concluded that "older subjects showed a much greater tendency than younger to produce answers in terms of past experience and pre-formed opinions, instead of organizing the data in the manner required by the instructions" (Welford *et al.*, 1951, p. 122). Still another reason for age differences in learning may be found in interests and motivation. In general, older persons are less likely to exert themselves in tasks which impress them as foolish or meaningless in terms of their experience —and such is likely to be the case in the typical laboratory tasks used in learning experiments.

Once we move away from such fuzzy concepts as intelligence, IQ, and general learning ability, and begin to study more clearly defined traits, we are able to provide more meaningful answers about aging. One important area of investigation concerns the relation between the specific activities in which adults have been engaged and the specific ability changes which occur with age. Some suggestive data on this question are to be found in a study of 100 persons awaiting hospital admission for surgery (Williams, 1960). Chosen chiefly because of their availability, these individuals ranged in age from 65 to over 90, although only a few were over 79. The group included no bedridden cases and none with suspicion of organic mental disorder. The subjects were quite heterogeneous in socioeconomic background and represented a variety of occupations. Their test performance as a whole showed them to be a fairly representative sample of the general population.

Each person in the study took a battery of seven tests, covering a wide sample of abilities. The analysis of results focused on the pattern or profile of scores in different abilities. Major discrepancies in relative performance on different tests were examined in relation to information about the individual's experiential background. The results led the author to conclude that significant differences in performance from test to test were related to past occupations and hobbies and that the selective deterioration of certain skills may result chiefly from disuse. For example, among the elderly persons who performed better on verbal than on spatial–perceptual tasks were a school teacher, a writer, and several high-level clerical workers; among those exhibiting the reverse pattern, with higher scores on spatial–perceptual and lower on verbal tests, were a carpenter, an engine driver, a skilled fitter, and a farmer. Similar relations were found with long-standing avocational activities, such as hobbies which had been pursued seriously for many years.

CONCLUSIONS

In summary: available research on the differential psychology of aging suggests three major conclusions. First, individual differences within any one age level are much greater than average differences between age levels. As a result, the distributions of scores obtained by persons of different ages overlap extensively. This simply means that large numbers of older persons can be found whose performance equals that of younger persons. Moreover, the best performers within the older groups excel the poorest performers within the younger groups. Nor is such overlapping limited to adjacent age levels; the ranges of performance still overlap when extreme groups are compared. Thus some 80-year-olds will do better than some 20-year-olds. Research on aging provides one more example of the current recognition of the preeminence of the individual as opposed to group stereotypes. An individual's chronological age is a poor indicator of his intellectual or emotional characteristics and an unreliable basis for major life decisions.

A second conclusion is that when considering factual data on the performance of older and younger persons, it is important to differentiate between age *differences* and age *changes.* Age differences, as found in cross-sectional group comparisons, may reflect educational and other cultural differences between generations rather than the physiological or psychological effects of aging as such.

The third conclusion follows from the growing body of research demonstrating the contribution of experiential variables. Whether abilities increase, decrease, or remain stable over any time period depends at least in part on the activities in which the individual has engaged during that period. Educational and vocational activities are major examples of organized and continuing experiences which influence the selective improvement of some abilities and the decline of others. How long a person has lived is less important than what he has been doing during those years.

REFERENCES

Anastasi, A. Age changes in adult test performance. *Psychological Reports,* 1956, *2,* 509.

Anastasi, A. *Differential psychology.* (3rd ed.) New York: Macmillan, 1958.

Anastasi, A. *Psychological testing.* (3rd ed.) New York: Macmillan, 1968.

Baller, W. R., Charles, D. C., & Miller, E. L. Mid-life attainment of the mentally retarded: A longitudinal study. *Genetic Psychology Monographs,* 1967, *75,* 235–329.

Bayley, N., & Oden, M. H. The maintenance of intellectual ability in gifted adults. *Journal of Gerontology,* 1955, *10,* 91–107.

Bell, A., & Zubeck, J. The effect of age on the intellectual performance of mental defectives. *Journal of Gerontology,* 1960, *15,* 285–295.

Birren, J. E. (Ed.) *Handbook of aging and the individual: Psychological and biological aspects.* Chicago: University of Chicago Press, 1959.

Birren, J. E., Butler, R. N., Greenhouse, S. W., Sokoloff, L., & Yarrow, M. R. *Human aging: A biological and behavioral study.* (DHEW Publ. [PHS] 63–986.) Washington, D.C.: Government Printing Office, 1963.

Burns, R. B. Age and mental ability: Re-testing with thirty-three years' interval. *British Journal of Educational Psychology,* 1966, *36,* 116.

Campbell, D. P. A cross-sectional and longitudinal study of scholastic abilities over twenty-five years. *Journal of Counseling Psychology,* 1965, *12,* 55–61.

Charles, D. C. Ability and accomplishment of persons earlier judged mentally deficient. *Genetic Psychology Monographs,* 1953, *47,* 3–71.

Charles, D. C., & James, S. T. Stability of average intelligence. *Journal of Genetic Psychology,* 1964, *105,* 105–111.

Doppelt, J. E., & Wallace, W. L. Standardization of the Wechsler Adult Intelligence Scale for older persons. *Journal of Abnormal and Social Psychology,* 1955, *51,* 312–330.

Eisdorfer, C. The WAIS performance of the aged: A retest evaluation. *Journal of Gerontology,* 1963, *18,* 169–172.

Eisdorfer, C., & Lawton, M. P. (Eds.) *The psychology of adult development and aging.* Washington, D.C.: American Psychological Association, 1973.

Husén, T. The influence of schooling upon IQ. *Theoria,* 1951, *17,* 61–88.

Jones, H. E., & Conrad, H. S. The growth and decline of intelligence: A study of a homogeneous group between the ages of ten and sixty. *Genetic Psychology Monographs*, 1933, *13*, 223–298.

Lorge, I. Schooling makes a difference. *Teachers College Record*, 1945, *46*, 483–492.

Miles, C. C., & Miles, W. R. The correlation of intelligence scores and chronological age from early to late maturity. *American Journal of Psychology*, 1932, *44*, 44–78.

Nisbet, J. D. Symposium: Contributions to intelligence testing and the theory of intelligence. IV. Intelligence and age: Retesting with twenty-four years' interval. *British Journal of Educational Psychology*, 1957, *27*, 190–198.

Owens, W. A. Age and mental abilities: A longitudinal study. *Genetic Psychology Monographs*, 1953, *48*, 3–54.

Owens, W. A. Age and mental abilities: A second adult follow-up. *Journal of Educational Psychology*, 1966, *57*, 311–325.

Schaie, K. W., & Strother, C. R. A cross-sequential study of age changes in cognitive behavior. *Psychological Bulletin*, 1968, *70*, 671–680.

Tuddenham, R. D., Blumenkrantz, J., & Wilkin, W. B. Age changes on AGCT: A longitudinal study of average adults. *Journal of Counseling and Clinical Psychology*, 1968, *32*, 659–663.

Wechsler, D. *The measurement of adult intelligence.* (3rd ed.) Baltimore: Williams & Wilkins, 1944.

Wechsler, D. *Manual for the Wechsler Adult Intelligence Scale.* New York: Psychological Corporation, 1955.

Welford, A. T. *Ageing and human skill.* London: Oxford University Press, 1958.

Welford, A. T., et al. *Skill and age; an experimental approach.* London: Oxford University Press, 1951.

Williams, M. The effect of past experience on mental performance in the elderly. *British Journal of Medical Psychology*, 1960, *33*, 215–219.

Psychopathology of Aging

ROBERT J. CAMPBELL

*Robert Jean Campbell, M.D., was, at the time
of the Institute, associate director, department of
psychiatry, St. Vincent's Hospital and Medical
Center, New York City. He had been in the department of psychiatry at St. Vincent's in various
capacities since 1956. As of July 1, 1973, however, he became medical director of Four Winds
Hospital, Katonah, New York. Dr. Campbell's
A.B. degree (1944) is from the University of
Wisconsin, his M.D. (1948) is from the College
of Physicians and Surgeons, Columbia University,
and his diplomate in psychiatry (1957) is from
the American Board of Psychiatry and Neurology.
Dr. Campbell is a fellow both of the American
Psychiatric Association and of the New York
Academy of Medicine. He is a frequent contribu-
tor to professional journals, and is the editor of
both the third and the fourth edition of Hinsie &
Campbell's* Psychiatric Dictionary.

As anyone can verify personally by the simple expedient of walking around
town, there are more persons under the age of 18 than ever before in New
York City. According to the 1970 U. S. census figures, they constitute 28%
of our population. What is not so noticeable, though, because they are
neither so physically active nor so vociferously involved, is that the number of older people has also increased. People over 65 account for 12%
of our population—947,878 of a total of 7,895,563 persons—and that number represents a 57% increase over the 1950 census figures.

New York City is by no means unique. As previous contributors to this

Institute have already observed, and as is evident from Table 1, the phenomenon is a national one, and at least insofar as Canada and the Western European countries are concerned, it is also an international one. Here in the United States, 4,000 persons reach the age of 65 every day, more than 3,000 over the age of 65 die each day, with the net result that about 1,000 persons are added each day to the age group with which we are concerned in this Institute. Sometimes overlooked is the fact that although the median age of the elderly is 73 years, there are about 8 million people in the U. S. over 75, and about one million over 85 years of age.

TABLE 1

PERSONS OVER 65 YEARS (USA)

Year	Total Number	Per Cent of Total Population
1900		4.1%
1950		8.2%
1959	14.4 million	8.6%
1972	21 million	10 %
2000	(?)29 million	(?)9–11 %

THE NEED OF THE AGED FOR HEALTH CARE

It is popularly believed that such figures as I am quoting are an expression of what has been termed medicated survival. In fact, though, the advances of modern medicine are not all that significant in keeping people alive. The things which science writers report generally benefit only tiny segments of the entire population, and even smaller parts of the aged population. How many of the 947,878 New Yorkers over 65 would be considered for a heart transplant, for example; and what kind of race could they run with a 25-year-old who needs renal dialysis? Even though many drugs have been developed over the last 30 years, none of them has any specificity for the multiple problems of aging. The reason our elderly population is increasing is the steady decline in infant mortality which obstetrical and pediatric groups have achieved; perhaps of equal importance is that antibiotics allow many young people to escape the plagues and epidemics which would have eliminated them a few decades ago, so they live to a riper old age than heretofore would have been their fate.

That fact alone has many implications for public-health planning. Once one recognizes that people are living who in times past would have died at a much younger age, and that no specific treatment for the illnesses of old age has yet been developed, one can easily predict that the elderly population will present a major challenge to every part of the health-services delivery system. The aged are more in need of health care than any other segment of the population in this country, and both their numbers and their needs are likely to rise. At the present time, that 10% of the population accounts for 27% of the nation's health expenditure. Numbers are a dull game to most of us, but they take on a distressing reality when one finds that three-quarters of the aged population are concentrated in 19 of the 50 states.

In the case of psychiatry, many of the problems issue from the rapid increase in mental disorders which accompanies the rise in age. While one-third of the aged have no real physical or mental problems, one-half are disabled to some extent by physical problems and one-sixth are severely disabled or bedridden. Mental impairment amounts to an almost ubiquitous plague for the elderly, 4% of whom are in mental hospitals, 15% to 25% of whom have some significant mental disability. Table 2 shows the enormous increase in hospitalized cases; what it does not show are the many who suffer unrecognized because they are alone, unaided because they cannot find a portal of entry into the complicated health-care system.

TABLE 2

INCIDENCE OF MENTAL DISORDER

Age	New Cases/100,000 population
under 15 years	2.3
25–34 years	76.3
35–54 years	93.0
over 65 years	236.1

Psychiatric illness is the largest single cause of chronic disability in the senium. That statement finds grim support in the statistics on suicide, which reaches a peak somewhere between the sixth and eighth decades of life. At ages 65–69, white males have a suicide rate 4 times as great as their female counterparts, and 3½ times the rate in the general population. When one gets to the 85-years-and-older group, one finds that white males have a rate 12 times that of white females, and more than 5 times that of the total population.

About 4,500 people over 65 commit suicide each year—and that figure comprises almost one-quarter of all suicides recorded. The highest rates of all are found among older men, living in the lowest socioeconomic areas of a city, alone or in social isolation, who have recently developed some physical illness and who have a history of a disturbed work role. Such people have little reason to ignore the possibility of suicide as an escape. Those with chronic diseases are not likely to improve; those who are lonely are unlikely to be able to resurrect dead friends, or to be able to attract active, supporting, and life-loving new acquaintances; those who are unemployed have little to sell on the open market; those on public assistance find help dwindling in inverse ratio to their mounting needs as they continue to live. The elderly person who tries suicide usually succeeds, and his attempt to end his life is not likely to be a distorted cry for help—which he would not get anyway in our youth-worshipping society (Rachlis, 1970).

FACTORS CONTRIBUTING TO PSYCHOPATHOLOGY IN THE AGED

In New York State, there has been a marked increase in senile psychoses and cerebral arteriosclerosis since the 1930s, and that increase largely accounts for the general increase in mental disorder (which thus is *not* due to any increase in those disorders we term "functional"—manic depressive disorder, involutional melancholia, the schizophrenias, or the psychoneuroses). The admission statistics of the last few years are not strictly comparable to earlier data, because of administrative decisions within the state-hospital system which have tended to bar admission of older patients, but, as of 1965, senile psychoses accounted for about 15% of all new admissions to mental hospitals, cerebral arteriosclerosis for about 20%. Even such clear-cut "organic" psychoses, however, are more than just degeneration of neural tissue. Studies over the past two decades have agreed that there is a high association between organic psychosis in the elderly and socioeconomic status, education, occupation, physical health, and living conditions (Busse, 1970). To phrase it differently: psychopathology in the elderly is over-determined; among the many factors to which it is related are the biologic effects of aging on mechanisms of resistance and defense, both physiologically and emotionally; socioeconomic conditions; the multiplicity of disorders; and the genetic determinants of disorders in the post-reproductive phase of life.

Genetic Factors

In general, all those diseases which appear for the first time in the post-reproductive phase of life are likely to be manifestations of genetically determined defects. The reason is that if an illness escapes detection throughout the reproductive phase it also avoids control by natural selection. Old age thus becomes "a dumping ground of the evolutionary process in which mutations detracting from full health and vigour have been deposited" (Mayer-Gross, Slater, & Roth, 1960, p. 478).

Socioeconomic Factors

Despite Social Security and Medicare, as of 1970 a quarter of over-65 families had incomes below $3,000 per year, while the median income of this group was $4,966. As Williams (1973) has pointed out, Medicare covers only 42% of the health costs of the aged, and this amount has been decreasing steadily under the current administration. The older person is now paying more out-of-pocket for health care than he paid the year before Medicare was introduced—$280 now as compared with $238 then. There has been a consistent erosion of benefits to the aged by reason of administrative restrictions on eligibility, the many gaps in coverage, and the cost of inflation. Among the vast social changes propounded by the administration, one is to increase premiums for the aged who will be expected to carry a larger percentage of the burden of their total health care; another is to have the elderly assume the cost of the first day of a hospital stay—always the most expensive day. The rationale behind all this is to encourage cost-consciousness—a kind of encouragement the elderly hardly need, and one based on a misconception of hospital utilization. The mode and timing of health-care utilization are determined not by the patient, but by the physician, for it is the doctor who is qualified to make that determination. It is the rare patient, no matter what his age, who tries to stay in the hospital any longer than he must (Cohen, 1973).

Multiple Medical Problems

Over 70% of the elderly have one or more *chronic* ailments; they have more severe illnesses than do the young, more of them, and once they fall ill they take about twice as long to recover. Persons over 65 account for 72% of all fatal falls, for 30% of all pedestrian fatalities (Butler, 1971). Age-related alterations in the physiology of most organ systems, the inflexibility or narrowed range of homeostatic mechanisms, and a general weakening of defense mechanisms contribute to their susceptibility to multiple disorders. A major complication in such a situation is that one disorder may profoundly affect the outcome of another, as in the elderly person with a colostomy who falls and dislocates his shoulder. How can he continue to manage his colostomy by himself if one of his arms must be immobilized (Agate, 1971b)?

The multiple problems of the aged cluster and interact in synergistic fashion. They require a degree of integration of health and social approaches which so far seems to exceed the capabilities of the system. Take, for example, the arthritic patient who becomes depressed by his infirmities: he has difficulty in dressing himself; he cannot easily go up and down the stairs; he finds it almost impossible to maneuver the two high steps into the bus which might take him to the clinic if he were more agile. Is this a psychiatric problem, because of his depression? Is it a health problem, because of his arthritis? Or is it a problem in income, a domestic problem, a problem in transportation, a problem in housing, or a problem in personal care? Actually, of course, it is all these problems, but, as anyone who deals with a bureaucracy knows, such a multiplicity of problems is likely to afford the different agencies a multiplicity of excuses, rather than provide the patient with a multiplicity of services.

Negative Expectations of the Culture

Still another problem is the role stereotypy into which the elderly person is forced by his culture, which defines success and fulfillment in terms of money, activity, and youth. The largely negative expectations held by other age groups—and even by older people themselves, who often will not complain of symptoms because they assume they are a product of senescence—constitute a series of self-fulfilling prophecies for the elderly (Kahn, 1971).

While persons of any age may have lapses of memory, the moment a grandfather forgets a name, the family prepares itself for his instant dementia. Yet what appears at first glance to be an intellectual deficit may in fact be something quite different. It has often been demonstrated that the apparent difficulty older people have in learning is more than anything else related to the stress of having to accomplish within a rigidly limited time span. When the time requirement is removed, not only do they perform as well as a younger group, but they succeed in doing it within the same length of time in which it had been impossible for them under rigid testing conditions.

Clinical depression is another case in point. At all ages, depression characteristically involves a slowing down of psychomotor processes; but when the depressed patient is over 65, the slowing is almost always perceived as an intellectual deficit, while the depression itself is overlooked. No matter what his degree of intellectual difficulty, the older person is viewed so critically by others in his culture that the functional effects of that difficulty are exaggerated.

Physiologic Factors

There are two kinds of age-related changes in functional capacity which create a new environment to which the older person must adjust. The first are perceptual changes, alterations in the capacity to secure stimulation, particularly through the eyes and ears. The second are motor changes, which alter the person's ability to manipulate his environment. The older person, in other words, must adapt to his environment with a reduction in both the quality and the quantity of information input, and with a reduced capacity to perform speedily, particularly when the tasks presented are complex ones (Kleemeier, 1959).

The most important reasons for the sensory decrements are neural changes, consisting of a reduction in nerve-cell populations and, consequently, a reduced channel capacity (Weiss, 1959). In order for the same amount of information to be transmitted when channel capacity is reduced, signals must be sent sequentially over the same elements—that is, the stimulus must be maintained for a longer time, or repeated. At the same time, since channel capacity is reduced, the elements involved in the transmission of any signal will necessarily represent a larger portion of the total capacity in the old than in the young, leaving a smaller reserve in the old.

According to Welford (1959), the sensorimotor performance of the elderly is largely limited by central mechanisms, with the result that there is a maximum which can be achieved at any one time and within any given period of time. The older person may compensate by taking a longer time, and this is the major cause of his "slowness." If the longer time is not allowed, accuracy suffers, particularly when movements have to be carried out in a continuous, coordinated series.

While all of the foregoing might seem to be of academic interest only, the fact that the aged population is increasing means that we shall increasingly be faced with the problem of how to make the retirement years a period of contentment and satisfaction, rather than a sentence of despair springing from sensory and social isolation and a conviction of uselessness. In order to achieve this, we must learn what the capacities of the aging organism are, what can be done to help it compensate for whatever the decrements are, and what we can do to alter the environment so as to minimize deficits. Thus in designing reading rooms, or books, or telephones, or houses, or industrial plants, the knowledge we have of the ways the sensory and motor processes of the aged operate can spell out for us some of the ways we might make life easier for them, at the same time as we make use of their experience for the betterment of society. Visual and auditory conditions can be modified so as to compensate for the older person's defects.

Even visual hallucinations may be an indication not strictly of psychopathology but of sensory impairment. Failing eyesight typically produces gradually decreasing mobility and domestic capability, leading to disinterest or unawareness which appears as disturbed orientation. Concomitant visual impressions, which frighten the person because he does not know how to interpret them, are labeled hallucinations by the ignorant professional (Agate, 1971a).

Impaired hearing leads to similar errors in diagnosis. It involves other people in effort and frustration and thus evokes little sympathy. It is more noticeable in group conversation, in committee meetings, or in social gatherings. In order to avoid the anger/disinterest/impatience of the people he might otherwise see, the elderly person withdraws from public work and from society. As it becomes harder and harder for him to hear, he responds to all questions with a blank expression or a polite smile. The clinician is likely to perceive this as evidence of retardation, dementia, or the like, when a single written question to the patient might have demonstrated the retention of full intellectual capacity.

NORMAL *vs.* PATHOLOGIC AGING

When senescence, or normal aging, becomes pathologic senility remains a matter of dispute, since there is no clear demarcation between normal functioning and distortions induced by disease. Instead, there is a gradual transition from one to the other, and we can sometimes reach a consensus that functioning is pathologic once it exceeds a certain degree. Never to be lost sight of, however, is that the degree of which we speak is determined not only by the patient's tolerance—that is to say, his symptoms reach a level at which he says to himself, "Something is wrong and I need help"— but that disease itself is to a very large extent determined also by society's tolerance, what the people around him can bear. In mental disorder, particularly, society's judgment can be crucial in determining what is to be labeled as sickness (Busse, 1959).

Take, for example, the "rigidity" of the older patient. In the midst of a culture moving at a pace more rapid than most of us can automatically adapt to, the elderly find that familiar scenes are changing, loved ones are disappearing, independence is waning (and along with it, their sense of security and feeling of usefulness); and rarely does a day fail to give evidence of the imminence of their own dissolution. What is labeled rigidity in such people is an attempt to hold on to a world which used to be, a world which provided some dignity, status, self-esteem, independence, and satisfaction. The culture, however, chaotic as it may be, demands that each of us move with it at breakneck speed, and those who do not we label sick.

Psychopathology is the study of the essential nature of mental disease— its causes, the structural and functional changes associated with it, and the ways in which it manifests itself. One could approach the psychopathology of aging in much the same way as one approaches psychopathology in general, in which case one would differentiate between functional and organic disorders, between psychoses and psychoneuroses and the behavior and personality disorders, and then go on to describe specific entities along with any accompanying structural alterations which have so far been identified. But aging is a complex process involving the interaction of many variables, and it is almost impossible to tease out a single one and say that it alone is the cause.

Indeed, in all age groups, modern science regards the mechanistic, reductionistic approach which hunts for a specific cause for any disease entity as outmoded, simplistic, and inexact. And certainly in aging we would be setting the stage for major disappointment were we to try to point our finger at a single cause for the many entities with which we deal. No matter what the symptom picture or the disease, each older person we see comes to us with difficulties arising not only from the effects of structural changes in his central nervous system which are part of the aging process, but from the equally important changes in the way society and his culture treat him, the changes in his relationships with his family and loved ones, the changes in his lifestyle as a result of enforced retirement, and a host of other alterations which are invariably overlooked in an attempt to find the right diagnosis to write on the Medicare slip.

PSYCHIATRIC DISORDERS OF THE ELDERLY

Rather than to attempt to deal with everything which could happen to the mental apparatus of the older person, it might be more to the point to describe the things which do happen to it. If one were to take a sampling of the older people identified as patients by reason of the fact that they end up in a mental hospital, or require consultation by a psychiatrist when they are in general hospitals or nursing homes, or seek help in a mental hygiene clinic, one would find that the problems could be subdivided into several general categories, each showing a relatively distinct pattern of outcome.

TABLE 3
TYPES OF MENTAL DISORDERS IN THE AGED

Disorder	After 6 months	After 2 years
Late paraphrenia	75% still in hospital	10–25% of total dead
Affective disorders	60% discharged	10–25% of total dead
Delirious states	50% discharged 40% dead	——
Arteriosclerosis (cerebral) often complicated by alcoholic encephalopathy	35% discharged 35% still in hospital 30% dead	70–80% of total dead
Senile dementia	60% dead	70–80% of total dead

Table 3 quite clearly demonstrates that the entire gamut of psychiatric disorders may be encountered for the first time in old age, and that not every psychiatric disturbance in an older person signals the inexorable progress of an organic dementia.

Late Paraphrenia

A case in point is late paraphrenia, a term more popular in Europe than in the United States, where the condition would be classified as paranoid schizophrenia first manifesting itself in old age. It is quite distinct from the organic psychoses, for true dementia is rare even after many years.

Late paraphrenia begins typically in the latter part of the seventh or the early part of the eighth decade, much more frequently in women, and both the women and the men affected are likely never to have married. Furthermore, about a third of the patients have severe defects in hearing or vision. Some paraphrenics appear to have had a forceful, outgoing premorbid personality and throughout their lives manipulated others in a cold and even ruthless way. Most, however, spring from a schizoid or paranoid pattern with a barely adequate social and sexual life, often protected by special circumstances from having to deal with the harsher demands of reality.

The condition itself develops rather rapidly, and the patient progresses from a suspiciousness, mistrust, and misinterpretation to a completely paranoid state with highly systematized delusions. The latter are of two types: in one, the patient accuses her neighbors of trying to get rid of her so they can steal her property or her money. This is the sort of woman who may arm herself with a gun which she turns on every unsuspecting and unexpected visitor, or the woman who withdraws completely from all but a single contact with the outside world. That contact may well be her clergyman, whom she expects to help her eliminate her diabolical persecutors.

In the other type, erotic themes predominate. The patient, convinced that a particular man is madly in love with her, begins to assemble a trousseau. Sometimes it is clear that she has never met her husband-to-be, and the delusional nature of her condition is quickly recognized. Just as often, however, her love object is someone she does know and see—her doctor, or her minister, for instance—and her vivid descriptions of his unbridled passion may fall on a host of overly receptive ears in the community.

The patient is alert, incisive, well-oriented, and even when hallucinations occur, they are in a clear intellectual field. Like other paranoids, the patient is shrewd in assembling her case, and quick to seize upon inconsistency or lapses in the logic of others. She is unreceptive to any suggestion that her own conclusions may be based on false premises, and she becomes increasingly difficult to manage or control. The difficulties of imposing any kind of restraint on such a person in these days of civil liberties need not be dwelled upon. The first goal in dealing with such a patient is to protect her, and her neighbors, from what could be tragic consequences of acting out her delusions. Specific treatments to modify or eliminate the delusions have not been very successful. Electroconvulsive treatment may erase them for a time, but the results are rarely permanent. Though rather out of favor in the United States at the present time, frontal lobotomy has been reported to be helpful in patients with a good premorbid history, a well-integrated personality, and a vigorous constitution. For some, phenothiazines or other tranquilizers may be of value in reducing the intensity of the delusions.

Senile Affective Disorders

Another group of disturbances which do not follow a downhill course of progressive dementia are the senile affective disorders. In 9 cases out of 10, the particular form of the disorder is a depression—by which is meant not simple sadness or unhappiness, but a distinctive clinical entity consisting of (1) feelings of painful dejection and concomitant decrease in self-esteem; (2) difficulty in thinking, which sometimes appears as slowed thinking and at other times as obsessive ruminations about wrongdoing, body functioning, or death; and (3) alterations in psychomotor reactivity, usually in the direction of retardation, but in the older age-group often manifesting an overlay of agitation, with pacing, restlessness, and breastbeating. Some of the older depressed patients are recognized as having a recurrence of the manic-depressive disorder which they have had since their early adult years, and in general their appearance and their response to treatment will follow the same pattern as episodes earlier in life.

Other depressions are simple retarded types, with body concern, constipation, insomnia, an inability to make decisions, general slowing down, and inefficiency being the most prominent symptoms sometimes mistaken for organic confusion. Most, however, have the appearance of involutional melancholia and would be so diagnosed were they not beyond the age limits generally specified for the involutional period. The challenges which life presents are much the same, however, and they include the effects of biologic aging on physical performance and response to physiological stresses; separation of children from the nuclear family and the definition of the grandparental role to the different nuclear families which one's children have founded; enforced retirement with idleness, boredom, and a feeling of uselessness; resultant changes in economic and social status; and enforced disengagement from activities which in the past might have occupied almost the whole of life, and from people important to one's emotional fulfillment. The agitated depression is typically precipitated by some kind of crisis arising from any of those life situations—the loss of a lifetime's savings in a plummeting stock market, the death of a spouse or of a close friend, the discovery of serious physical illness, rejection by or merely the indifference of a child, to name a few.

Whatever sparks the depression, the clinical picture tends to unfold with remarkable similarity. In the beginning appear vague feelings of discontent and uneasiness, an uncertainty about one's worth or competence, and a feeling of not being up to par. Minor physical conditions, such as a back-ache or indigestion, become major concerns. The person becomes increasingly tense, irritable, fidgety, and jumpy; almost totally preoccupied with concern about his physical health, he overreacts to whatever gets through to him from the outside world. He becomes inordinately sensitive to criticism; a minor disappointment brings a flood of tears, and while he clings stickily to others in his search for reassurance, his continuing complaints are an accusatory reminder that people and life are failing him. He has more and more trouble sleeping, and his thoughts both day and night are tormenting questions: what really is wrong, what really is going to happen, what should I do, what have I done to deserve this?

Drugs and Alcohol

At this point, many seek respite from anxiety and insomnia in drugs. In an age accustomed to find relief for anything in the form of one or another pill, tranquilizers afford the promise of instant relief. They may help for a time, but they rarely control symptoms at a dosage level compatible with functioning, particularly since the older person is likely to be overly sensitive to almost every kind of psychopharmacologic agent. What generally happens is that the medications themselves further impair concentration, motor skills, and general performance, and what was taken at first as a short-term ally in the battle against fear and dejection becomes finally another enemy adding more failures to the patient's mounting list of self-accusations. Increasingly, he feels worthless and useless, and may turn to alcohol in an attempt to dilute his despair.

While it would be incorrect to claim that depression is always the basis of alcoholism, there is no doubt that heavy and pathologic drinking is often a mask behind which loss of self-esteem hides. Sometimes, in fact, drinking to excess may be the only obvious symptom in a depressed person. A fairly rapid increase in the amount of alcohol consumed and/or in the frequency of drinking to the point of intoxication is highly suggestive of an underlying depression, particularly in someone over the age of 50.

Alcoholism has long been recognized as a major public health problem in the United States. Not so well known, however, is the extent of alcoholism in the elderly. If one were to look at the people over 65 years of age admitted to psychiatric observation units, one would find that at least one-quarter of them had alcoholism as a complicating factor in their hospitalization, if not, indeed, the sole reason for their admission (Simon, 1970). In other words, of that age group arrested in metropolitan areas, over 80% are charged with drunkenness—a much higher proportion than in any other age group (Epstein, Mills, & Simon, 1970). Of considerable interest from the therapeutic point of view is that most workers have found such alcoholism to be clearly reactive in nature. It responds readily to a combination of antidepressant treatment (usually with thymoleptic agents) and resocialization efforts.

Addicting drugs may also be a problem for the aged, and in some depressed patients drugs are used as people substitutes. Other drug problems in the aged are the continuation of a dependency or an addiction which began anywhere from 15 to 40 years earlier. Their craving has not diminished with age, but their access to money has, and inflation has not spared the drug market. The older addict nowadays is caught in the vise of less income, more expensive drugs, and less potent preparations than he probably was accustomed to. Older addicts as a rule do not like methadone maintenance; nor can they tolerate a drug-free existence. What generally happens, as a result, is that they go on to other drugs—more easily procurable opiates such as codeine or paregoric, or substitutes such as barbiturates—or into multiple drug abuse such as is characteristic of our very young population.

Ordinarily, of course, neither tranquilizing drugs nor alcohol will hold depressive symptoms in check indefinitely, and if the condition is allowed to continue, anxiety will soon be translated into action—in the form of general restlessness, tremulousness, floor-pacing, hand-wringing, etc. Tormented by self-doubts, unable to see anything but failure around him and gloom before him, increasingly certain that his multiple physical symptoms portend some dread and fatal illness, the patient broods about what share he himself might have had in weaving the wretched web which ensnarls him.

What was at first a disquieting notion of self-blame becomes a conviction that earlier failures or sins are responsible for his current plight. He pores over his past life in an unceasing search for maleficence, and the peccadilloes he might uncover assume an importance to him which is totally out of proportion to their objective significance. He makes his environment a confessional by proclaiming guilt for his misdeeds—or even for only his "evil" thoughts—to all who will listen. He looks for ways to expiate and atone, but he is rarely successful in trying to undo his imagined crimes. While such attempts may appear almost comical to the observer, they must nonetheless be recognized as of fateful importance for the patient himself.

Some patients, instead of becoming almost delusionally convinced of guilt, express their inner feelings of worthlessness as protestations about their lack of material worth. Despite a more than adequate bank balance, the patient becomes convinced that he is poor—too poor to afford any kind of treatment, too poor even to live. Still others become obsessed with the idea of death, and their only thoughts revolve about how and when they will die. For some, the already noted hypochondriacal trends continue to dominate the clinical picture, and complaints about the digestive tract—

particularly about bowel function—occupy almost every waking moment of the patient's day.

Whatever the course taken by a particular patient, as guilt and depression deepen he feels trapped and hopeless, and he may turn to ideas of doing away with himself as the only way to escape his misery. Some may plan artfully to kill themselves, while others seem to act impulsively. For some, suicide is their conscious goal; for others, the aim instead is to mutilate themselves, perhaps as a way to atone for their imagined misdeeds. The possibility of such action must never be ignored in a seriously depressed person, particularly since as age increases, so does the likelihood of suicide.

Manic Episodes

The remaining 5% to 10% of affective disorders in the elderly consist of manic episodes—with a sudden onset of hyperactivity, flight of ideas, extravagant notions of power, wealth and grandeur, and an elated, euphoric, triumphant mood. As with mania in younger people, such patients have a poorer prognosis than the depressives. About half of them may continue for years in their unbridled and often puerile ebullience, but the interesting thing is how well integrated they remain insofar as their sensorium, mental grasp, and capacity are concerned.

Senile Delirium

A different and important category of disorder is senile delirium. The delirious states are non-specific in their etiology and may be caused by, or related to, any number of physical factors, such as: (1) infections (in any part of the body) with accompanying toxic states; (2) drug reactions;* (3) head trauma related to a fall; (4) post-operative reactions; (5) short-lived cerebrovascular or general cardiovascular irregularities; (6) deficiency states;† or (7) any kind of sudden stress—somatic or psychic. The clinical picture is similar, no matter what cause may ultimately be identified, if any.

The clinical picture is one of sudden onset of clouding of consciousness, often with visual or, less commonly, auditory hallucinations. The patient feels mixed up, unsure of himself, lost, uncertain about the identity of the

---

* A not-unknown occurrence today because of the incompatibility of the many different drugs with which a person is treated. Because the older person tends to have multiple ailments, his physicians tend to give him multiple treatments. The average number of different drugs which a person over 65 receives in today's hospital is 10, yet very little is known about the interaction of more than two drugs.

† These are very common because of poor eating habits. The single person finds it difficult to cook for one, and the poor person finds it difficult to afford a balanced diet. The elderly person more often than not is both, but even if he is not poor, his depression may make him convinced that he is worthless in a material sense; in either case, he often ends up not eating.

people around him, vague about time, and unclear in his recall of recent events. The clouding and hallucinations may be intermittent, or they may continue uninterruptedly for many weeks, even after the precipitating cause has subsided. While confused, the patient is restless, resistant to any attempts to intervene, often wanders aimlessly without knowing where he has started from or where he has ended, and is unable to sleep. The chief physical danger is exhaustion and cardiovascular collapse.

Whatever the underlying condition, about half of those affected die, and about half recover completely; very few go on to a progressive cerebral degeneration. An attack of delirium in an older person should thus be regarded as a medical emergency which demands an intensive workup to track down the specific agent or constellation of factors which has produced the episode. If those underlying factors can be identified and treated, the chances are high that the patient will end up in the completely recovered group, and will return to the same level of functioning he held before the incident.

Cerebral Arteriosclerosis

The progressive disorders of old age include senile dementia, or simple senile deterioration, which accounts for about 20% of the group; cerebral arteriosclerosis, accounting for about 30%; and mixed senile-arteriosclerotic forms which make up the other half.

It is assumed that the same factors which influence coronary atherosclerosis probably predispose to cerebral arteriosclerosis. In this connection, see Table 4.

TABLE 4

FACTORS PREDISPOSING TO ARTERIOSCLEROSIS

1. hypercholesteremia
2. hypertension
3. obesity
4. diabetes
5. heavy smoking
6. hypothyroidism
7. renal damage
8. physical inactivity
9. personality makeup
10. family history
11. gender (males 3:1)

In general, within the arteriosclerotic group there are two routes of progression, determined by the type of pathology within the cerebral circulatory system. In one, hyperplastic degeneration of the vessels produces focal lesions within the parenchyma of the brain, and mainly neurologic symptoms result, depending upon the particular sites attacked. Fits, aphasia, agnosia, apraxia, upper-motor-neuron paralyses, tremors, chorea, athetosis, Parkinsonism, drowsiness, and finally coma may all be seen, with relatively few manifestations in the mental/psychologic/interpersonal/social parameter. In the other, hypoplastic degeneration of the walls of the small vessels results in collapse of the vessels and gross hemorrhagic softenings of areas of the brain. The symptoms are then mainly in the mental sphere, their specific type again depending upon the particular sites of brain affected. Predominant frontal lobe involvement, for example, manifests as *Witzelsucht* (facetiousness), lapses in moral or ethical standards, a callous euphoria, and a general deterioration in interest and attention. Lesions in the basal ganglia may produce a petulant, whining attitude, with impulsive behavior outbursts.

Temporal lobe involvement generally brings depression, often with visual hallucinations, while parietal lobe involvement often produces somatic preoccupation and hypochondriasis. On the physical side, the patient begins to complain of headaches, dizziness, or feelings of discomfort in the head and neck. His family may note that he has a decreasing tolerance to alcohol. His general physical maneuverability may be embarrassed by recurrent episodes of fleeting loss of power in the arms and legs, or of paresthesiae (such as numbness) in those areas. Transitory aphasias or apraxias may also be noted early, and stance becomes insecure, with a short and spastic gait, transitory tremors of the upper body, and inequalities of the pupil.

On the mental side, among the earliest symptoms are mental fatigability and impaired creativity. The patient's memory has an uncertain quality about it, and the irritability he shows—often combined with some effective lability —may be misdiagnosed as an anxiety state. He may show transitory ideas of persecution or extreme jealousy at an early stage, and at least half of the patients have acute confusional episodes before dementia becomes profound. Some workers have distinguished pseudoneurasthenic, affective, and confusional syndromes in the early phase of cerebral arteriosclerosis, but the usual picture is a combination of them all.

As the disorder progresses, discontinuity of the thought processes becomes more marked. Memory is fluctuating and capricious—what could be recalled yesterday seems to be lost today, and the sensorium accordingly becomes spotty and undependable. The patient cannot think quickly or accurately; nor can he progress readily from one topic to another. Instead, he clings to what has already been elaborated, and his perseverative tendencies are the bane of his children and visitors. He becomes increasingly egocentric; since he can only poorly appreciate what is going on outside him, he loses initiative and energy; he neglects his personal appearance. Antisocial or unethical behavior is fairly frequent, probably not an uncovering of long-latent psychopathic traits but rather an outgrowth of defects in comprehension. The befuddled man of 70 with urinary frequency and an intention tremor may really be trying only to undo his zipper when he thinks he has found a safe spot to void, not seeing the rapt attentiveness of the middle-aged spinster 30 yards away who will later tell the judge that he touched himself obscenely for a full five minutes before he finally exposed himself to her.

The nucleus of the personality is generally retained, and depending upon what that personality was, the patient may become suspicious and distrustful, or quarrelsome and fault-finding, or explode in emotional outbursts with minimal provocation. He retains his capacity for normal and appropriate affective responses, and his face often has an expression of perplexed distress, an expression which is disconcertingly appropriate to the altered reality with which he must deal. The overall course of the disorder is irregularly downhill, with retention of some insight and some ability to relate socially to others, but with an instability of mood and unpredictable acute episodes of neurologic signs (including convulsions).

Senile Dementia

Senile dementia is similar in many respects, but there are some notable differences. One must make a clear distinction between senile dementia and normal aging, for senile psychosis causes not only a quantitative impairment of some attributes of the personality but a rapid disorganization of the personality as a whole. It is a disease with a fairly well-defined course, and when the diagnosis is made it implies death within a few years. On the average, the patient will be dead within two years after hospitalization has been deemed necessary.

Few cases begin under the age of 70, although the pathologist can identify the neural changes in many under the age of 60. There is no direct correlation between the degree of brain tissue damage and the degree of functional impairment, a finding which strongly supports the theory that tissue damage alone is not responsible for the symptoms. Females are more often affected than males, the reverse of the situation with cerebral arteriosclerosis.

Usually the condition begins insidiously and thereafter advances evenly and rapidly. In a few, an acute delirium may signal the onset of the condition, with restlessness, auditory and visual hallucinations, and paranoid suspicions leading to a violent assault. Recovery from the episode is never complete, and what remains is a dementia far more severe than the history shows was present before.

Perception, registration, and impressionability are impaired early, and mental processes in general are hindered in their activation. As a result, the patient requires a simplification of anything he is to understand, and at best he will borrow a solution from the past to work on a problem in the present. His memory becomes faulty—first to go is his memory for recent, concrete events, then his memory for names, later his memory for the names of abstract objects, and finally his memory for the names of things.

In contrast to the aphasic, he will admit his lapses without resentment, and unlike the arteriosclerotic he can accept them without apparent distress. In any event, his failing memory in combination with his multiple sensory impairments can no longer support an adequate orientation. He becomes confused about time and space, and may develop amnesic crises and an inability to differentiate between facts and imagination, between perceptions and hallucinations. He calls the hospital a hotel or butcher shop, gives it an address close to his home, and dates everything prior to his own illness.

Often there is a depressive coloring with delusions of guilt; but the mood is shallow, and the depressive shifts are transient. As the condition progresses, more and more of the past is blotted out, leaving only islands of memory about vivid experiences in the patient's past life. The term dementia is ordinarily used when the patient's sensorium and mental grasp are so disturbed that his relationship to his surroundings is completely falsified or at best fragmentary. The patient tires easily and cannot follow an argument. He is slow and perseverative, and even familiar and habitual tasks confuse him. Until early habits disappear completely, they are insistently repeated, leading to misoneism, obsessiveness, and stereotypy. Thought and speech disorganize until all that remains is an unintelligible babble.

Along with the changes in sensorium are changes in social and interpersonal relationships. The ethical obtuseness so often reported in the senile psychotic springs from a combination of cerebral disinhibition on an organic basis, loneliness, absence of any usual or acceptable means of gratification, and impairment of finer discriminatory sensibilities. One must recognize that age does not obliterate sexual interest—65% of men in their 60s are still having intercourse (Pearlman & Kobashi, 1972). Not only may unusual or so-called perverted sexual behavior occur, but the patient may also become dirty, greedy, thieving, foul-mouthed, etc.

MENTAL AND LEGAL COMPETENCY

For the senile psychotic, be he suffering from senile dementia or cerebral arteriosclerosis, the question of mental capacity and competence often arises. The presence of squandering, hoarding, and gullibility are typical indicators of such marked impairment in judgment, insight, and general intellectual functioning that the examiner can advise the court that the patient cannot function totally independently in such and such a way, or in such and such an area. There are many areas in which mental capacity and competence can be called into question, and Table 5 gives a list of most of them.

PROGNOSIS

The later changes in the patient's affect correspond with the delusions he develops—be they self-accusatory, hypochondriacal, persecutory, or sexual.

TABLE 5

LEGAL AREAS INVOLVING COMPETENCY

1. Making a will
2. Making a contract, deed, sale
3. Marrying or divorcing
4. Adopting a child
5. Being a fit parent
6. Suing and being sued
7. Receiving or holding property
8. Making a gift
9. Operating a motor vehicle
10. Voting
11. Responsibility for criminal act or tortious civil wrong
12. Standing trial for criminal charge
13. Being punished for criminal act
14. Having a guardian, committee, trustee appointed
15. Commitment to or discharge from mental institution
16. Being paroled or put on probation
17. Giving valid consent, binding release, waiver
18. Being a witness (testimonial capacity), judge, or juror
19. Professional practice: physician, lawyer, teacher
20. Representing public: governor, etc.
21. Acting in fiduciary capacity: trustee, executor, etc.
22. Business practice: director, stockholder, etc.
23. Receiving compensation for inability to work as a result of injury
24. Fitness for military induction or discharge

[Mezer & Rheingold, 1962, p. 827.]

Ordinarily, the delusions are fleeting, unsystematized, uncolorful, and are related more to the patient's inability to grasp the nature of reality rather than any premorbid paranoid or depressive trend. The hallucinations seen are most often visual, less commonly auditory, and only rarely of smell or taste unless there is major involvement of the temporal lobe and the uncinate area. Overall, most patients show a picture of simple dementia, about 20% develop a predominantly paranoid picture, and about 10% have mainly affective manifestations. Physical changes proceed apace with the mental deterioration. The vibratory sense is impaired early, then touch and pain. Reflexes become more and more sluggish, and focal neurological signs appear if arteriosclerosis begins to complicate the picture. Sphincter control is often impaired early, although in general it is taken as an indicator of a poor prognosis for survival.

For the more clearly organic disorders of the senium—and particularly senile dementia and cerebral arteriosclerosis—there are four criteria suggestive of early mortality: the severity of the mental impairment and the brain syndrome; the severity of physical dependence on others; the presence of incontinence; and the number of errors on the mental status questionnaire [Table 6]. More than half of patients with all four will be dead within one year.

TABLE 6

MENTAL STATUS IN AGED

1. What is the name of this place?
2. Where is it located (address)?
3. What is today's date?
4. What is the month now?
5. What is the year?
6. How old are you?
7. What month were you born in?
8. What year were you born in?
9. Who is the president of the United States?
10. Who was the president before him?

[Kahn, Goldfarb, Pollack, & Peck, 1960, p. 326.]

REFERENCES

Agate, J. Common symptoms and complaints. In I. Rossman (Ed.) *Clinical geriatrics.* Philadelphia: Lippincott, 1971. Pp. 357–368. (a)

Agate, J. The natural history of disease. In I. Rossman (Ed.) *Clinical geriatrics.* Philadelphia: Lippincott, 1971. Pp. 115–120. (b)

Busse, E. W. Psychopathology. In J. E. Birren (Ed.) *Handbook of aging and the individual: Psychological and biological aspects.* Chicago: University of Chicago Press, 1959. Pp. 364–399.

Busse, E. W. Research and training in clinical gerontology: Psycho-social. *Interdisciplinary Topics—Gerontology,* 1970, *5,* 14–22.

Butler, R. N. Clinical psychiatry in late life. In I. Rossman (Ed.) *Clinical geriatrics.* Philadelphia: Lippincott, 1971. Pp. 439–460.

Cohen, E. S. Problems of older people: Integration of health and social services in federally funded programs. *Bulletin, New York Academy of Medicine,* 1973, *49,* 1038–1050.

Epstein, L. J., Mills, C., & Simon, A. Antisocial behavior of the elderly. *Comprehensive Psychiatry,* 1970, *11,* 36–42.

Kahn, R. L. Psychological aspects of aging. In I. Rossman (Ed.) *Clinical geriatrics.* Philadelphia: Lippincott, 1971. Pp. 107–114.

Kahn, R. L., Goldfarb, A. I., Pollack, M., & Peck, A. Brief objective measures for determination of mental status in aged. *American Journal of Psychiatry,* 1960, *117,* 326–329.

Kleemeier, R. W. Behavior and the organization of the bodily and the external environment. In J. E. Birren (Ed.) *Handbook of aging and the individual:*

Psychological and biological aspects. Chicago: University of Chicago Press, 1959. Pp. 400–451.

Mayer-Gross, W., Slater, E., & Roth, U. M. Aging and the mental diseases of the aged. In W. Mayer-Gross, E. Slater, U. M. Roth (Eds.) *Clinical psychiatry.* (2nd ed.) Baltimore: Williams & Wilkins, 1960. Pp. 477–543.

Mezer, T. R. & Rheingold, P. D. Mental capacity and incompetence: A psycho–legal problem. *American Journal of Psychiatry,* 1962, *118,* 827–831.

Pearlman, C. K. & Kobashi, L. I. Frequency of intercourse in men. *Journal of Urology,* 1972, *107,* 298–301.

Rachlis, D. Suicide and loss of adjustment in the aging. *Bulletin of Suicidology,* 1970, *7,* 23–26.

Simon, A. Physical and socio-physiologic stress in the geriatric mentally ill. *Comprehensive Psychiatry,* 1970, *11,* 242–247.

Weiss, E. Sensory functions. In J. E. Birren (Ed.) *Handbook of aging and the individual: Psychological and biological aspects.* Chicago: University of Chicago Press, 1959. Pp. 503–543.

Welford, A. T. Psychomotor performance. In J. E. Birren (Ed.) *Handbook of aging and the individual: Psychological and biological aspects.* Chicago: University of Chicago Press, 1959. Pp. 562–613.

Williams, H. A. Problems of older people: The Congressional outlook. *Bulletin, New York Academy of Medicine,* 1973, *49,* 1028–1031.

IV
RETIREMENT:
CENTER OF THE AGING
CHALLENGE

Retirement: The Emerging
Social Pattern

R<small>UTH</small> G. B<small>ENNETT</small>*

Ruth Granick Bennett received her A.B. degree in 1955 from Brooklyn College of the City University of New York, and her Ph.D. (in sociology) from Columbia University in 1962. She is currently principal research scientist in the Gerontology Unit of Biometrics Research, New York State Department of Mental Hygiene, a post which she has held since 1969. She is also adjunct associate professor, Program in Services to the Aging, Teachers College, Columbia University, and research associate, department of psychiatry, College of Physicians and Surgeons, Columbia University. Dr. Bennett is the author or co-author of more than 25 articles in scientific and professional journals, and was the co-chairman, Workshop on the Institutionalized Aged, International Congress of Gerontology, held in Washington, D.C., in August, 1969. She is a member of the American Sociological Association and the Gerontological Society.

Retirement refers to a life stage, an event, and a process of adjustment (Shanas, 1972). As a life stage, it is a period of economic inactivity socially prescribed for workers in later life. As an event, it is characterized by the

* The author wishes to acknowledge the collaboration of Holly Wright, research assistant, Dr. David E. Wilder, associate research scientist, and Elizabeth Sanchez, research scientist, all in biometrics research, New York State Department of Mental Hygiene.

"separation from paid employment which has the character of an occupation or a career over a period of time" (Donahue, Orbach, & Pollak, 1960, p. 330). Finally, as a process of adjustment it "begins when retirement is first considered by the individual and abates when the individual has achieved a new distribution of his energies and new modes of behavior" (Shanas, 1972, p. 236) in the absence of his work role. Thus, retirement can be viewed both as an institutional arrangement in society and as an experience of the individual.

RETIREMENT AS AN INSTITUTIONAL ARRANGEMENT

The social and economic forces which have led to the emergence of retirement as an institutional arrangement within industrial societies have been described by Donahue, Orbach, and Pollak (1960). They discuss the capacity of industrial societies to support retirement as a life stage made possible by an economy in which adequate production of goods and food has been achieved. In their view, such a capacity to support retirement can be a liberating force: individuals are allowed increasing amounts of leisure time, and in their later years, an alternative to a work-centered lifestyle becomes available to them. But these same authors are quick to draw attention to the pressures within the economic system to meet the demands for employment under conditions of job scarcity and to achieve sufficient consumption (as opposed to sufficient production), and they cite these pressures as factors which turn retirement into a coercive force prescribing unemployment for the older segment of the population. Indeed, Kreps (1968) has suggested that retirement relates more to the state of the economy than to the state of the aging.

According to Gordon (1960), changes in occupational structures and in technology have made it increasingly difficult for older persons to compete in the job market, the result being a decline in their participation in the labor force. Slavick (1966) suggests, too, that the declining importance of agriculture, the increasing availability of financial-support systems, and the institution of hiring-age limits and compulsory retirement practices have also contributed to a continuing decrease in the labor-force participation of the aged since the turn of the century. The proportion of males 65 and over in the labor force has decreased from 68.3% in 1900 to 41.4% in 1950, from 30.5% in 1960 to 24.8% in 1970 (U. S. Bureau of the Census, 1970).

Coincidental with this decrease is the rising proportion of aged persons in the population. In 1970, persons 65 and over constituted 10% of the population in the United States, and it is projected that the proportion may increase to 13% in 2020 (U. S. Bureau of the Census, 1971a). According to Schulz (1973), the key issues posed for any society by an aging population are the effect the aging of the population has on the capacity and desire of that population to provide income protection in retirement for succeeding generations of older persons, and the way in which the cost of retirement support should be apportioned among groups within one generation and among generations.

That elderly persons account for 17% of the poverty population and only 9% of the above-low-income population (U. S. Bureau of Census, 1971b) indicates that the issues Schulz raises are yet to be seriously faced. In the light of the economic circumstances which these percentages imply, Kreps' (1968) observation is well taken that if the older person is alloted an increasing span of leisure without sufficient income with which to enjoy it, retirement becomes merely a euphemism for unemployment.

The disparity between the economic circumstances of the younger, working generation and the retirees has developed because retirement-support programs have been inadequate and because, as the economy has expanded and the cost of output decreased, workers have benefited with increased wages, and investors with greater returns on their investments, but there has been no benefit to consumers in the form of a general decrease in prices. As a result, the position of the economically inactive retirees who are on fixed incomes worsens in relation to the economically active, even if price stability is maintained (Spengler & Kreps, 1963).

Kreps (1968) observes that arguments for higher transfers of income to the aged generally rest upon the disparity between the incomes of the aged and those of younger persons and on the scarcity of jobs and the relative disadvantage of the elderly for securing jobs. She suggests, however, that the significance, for the broader interests of society, of the economic plight of the elderly and of their ever-increasing proportion in the population should not be obscured. One important consequence of the exodus of older workers from the labor force is the burden of financial support for retirees borne by current generations of workers, a situation exacerbated by compulsory-retirement practices and the current pressure for early retirement.

In a review of the arguments for compulsory and flexible retirement, Palmore (1972) suggests that the major arguments for compulsory retirement are that it is easy to administer; prevents discrimination against individual workers; provides predictability; forces management to provide retirement benefits at a determined age; reduces unemployment by reducing the number of workers competing for limited jobs; prevents seniority and tenure provisions from blocking the hiring of younger workers; and, in any case, forces retirement in only a few instances since most workers 65 and over want to retire or are incapable of continuing to work. Palmore refutes each of these arguments and, in support of flexible retirement, maintains that compulsory retirement is unfair to the productive worker, damaging to individuals and to groups psychologically and socially, and economically wasteful.

Palmore (1972) reviewed Social Security surveys, which reflect the pervasive impact of compulsory-retirement policies, and found that 11% of male beneficiaries in 1951 and 21% in 1963 had retired because of compulsory-retirement practices (Palmore, 1967). According to the 1969 Social Security survey of newly entitled beneficiaries, 52% of the non-working beneficiaries, who had been wage or salary workers and who had become entitled at age 65, retired because of compulsory-retirement practices (Reno, 1971). Early retirement appears to be on the increase as well. Katona and Morgan (1967), in a national sample study, found that a large proportion of American men plan early retirement, a trend also reflected in a study by Palmore (1964). A number of problems are commonly raised in the literature on the economics of retirement. The economic problem which early retirement poses for the individual is that it limits his work-life earnings and the amount of his retirement benefits, and this means that smaller amounts of savings and lower monthly benefits must be spread over a longer retirement period. The implications of early retirement and of compulsory retirement for the broader interests of society are that the burden of financial support of retirees for extended numbers of years becomes heavier, and the weight of the burden of the older generation on the younger, working generations may lead to the exacerbation of intergenerational tensions and, possibly, to a worsening of the relative economic circumstances of the elderly if adequate sacrifices by the working generations are not forthcoming.

Schultz (1973) has suggested a number of incentives to individuals and organizations which would encourage flexible retirement and later retirement and, by limiting the number of those retired, would minimize the problem created by a high proportion of dependent or economically inactive persons who must be supported at the expense of the consumption of current wage-earners. He recommends requirements for Social Security; exempting workers over the normal retirement age from Social Security taxes; removing tax-exemption privileges for employers' private pension contributions to finance early-retirement pension incentives; outlawing or liberalizing mandatory-retirement-age policies; making work experiences for workers more enjoyable; and developing "flexible" retirement job opportunities. In other words, his aims are to discourage rather than encourage movement out of the labor force. Kreps (1968) suggests that two possible goals for policy might be to create "part-time employment" in the place of full-time unemployment for the elderly, and to spread leisure time among all age groups. She contends that such a policy would have the advantages of providing longer vacations earlier in life and a more even distribution of earnings over the life span.

PSYCHOSOCIAL IMPLICATIONS OF RETIREMENT

Empirical investigations into the psychosocial implications of retirement have primarily addressed themselves to the following areas: (1) attitudes toward retirement; (2) reasons for retirement; (3) predictors of adjustment to retirement; (4) effects of retirement; and (5) effects of living in retirement communities. A discussion of some studies in these five areas follows.

Attitudes Toward Retirement

Early investigations regarding pre-retirement attitudes toward retirement, such as the one by Friedman and Havighurst (1954), have shown that to the extent that one's occupation is time-filling or merely a means of earning a living rather than intrinsically satisfying, one's attitude toward retirement prior to retirement will be favorable. In a more recent investigation, Lehr and Dreher (1969) analyzed data from a cross-national study and concluded that while attitudes toward retirement during the period immediately after retirement appear to be determined by the worker's attitude toward his work history, attitudes toward retirement during the period just prior to retirement appear to be determined by his attitude toward his immediate job situation. The Cornell longitudinal study of retirement found that anticipating adequate financial circumstances in retirement was associated with a favorable anticipation of retirement (Streib & Schneider, 1971). Schneider's (1965) analysis of data on white-collar women in the Cornell study suggests that marital status may be a predictor of retirement anticipation: those white-collar women who are single, then married, then widowed were likely in that order to anticipate retirement favorably.

Studies have been conducted to see whether the retirement period is thought about and planned for by workers prior to retirement. Fillenbaum (1971) found that thinking or worrying about retirement was inversely related to the occupational status of workers and their level of education, but that planning for retirement was positively related to their occupational status and level of education. Simpson, Back and McKinney (1966) found that planning for retirement was associated with exposure to information on the subject. Thinking about and planning for retirement appear to increase as the worker approaches retirement age (Fillenbaum, 1971).

Reasons for Retirement

The occasion of retirement has been investigated in terms of the reasons for retirement and the time retirement occurs. Researchers have been interested in the incidence of compulsory retirement as compared with the incidence of voluntary retirement, and in the specific motivations of those who retire voluntarily. One such investigation is Palmore's (1965) analysis of a national survey conducted in 1963 in which he found that a majority of the men and women surveyed had retired for involuntary reasons. Of the reasons given for voluntary retirement, preference for leisure was mentioned more often by women than by men, but few in either group mentioned job dissatisfaction as a reason for retiring.

The question of the time of retirement has received increasing attention as the incidence of early retirement increases, and it would appear that, as in other aspects of retirement, socioeconomic status is of some significance. In the Cornell study, Streib and Schneider (1971) found that men and women with lower incomes, lower education, and lower occupational status were more likely to retire early than were others.

Predictors of Retirement Adjustment

Adjustment to retirement has been measured in terms of attitude toward retirement, feelings of job deprivation (what, if anything, is missed about having a job), and general measures of life satisfaction and morale in retirement. The level of role activity, evaluation of present roles and any change in role activity accompanying retirement have been used as measures of adjustment (Havighurst et al., 1969).

Since retirement may be defined as a loss of work role, feelings of job deprivation in retirement have been studied. Occupational status has been shown to be predictive of the satisfactions individuals derive from their jobs (Friedman & Havighurst, 1954) and, in turn, of the kinds of job deprivation, or loss, which retirees experience (Lehr & Dreher, 1969). Shanas (1972), in a review of retirement literature, cites the findings of numerous studies which show that the aspect of having a job which is missed the most is income and that missing income is inversely related to occupational status. Furthermore, certain selected job characteristics of the occupation from which the individual retires, such as rank, prestige, and control over job, seem to have an impact on how the retiree adjusts to retirement. Pollman (1971), for example, found that morale in retirement was positively associated with precisely these characteristics.

Impact of Retirement

Hearnshaw* investigated the multiple effects of retirement on the psychological, social, and health states of industrial workers in northwest England.

---

* This study, by L. S. Hearnshaw, entitled: The effects of retirement on industrial workers, is available only in a four-page mimeographed form. It was issued at the University of Liverpool, and is without a date.

All his subjects were male, pre-retireees aged 55–65, and retirees aged 65–75 (N = 685), and his purpose was to compare their circumstances both before and after retirement. The subjects were interviewed, at home, on matters of housing, health, attitudes, income, social life, and psychological state.

The following findings were obtained: (1) *Attitude toward retirement*: half of the retirees would like to have continued some kind of work on a part-time basis; pre-retirees were apprehensive and preferred not to talk about retirement. (2) *Health*: Illness frequency differed between the shop-floor workers and the office workers. Among the shop-floor pre-retirees, as retirement approached, the frequency of treatment for illness increased; among the office workers, there was a decrease in the treatment of illness. Among the shop-floor retirees, there was a temporary health improvement with a return to equal frequency of illness after five years. Among the office workers, there was an increase in illness immediately after retirement. Hearnshaw attributes the differences in health prior to retirement to the differences in attitude toward work and social status. Post-retirement health decline was attributed to the aging process. (This conclusion seems to be more intuitive than factually based.) (3) *Social life*: Office workers were more worried about social deprivation than were shop workers. The former counted on colleagues and friends while the latter relied on family. (4) *Psychological state*: No serious problems were found, but upon retirement for both groups, there was an immediate loss of confidence followed by some recovery and readjustment. The two main perceived disadvantages of retirement were inactivity and social deprivation rather than financial loss. Hearnshaw recommends more preparation for retirement, the provision of opportunities to develop new interests and activities, and a fundamental reconsideration of forced retirement based on chronological age alone.

The social impact of retirement was investigated by Blau (1961) who conducted a study of men and women 60 years of age and over in Elmira, N.Y., and the Kips Bay Health District in New York City. She looked at the effects changes in two major roles have on friendship patterns, since friendships play such an important part in adjustment to old age. The roles considered were widowhood and retirement. She divided the groups by the level of friendship participation, sex, class, and age (60–70, and over 70).

The major finding was that:

In those high friendship participation groups where widowhood and retirement are relatively rare, either change in status places the individual in a deviant position among his peers, differentiates his interests from those of his associates and thereby exerts a detrimental effect on friendships [Blau, 1961, p. 429].

Actually, the emphasis of Blau's study was on the effect of widowhood on friendship participation. The analysis of change in the work role was used as an additional test of the above findings, which it confirmed. For women, retirement had no adverse effect on friendship participation since employment was only a secondary role. Blau did not combine the two independent variables of widowhood and retirement to look at their joint effect.

This rather early study is interesting in that it considers the effects of role loss within an environmental setting as having implications for adjustment to aging. Although widowhood and retirement are prevalent states in the over-70 age group, Blau raised the question of the amount of damage (cognitive impairment, de-socialization) which takes place when the elderly individual holds a deviant position in relation to his own social setting or peer group.

Effects of Retirement Housing

The final group of studies reviewed compares individuals living in retirement housing with their peers who do not. It is not clear how many people currently live in retirement housing and at what rate their numbers are increasing, but this seems to be a growing group.

Much of the information about retirement housing comes from "spinoff" studies of the five-year California Survey of Retirement Housing, the intent of which was to provide base-line information about the status of development of special housing facilities for elderly in good health (Sherman, 1971, 1972; Sherman, Mangum, Dodds, Walkley, & Wilner, 1968; Walkley, Mangum, Sherman, Dodds & Wilner, 1966).

Sherman, Mangum, Dodds, Walkley, and Wilner (1968) selected six representative sites from the more than 3,000 originally surveyed to look at the consequences of residence in retirement housing. The sites selected were (1) a retirement hotel in downtown Los Angeles; (2) a low-cost rental retirement village in central California; (3) a high-rise apartment in the downtown section of a city in southern California; (4) a retirement village where houses were purchased in a desert area of California; (5) a retirement village selling co-op apartments; and (6) a life-care institution for the aged in a college town near Los Angeles. One hundred subjects were selected at each site with a range SES,* age, and marital status. Subjects were asked about interaction with the younger generation, about friends and neighbors as sources of nurturance, use of leisure time, pressures and privacy, satisfaction with the site, and general morale. On the basis of the obtained data, the authors concluded that the negative characteristics at-

* Socioeconomic status. This is defined in Zadrozny's *Dictionary of social science* as follows: The status or amount of prestige in a society, which is associated with the amount of income, wealth, or type of occupation.—Ed.

tributed to age-segregated housing did not adversely affect individuals residing there, and that though not all, at least several, of the possible positive characteristics were present, along with a high degree of general satisfaction.

In a subsequent publication, Sherman (1971) examined the motivation behind the choice to live in retirement housing. To the original 600 residents of the six housing sites listed above, she added a control sample of an additional 600 elderly living in dispersed housing in California. The control sample matched the test sample on ten demographic characteristics but differed in type of housing. Besides examining the motivations behind the choice, she sought information on expectation fulfillment, the attitudes on the part of dispersed-housing elderly toward retirement housing, and their reasons for choosing not to live there.

Each test subject and each control respondent were given an initial interview and a follow-up interview after a two-year interval. Of the original 1,200, 952 responded to the follow-up interview.

It was found that motivations behind the choice to live in retirement housing included:

provisions of meals and other services in an urban environment; improved living quarters in close proximity to age peers; attractive quarters in an urban environment; good value in housing and recreation facilities with agreeable climate and suburban atmosphere; easy maintenance and recreation facilities; and security. [Sherman, 1971, p. 135].

The control group liked several of the features which had attracted the others—namely, easy maintenance and recreation facilities—but disapproved of age segregation, and feared regimentation and boredom.

In the follow-up interview, there was found to be reasonable agreement between the test group's expectations and their actual experiences. Moreover, they did not object to those features which hindered the in-moving of those in the control group: age segregation and regimentation.

In a further refinement using these same subjects, Sherman (1972) studied satisfaction with retirement housing, measuring it in three ways: (1) direct attitudinal questions; (2) projective questions concerning the respondent's recommendations for others; and (3) a behavioral measure—e.g., moves away from the site.

In response to the direct attitudinal questions, 55%–70% greatly approved the site, the percentage varying little from one time to another. The projective questions revealed that nearly all experimental and control subjects felt they should not live with their children. There was a large difference between the test group and the controls, and from site to site, in the proportion recommending special retirement housing. There were also differences from site to site with regard to satisfaction with the location and financial arrangements.

In general, it appears that residents of urban sites are more satisfied with their location than those in suburban or desert areas; the younger-aged prefer closeness to the amenities of the city, while the older-aged in the suburbs recommend their location more than the younger-aged in suburban housing sites.

Sherman's final conclusion is that there is

> no one right kind of housing; rather, the person will be most satisfied with the housing that best fits his requirements and condition . . . each individual [should] be aware of the range of housing alternatives and the various dimensions on which a site can be rated, and . . . match these to his own needs and abilities [Sherman, 1972, p. 363].

Lipman (1967) looked at 71 matched pairs of low-income elderly in Florida. Half of the group resided in a low-income public-housing project for the elderly, and the other half, denied acceptance into the project, lived in conventional housing. The group was matched on seven traits: race, sex, age, perceived health, source of income, marital status, and education.

Lipman tested the hypothesis that low-income elderly in a low-income public-housing project would show lower morale, be less trusting, show less responsibility and lower life-satisfaction, and be more willing to disengage, than low-income elderly in conventional housing.

Six scales were administered to the 71 pairs: disengagement, life satisfaction, faith in people, anxiety, morale, and norm of responsibility (achieving or retaining autonomy). There were no significant differences between the groups on any of the scales except morale and norm of responsibility, though the test group scored higher than the controls on all scales. Further examination of the data revealed no relationship between either higher morale or norm of responsibility, on the one hand, and club membership and friends, on the other. The only clarifying factor was that those in the project approved their current home significantly more often than those in dispersed housing.

Though these findings cannot be generalized because of the non-random nature of the sample, Lipman concludes that a consequence of low-cost government housing is increased personal morale and an increase in attitudinal adherence to the norm of responsibility.

Rosow (1967) conducted a well-known study of the impact of age density on the elderly in community housing-developments in Cleveland. He studied a large number of elderly residents of apartment buildings whose old-age concentrations were classed as dense, concentrated, and normal. He found that social integration was associated with residence in buildings of high density of older people, and that the social responsivity to the degree of local concentration of older people was greater among working-class than among middle-class people. The compensatory replacement of missing or lost reference groups with neighbors as a reference group occurred most easily among disadvantaged people living in dense concentrations of older people. People with varying patterns of social interaction—groups which Rosow named the Isolates, the Sociables, and the Insociables—react to high concentrations of elderly people in their immediate environments with decreased, unchanged, and increased morale respectively. Similarly, Messer (1967) found that residence in an age-integrated environment appeared to foster a correlation between low morale and low level of social interaction, as compared with the absence of a positive correlation between the two in an age-segregated environment. The basis for friendship-formation and other forms of social interaction in community housing for the aged is usually proximity. Next-door neighbors tend to become friends in housing for the aged (Carp, 1966; Friedman, 1966; Simon & Lawton, 1967; Lawton & Simon, 1968).

The issue of the impact of age segregation always arouses discussion whenever the subject of retirement housing is raised. In Lawton's (1970) housing study, applicants to such housing preferred or were indifferent to age segregation, while community residents who had not applied for such housing showed a plurality but not a majority favoring age integration. Almost no tenant actively objected to living in an age-segregated environment after having been in one for a year, and relatively few indicated a desire to have children or teen-agers there. A sizable majority, however, would have liked younger adults without children. In one age-integrated housing site the same preference for age-segregated living was expressed. To this clear preference for age peers was added the fact of an almost non-existent degree of visiting between older tenants and teen-agers or children, and an age-segregated limitation of within-building friends named in a sociometric survey of age peers.

Lawton (1970) found, also, that where many on-site services are offered, the population applying to that site tends to be somewhat more dependent—that is, older, less healthy, and, perhaps, less competent in other areas of behavior—than those who apply to sites without services. Thus, it may be concluded that when old people apply to old-age housing units they usually know what they need and want.

DISCUSSION AND CONCLUSIONS

The literature reviewed reflects three types of studies done on the retirement process: (1) analytic and descriptive studies in which an approach to conceptualizing retirement is made; (2) studies of the reasons for and attitudes toward retirement; and (3) studies of the impact of retirement and retirement housing.

Recently Fuelgraff (1972) proposed an analytic model to facilitate cross-cultural comparison of the retirement process for use in countries of comparable but varying degrees of industrialization. She conceptualizes retirement as a new developmental stage in the life cycle, and writes that it is crucial to understand the forces behind this evolving life phase and the factors which influence it. Since there are similarities of development in industrial nations, cross-cultural comparisons and a common model in which to make them would help deal with present and future problems and assist developing countries to avoid them.

The model proposed takes into account the interrelationship between biological and environmental factors on the one hand and societal and cultural patterns on the other. It includes the following factors: (a) politicoeconomic system of a society which determines (b) the social chances of individuals, (c) the cultural patterns being maintained within a society, and (d) the physical condition to which human beings are exposed.

Clearly, in the United States factors, such as attitudes, health, sex, marital status, SES, income, and education, make a difference in the way one anticipates and adjusts to retirement. There is some evidence that pre-retirement counseling and information is helpful in the post-retirement adjustment.

Past research has produced some findings which raise questions only additional, more detailed research can answer. For example, several studies report that both early retirement and involuntary retirement are increasing; but early retirement occurs disproportionately among lower socioeconomic groups who generally are less prepared for retirement and who adjust less satisfactorily to it. Yet, in spite of recent claims of high rates of work dissatisfaction in the United States, research reports indicate that few retire early because of dissatisfaction with their jobs. To be sure, many married women retire early to join their husbands, and liberal pension plans can sometimes make early retirement attractive; but it may be that substantial early retirement is also involuntary retirement.

A number of issues about retirement emerge which require both more research and further conceptualization. For the average retiree, approximately fifty hours per week were previously occupied by work schedules and going to and from work. Upon retirement this may be free or leisure time or enforced unemployment. The average retiree's job may have provided in addition to income (1) a sense of responsibility, productivity, and usefulness; (2) a daily schedule and living pattern; (3) a spirit of competition with incentives to move ahead; and (4) a position in society which yielded some degree of security.

A challenge before us is to develop and institutionalize roles or activity substitutes which can be found to replace the important components associated with work.

There have been many suggestions for filling the leisure time of retirees, but few have been evaluated systematically. Studies comparing elderly persons working at either first or second careers with their counterparts engaged in leisure-time activities are virtually nonexistent. The question whether any activities or program of activities including work activities can be found or developed which will afford the retiree a sense of purpose, well-being, and a secure position in society remains unanswered.

Another, more dramatic approach, suggested by Lee and others, is to think of retirement as an environmental stress imposed upon a vulnerable population with the following traits:

1. Changed ability to compensate for applied stress.
2. Changed tolerance for functional displacement.
3. Cumulation of deleterious material or progressive shift toward a tolerance level.
4. Changed exposure through changed activity patterns.
5. Changed acceptance of environmental effects [Lee, 1969, pp. 179–180].

Looking at the aged as a group more vulnerable to changes and environmental stresses of any sort, we find the need to reduce the impact of retirement and to develop adequate substitutes for work-related activities even more apparent.

The advantage of this approach is that it does not necessarily assume that the work ethic has been equally shared by all who retire. Indeed, it is entirely conceivable that leisure has been eagerly anticipated by many who are no longer able to handle the stress induced by the changes in long-established patterns of daily living which retirement leisure implies. Thus, there is the need not only to find a satisfactory variety of roles and activities for retirees, but to ensure that the impact of retirement-induced changes can be adequately met by those who face them.

REFERENCES

Blau, Z. S. Structural constraints on friendships in old age. *American Sociological Review*, 1961, *23*, 429–439.

Carp, F. *A future for the aged*. Austin: University of Texas Press, 1966.

Donahue, W., Orbach, H. L., & Pollak, O. Retirement: The emerging social pattern. In C. Tibbits (Ed.) *Handbook of social gerontology: Societal aspects of aging*. Chicago: University of Chicago Press, 1960. Pp. 330–406.

Fillenbaum, G. G. Retirement planning programs—At what age, and for whom? *The Gerontologist*, 1971, *11* (Pt. I), 33–36.

Friedman, E. Spatial proximity and social interaction in a home for the aged. *Journal of Gerontology*, 1966, *21*, 566–570.

Friedman, E., & Havighurst, R. J. *The meaning of work and retirement*. Chicago: University of Chicago Press, 1954.

Fuelgraff, B. A retirement process. Paper presented at the Seventh International Congress of Gerontology, Kiev, 1972. Mimeographed.

Gordon, M. S. Aging and income security. In C. Tibbits (Ed.) *Handbook of social gerontology: Societal aspects of aging.* Chicago: University of Chicago Press, 1960. Pp. 208–260.

Havighurst, R. J. *et al.* (Eds.) *Adjustment to retirement: A cross-national study.* Assen, The Netherlands: Roval Van Gorcum, 1969.

Katona, G., & Morgan, J. Retirement in retrospect and prospect. In *Retirement and the individual.* (Hearings before the Subcommittee on Retirement and the Individual of the Special Committee on the Aging, U. S. Senate, 90th Congress, July 26, 1967.) Washington, D.C.: Government Printing Office, 1967. Pp. 587–598.

Kreps, J. M. Economic policy and the nation's aged. *The Gerontologist,* 1968, *8* (2), 37–43.

Lawton, M. P. Ecology and aging. In L. Pastalan & D. H. Carson (Eds.) *The spatial behavior of older people.* Ann Arbor: University of Michigan Press, 1970. Pp. 40–67.

Lawton, M. P., & Simon, B. The ecology of social relationships in housing for the elderly. *The Gerontologist,* 1968, *8* (Pt. I), 108–115.

Lee, D. H. K. Significance of aging in response to environmental stress. In *Proceedings of seminars 1965–69.* Durham, N.C.: Center for Aging and Human Development, Duke University Medical Center, 1969. Pp. 177–183.

Lehr, U., & Dreher, G. Determinants of attitudes toward retirement. In R. J. Havighurst *et al.* (Eds.) *Adjustment to retirement: A cross-national study.* Assen, The Netherlands: Roval Van Gorcum, 1969. Pp. 116–135.

Lipman, A. Public housing and attitudes adjustment in old age: A comparative study. Paper presented at the 20th Annual Meeting of the Gerontological Society, St. Petersburg, Fla., November 10, 1967.

Messer, M. Possibility of an age-concentrated environment becoming a normative system. *The Gerontologist,* 1967, *7,* 247–251.

Palmore, E. Retirement patterns among aged men: Findings of the 1963 survey of the aged. *Social Security Bulletin,* 1964, *27* (8), 3–10.

Palmore, E. Differences in the retirement of men and women. *The Gerontologist,* 1965, *5,* 4–8.

Palmore, E. Retirement patterns. In L. Epstein & J. Murray (Eds.) *The aged population of the U. S.* Washington, D.C.: Government Printing Office, 1967. Pp. 101–112.

Palmore, E. Compulsory versus flexible retirement: Issues and facts. *The Gerontologist,* 1972, *12,* 343–348.

Pollman, A. W. Early retirement: Relationship to variation in life satisfaction. *The Gerontologist,* 1971, *11* (Pt. I), 43–47.

Reno, V. Why men stop working at or before age 65: Findings for the survey of new beneficiaries. *Social Security Bulletin,* 1971, *34* (6), 3–7.

Rosow, I. *Social integration of the aged.* New York: Free Press, 1967.

Schneider, C. J. *Adjustment of employed women to retirement.* (Doctoral dissertation, Cornell University) Ann Arbor, Mich.: University Microfilms, 1965. No. 65–3352.

Schultz, J. H. The economic impact of an aging population. *The Gerontologist,* 1973, *13,* 11–118.

Shanas, E. Adjustment to retirement: Substitution or accommodation? In F. M. Carp (Ed.) *Retirement.* New York: Behavioral Publications, 1972. Pp. 219–243.

Sherman, S. R. The choice of retirement housing among the well-elderly. *Aging and Human Development,* 1971, *2,* 118–138.

Sherman, S. R. Satisfaction with retirement housing: Attitudes, recommendations and moves. *Aging and Human Development*, 1972, *3*, 339–366.

Sherman, S. R., Mangum, W. P., Dodds, S., Walkley, R. P., & Wilner, D. M. Psychological effects of retirement housing. *The Gerontologist*, 1968, *8* (Pt. I), 170–175.

Simon, B., & Lawton, M. P. Proximity and other determinants of friendship formation among the elderly. Paper presented at the 38th Annual Meeting of the Eastern Psychological Association, Boston, April 1967.

Simpson, I. H., Back, K. W., & McKinney, J. C. Work and retirement. In I. H. Simpson & J. C. McKinney (Eds.) *Social aspects of aging*. Durham, N.C.: Duke University Press, 1966. Pp. 45–54.

Slavick, F. *Compulsory and flexible retirement in the American economy*. Ithaca, N.Y.: Cornell University (New York State School of Industrial and Labor Relations), 1966.

Spengler, J. J., & Kreps, J. M. Equity and social credit for the retired. In J. M. Kreps (Ed.) *Employment, income and retirement problems of the aged*. Durham, N.C.: Duke University Press, 1963. Pp. 198–229.

Streib, G., & Schneider, S. J. *Retirement in American society: Impact and process*. Ithaca, N.Y.: Cornell University Press, 1971.

U. S. Bureau of the Census. *1970 census of population*. Washington, D.C.: Government Printing Office, 1970.

U. S. Bureau of the Census. *Current population reports*. (Series P-25, No. 470) Washington, D.C.: Government Printing Office, 1971. (a)

U. S. Bureau of the Census. *Current population reports*. (Series P-60, No. 86) Washington, D.C.: Government Printing Office, 1971. (b)

Walkley, R. P., Mangum, W. P., Sherman, S. R., Dodds, S., & Wilner, D. M. The California survey of retirement housing. *The Gerontologist*, 1966, *6*, 28–34.

Pre-Retirement:
Planning and Programs*

VITO A. GIORDANO

Vito A. Giordano received his B.S. degree from Fordham University in 1956, and his M.S. in education in 1964. He has held a series of administrative positions in Westchester County, including those of Supervisor of Senior Activities, City of New Rochelle, and Supervisor of Senior Services, County of Westchester. At the time of the Institute, Mr. Giordano was Assistant to the County Executive (of Westchester) for Special Services, including Youth Services and Senior Services. Currently, he is Director of Manpower Services in the Department of Social Services of Westchester County. From 1967 to 1969 he was Project Director of a pre-retirement leadership training program in the School of General Studies at Fordham University. In 1967 Mr. Giordano received the Certificate of Appreciation "for outstanding contribution and service to the field of aging in Westchester County." And in 1968 the American Association of Industrial Management presented him with an award "in recognition of leadership and outstanding service in management education and pre-retirement training."

Retirement on a mass scale has been characterized as a relatively new phenomenon in American life, in large measure an outgrowth of our highly

* The author extends his appreciation to Marc Gertz of the University of Connecticut for his assistance in the research connected with this paper.

productive and industrialized economy. We are reaping the benefits derived from the advances in technology, medicine, the physical sciences, and nutrition. Today, one out of every twelve Americans is aged 65 or more, more than 50,000 pension and deferred-profit-sharing plans have been approved under the Internal Revenue Code, and over 90% of all those in paid employment are covered under Social Security.

> The Census Bureau and other statistical sources estimate that out of a population of 300.8 million in the year 2000, the number of persons 48 years and over will be 82.5 million. . . . If there is a significant extension of private pension coverage and one third of those between 48 and 64 elect early retirement, . . . they would join the expected 28.2 million past age 65 to create a retired population of about 46 million [The early retirement time bomb, 1971, p. 24].

Even newer than the accomplished fact of mass retirement, however, is the concept of helping people anticipate and prepare for such things as the changed economic status, health problems, increased leisure time, and shifting social and family relationships which accompany aging and retirement.

One technique for solving some retirement-adjustment problems is the use of a pre-retirement planning program. A ten-year study of retirement, initiated by the Social Security Administration and based on an analysis of Social Security records and data from a mail survey of newly entitled beneficiaries, revealed that both the timing of retirement and the quality of retirement living are fundamentally affected by the character of the years immediately before retirement (Irelan, 1972).

The term "retirement planning" or "retirement counseling" as used in this paper describes the various forms of assistance which any employing organization may provide for its employees to enable them to make a better adjustment to retirement.

PREVALENCE OF PRE-RETIREMENT PROGRAMS

There has been a steady increase in the number of pre-retirement programs, although there is as yet no clear definition of what constitutes pre-retirement planning. The National Industrial Conference Board reports that:

> According to a 1950 survey made by the Equitable Life Assurance Society, only about 13% of the 355 companies questioned had formal or informal programs of indoctrination and preparation for retirement [Brower, 1959, p. 31].

In its own survey conducted in 1964, The National Industrial Conference Board (consisting of 1,000 companies including 700 manufacturing firms and 300 other kinds of companies) found that 65% of the companies polled had instituted some kind of pre-retirement counseling program, although most were reported to be informal (How to prepare your employees for retirement, 1966, p. 54). One-half of the programs were limited to financial discussions, but in 25% retirement-planning literature was distributed, and 21 companies allowed their employees to taper off the number of working hours as they approached retirement age. The report went on to state that

> A survey of 80 Chicago area companies, made in 1964–65 by the Mayor's Commission for Senior Citizens, determined that 80% of these companies had instituted some sort of pre-retirement employee contact [How to prepare your employees for retirement, 1966, p. 54].

Similarly, in a survey conducted by the Management Information Center of Miami for *Administrative Management* magazine, it was reported that of the 200 companies polled, 86% had no formal (again, without precise definition) pre-retirement programs (Most firms neglect retirement counseling, 1971).

What has prompted this rapid growth in retirement planning? Of first importance is the increase in the proportion of older people in our population, and the rapidly growing recognition of the political, social, and economic importance of the elderly. Scientific inquiry into the social and physical aspects of aging has been accelerated, and, stimulated by advances in the field of medicine, striking developments are taking place in the field of social gerontology, the area of research and teaching concerned with the psychological and sociological aspects of aging. Of comparable importance are the expansion of the federal Social Security system and the widespread adoption of pension systems by employers throughout the nation. The universities, too, have made a contribution, by producing a number of important studies on aging. Similarly, commissions on aging, and state and local offices of aging, are beginning to appear in all areas of the country.

This general interest in the aged and in aging itself has given impetus to questions relating to the adjustments attendant upon retirement from work, and the subject of retirement was a major area of study and discussion at the White House Conference on Aging in 1971.

For the employed worker, retirement is a pivotal point in the process of growing older. The Cornell Study of Occupational Retirement points out that:

> Many aspects of aging are a matter of gradual change or deterioration. However, retirement is a status change which is relatively clear cut, and as a consequence has a significant impact upon the persons involved [Streib, Thompson, & Schuman, 1958, p. 5].

When an employee is retired, he is detached not only from his job, but from a role which helped form the pattern of much of his life. This may in part explain why there is some evidence to show that the closer some workers come to the time of retirement, the more they wish to remain at work. Since there is no clear-cut established social role for retired people in our society, retirement, in a very real sense, is what one makes of it.

Furthermore, retirement can be a time of economic deprivation for many older people. The changed financial status which accompanies retirement may have a major effect on adjustment. The mobility of younger family members and the loss of a life partner may create a lonely life for a once busy person. Thus, many powerful social and personal factors are behind the current surge of interest in retirement planning; and there is every reason to believe that this interest will become even stronger in the ensuing years. It is not surprising, therefore, that this growing concern has prompted employers to prepare workers for retirement.

There are many reasons for instituting a pre-retirement program. W. G. Caples, Vice President of Industrial and Public Relations at the Inland Steel Corporation, has stated, "A retired employee enjoying his retirement years is a living advertisement for his employer" (How to prepare your employees for retirement, 1966, p. 54). Other reasons include: increasing the effectiveness of pension plans, improving employee and labor relations, fostering good community relations, and extending corporate responsibility.

Practical business considerations, too, have contributed to company interest in retirement planning. Companies with mandatory-retirement ages have felt that retirement preparation would soften the abrupt break· in employment. Some companies with flexible retirement planning may help encourage employees whose productive capacity has dwindled, but who may be reluctant to retire voluntarily, to give more favorable consideration to making the decision to retire.

Yet by no means is there general agreement that employer organizations should conduct retirement-planning programs. Employer opinions on this subject run the gamut from enthusiasm to complete rejection of the concept. Some feel that encouraging workers to think about retirement injures their usefulness as employees. Others feel that any program which goes beyond an explanation of benefits available from the company is paternalistic and constitutes unwarranted interference in the private affairs of individuals.

TYPES OF PRE-RETIREMENT PROGRAMS

So far in this paper pre-retirement programs have been discussed for the most part in terms of the formality or informality of the programs. It should be recognized that most pre-retirement programs operate in companies which have already established retirement benefit plans. Retirement is either discretionary or mandatory (compulsory). The advantage of a compulsory-retirement program is that it creates an orderly method for the retirement of workers. "The disadvantage of mandatory retirement listed most frequently is the loss of employees who are still efficient and the difficulty of finding replacements for experienced personnel" (Brower, 1959, p. 12). Discretionary programs present the opposite problem. Many companies find it difficult to retire unsatisfactory workers who want to continue working. The workers, however, seem to favor the options afforded by discretionary-retirement policies.

A number of pre-retirement plans operate within the available retirement options. These programs may be classified as general (comprehensive), benefit, or gradual, and the classifications further subdivided according to the approach utilized: individual counseling, group counseling, and/or self-study.

Most comprehensive programs devote a substantial amount of time and effort to the presentation of information on the physical and mental health of the aged, on leisure-time activities, and on planning for family relationships and living arrangements after retirement. These three topics are interrelated, and each invites a consideration of the physical, psychological, and social implications and requirements of life in retirement.

Gradual-retirement plans function in one of three ways: extended vacation with pay, time off without pay, or reduced work weeks. "Basically, a gradual retirement program is one which gives an employee increasing amounts of time off, in addition to regular vacations, in the year or two preceding his retirement" (Gradual retirement plan eases transition, 1967, p. 24).

The benefit plans, the least organized of the programs, give information to retirees dealing exclusively with limited financial matters. A benefit-plan program usually discusses the amount of company benefits, the options for retirement under the company plan, and the procedures to follow in filing for OASI benefits.

The timing, frequency, and duration of pre-retirement programs vary from company to company. The National Industrial Conference Board conducted a survey of 214 companies with reference to their pre-retirement programs. The results of the survey, showing the variety of topics dealt with in such pre-retirement planning programs, are presented in Table 1 (Brower, 1959, p. 32).

In 39% of the 180 companies with informal pre-retirement programs, the beginning date of counseling varied at the option of the employee. In 25%, counseling did not begin until one year or less before retirement, but about one out of five programs began counseling five years before retirement. Conversely, all but one of the 34 formal programs had fixed beginning dates. In 6% of these programs, counseling began ten years

TABLE 1

SUBJECT MATTER OF PRE-RETIREMENT COUNSELING IN 214 COMPANIES

	Companies	
Subject Matter	*Number*	*Percent*
Amount of benefits	213	99.5
Assistance in filing for OASI	190	88.8
Options under company plan	178	83.1
Financial problems	144	67.3
Health advice	107	50.0
Hobbies	104	48.6
Leisure-time activities	93	43.4
Finding other work	92	42.9
Opportunities for civic and religious work	52	24.7

before retirement; in 41%, five years; and in 18%, two to four years in advance of retirement.

MANAGEMENT, UNION, AND UNION–MANAGEMENT PROGRAMS

One of the first pre-retirement plans in the country was developed by the Owens–Illinois Glass Company in 1942. It included a physical examination by the plant doctor in the final year of employment and company-sponsored meetings for discussions of the health problems of older persons, Social Security matters, and other money problems. Booklets concerning retired Owens–Illinois personnel were distributed at these meetings, and a column dealing with retired people appeared in the plant newspaper. The company sponsored a club for retirees, as well as company parties and picnics, and an annual luncheon. Much of the Owens–Illinois program dealt not so much with preparing for retirement as with providing information and activities once employees were no longer working. The Inland Steel Corporation affords us an example of an individual, pre-retirement program (How to prepare your employees for retirement, 1966). As employees reach age 55, they are contacted by members of the personnel staff for a discussion of finances. The procedure is repeated when the employee reaches 60, and again at 64. To the two latter sessions the employee's spouse is invited, and they are given materials, including a free subscription to *Harvest Years*.* The employee retires at age 65, and five months later receives a personalized "How are you doing?" letter.

This program is effective because it is friendly and shows a direct ex-

* Published monthly by the Harvest Years Publishing Company, 150 East 58th St., New York, N.Y., 10022.—Ed.

pression of the company's personal concern. James Haley, President of Chicago's Retirement Resources, Inc., is a booster of these individualized counseling programs and has been quoted as saying: "No two people have the same retirement problems, so no two people should get the same counseling" (A poor retirement program is the most expensive kind, 1971, p. 52). Two of the major drawbacks of such individual plans are that they consume a considerable amount of time and require a trained counseling staff.

Group programs offer an interesting contrast to individual counseling methods, as the program of the Abbott Laboratories illustrates (How to prepare your employees for retirement, 1966). Abbott uses the University of Chicago's course "Making the Most of Maturity" in which ten topics are explored in ten weekly, 90-minute sessions. Before starting the program, each participant is sent an informal explanation of what to expect. The company provides study booklets before each session, and if an employee attends at least 80% of the sessions, he receives a subscription to *Harvest Years*. The value of the group-counseling program lies in its emphasis on the similarities in the problems of retirees; and overall company time is saved since employees meet in groups. There are difficulties, of course, since, in any group, some individuals are reluctant to discuss personal problems, and employees working at different levels may not want to meet together. In the Abbott program, training sessions were held during working hours, and consequently there was some loss of time on the job; but this problem could be eliminated by scheduling the sessions after hours.

A study by Wermel and Beideman identified 161 companies with individual or group-counseling pre-retirement programs. Table 2 indicates the subjects covered in these counseling sessions (Wermel & Beideman, 1961, pp. 80–81):

TABLE 2

RETIREMENT SUBJECTS COVERED IN GROUP AND INDIVIDUAL PROGRAMS IN
161 COMPANIES

Retirement Subject Covered	Percent of Pre-Retirement Programs Including	
	Group	Individual
Use of leisure time	100	87
Figuring retirement income	97	93
Financial planning and family budgeting	92	66
Ways of adding to retirement income	83	64
Housing and living arrangements	81	50
Finding new work activities	75	57
How to live with health problems	70	52

An inspection of the above table indicates that the group sessions tend to be much more comprehensive than individual programs.

There are relatively few self-study pre-retirement programs. One currently in operation is available at North American Aviation, developed in conjunction with the California Institute of Technology (How to prepare your employees for retirement, 1966, p. 55). This program contains a review of the company retirement plan at ages 55, 60, and 62. At age 63, the employee is invited for a personal conference, and at age 64 he is given Social Security information. After retirement, he receives booklets on home safety and finance, and "a personal inventory sheet that he may use to determine what heretofore extracurricular skills can be turned into remunerative work" (How to prepare your employees for retirement, 1966, p. 56).

From the company's point of view, this plan is good because it is easy to administer. But material must be constantly updated, and there is no way of determining if the information is being properly assimilated by the retirees. Self-study programs are characteristic of the following, not atypical, response to company responsibility:

> Pre-retirement counseling by designated members of the company staff walks the thin line between paternalism (or meddling) and the performance of a real service to employees [Wermel & Beideman, 1961, pp. 44–45].

The growth of pre-retirement programs sponsored by unions is increasing. The International Brotherhood of Electrical Workers, Local 1859, and Roosevelt University in Chicago established a continuing eight-week program in 1955 (How to prepare your employees for retirement, 1966). District 31 of the United Steelworkers cooperated with the University of Chicago's Union Research and Education Project to begin a pre-retirement program in 1956 (Wermel & Beideman, 1961). This program provided for the training of union members to carry out the plan.

The National AFL–CIO Community Services Activities Project began a pilot pre-retirement program in Lansing, Michigan, in 1955.

> The objective of the project was to develop a program within the framework of a local community's resources which would assist retired persons to satisfy their needs for companionship and social belonging and help those nearing retirement age understand more fully what was involved in retirement [Wermel & Beideman, 1961, p. 16].

The program includes: a drop-in center, counseling, pre-retirement education, and the mailing of pre-retirement literature to members between the ages of 50 and 65.

The United Auto Workers has been involved in a number of interesting plans, developed jointly by union and management. In 1963, the Scoville Manufacturing Company and Scoville Local 1604, UAW, developed a program in conjunction with the University of Michigan (How to prepare your employees for retirement, 1966). The program is called: "Looking Forward to Retirement," and a company spokesman, commenting on the program, said:

> We know of no other service program that has received such spontaneous approval and acceptance in our plant. It has indeed filled a vital need. We like the program. We use it. We recommend it [How to prepare your employees for retirement, 1966, p. 56].

The UAW has also developed a pre-retirement program with the Chrysler Corporation. Called "Planning Your Retirement," it was originally created by the University of Michigan's Department of Gerontology in 1965, and since that time has seen more than 8,000 employees and their spouses participate. Employees "are offered a free seven-week course in which they are taught everything from how to figure out a retirement budget to making a will. Cost of the program is shared by the company and the U.A.W." (Louviere, 1972, p. 11). Classes are held wherever it is convenient—in churches, schools, community centers, or union halls. Doctors, lawyers, Social Security officials, and other retirement experts are guest speakers. Freewheeling discussions are encouraged in sessions which are led by two trained leaders, one representing the company, the other, the union.

THE FORDHAM PRE-RETIREMENT LEADERSHIP TRAINING PROGRAM

In 1967, the School of General Studies at Fordham University developed a pre-retirement leadership training program, supported by a grant under Title v of the Older Americans Act. Students nominated by companies, unions, and other organizations were trained in retirement topics and basic conference and group-discussion skills. The course included practical training in conducting pre-retirement education sessions and an opportunity for the enrollees to evaluate on-going programs.

The objectives of the program were twofold: (1) to stimulate positive planning for the later years; and (2) to encourage action before retirement through educational programs. Once trained, the participants would organize and develop pre-retirement programs in their respective companies or organizations. Practical seminars were conducted for those who successfully completed the course. The seminar was designed primarily for those trainees who had organized or were planning to organize pre-retirement programs for their employers.

Phase one of the project exposed the students to a curriculum which included the following topics: Health Care, Where to Live in Retirement, Legal Affairs and Taxes, Financial Planning, Social Security and Medicare, Use of Time, Supplementing Retirement Income, Community Service, and the Meaning of Work. During this phase, the participants also received training in Conference Leadership, Group Dynamics, and Techniques for Organizing a Pre-retirement Program.

The second phase was practical in its design as it afforded each student an opportunity to plan, organize, and lead one session relating to the meaning of and possible consequences resulting from retirement. Each session during phase two was evaluated by the students, who offered critiques of the sessions conducted by their fellow-students.

To create an atmosphere of authenticity and to test attitudes, persons approaching retirement were invited to audit a series of sessions planned, organized, and presented by the participants. To evaluate the effectiveness of the sessions offered during phase two, pre- and post-course questionnaires were completed by the retirees.

Phase three was designed as the support element, in which members of the staff provided technical assistance to the trainees in helping them institute pre-retirement education programs in their home organizations.

In the second cycle of training, students enrolled in the course met with trainees from the first cycle who, prior to the course, had had some experience with pre-retirement programs, to share concerns, exchange views, and learn various techniques.

The program was terminated in 1970 with almost 50% of those successfully completing the course instituting some type of pre-retirement program in their employer's organization.

CONCLUSION

The diversity manifest in these pre-retirement programs points to the fact that there is as yet no acceptable paradigm for the development of an appropriate model to meet the diverse needs of the increasing number of individuals who are approaching retirement. These differences are healthy, because without effort there will be no progress. There is need for further experimentation and evaluation, because of the scarcity of objective information on the relative effectiveness of various programs, and the dearth of research evidence on the long-range significance of retirement-planning activities.

The signs are many, however, that retirement planning is a matter of increasing general interest. The 1971 White House Conference on Aging, in its recommendations for action in the section on Employment and Retirement, had this to say about pre-retirement preparation:

Too many individuals fail to plan for retirement or plan too late. Preretirement education and counseling should be provided locally throughout the nation by trained instructors, starting at least five years before normal re-

tirement age. Information on problems and opportunities involved in retirement should be included in all family living and other pertinent courses
at all educational levels. . . . Special courses for those nearing retirement
are urgently needed [1971 White House Conference on Aging, 1973, Vol. 2,
p. 14].

The challenge to the individual as he approaches the retirement phase of
life is to re-think the role of traditional types of work in his life, to investi-
gate the changing financial needs and opportunities of the retirement period,
to adjust to his changing health conditions, and to explore the potential
of available free time. Well-planned and effectively coordinated pre-retirement education programs developed through a total community effort can
help promote a positive attitude toward retirement, so that where science
has added years to our lives, we may add life to these years.

REFERENCES

Brower, B. *Retirement of employees: Policies–procedures–practices.* (Studies in
    personnel policy, No. 148). New York: National Industrial Conference Board,
    1959.
The early retirement time bomb. *Nation's Business,* 1971, *59* (2), 20–24.
Gradual retirement plan eases transition. *Administrative Management,* 1967, *28*
    (9), 24–30.
How to prepare your employees for retirement. *Business Management,* 1966, *30*
    (8), 53–66.
Irelan, L. M. Retirement history study: Introduction. *Social Security Bulletin,*
    1972, *35* (11), 3–8.
Louviere, V. Panorama of the nation's business: Chrysler's road map for retire-
    ment. *Nation's Business,* 1972, *60* (8), 16.
Most firms neglect retirement counseling. *Administrative Management,* 1971, *32*
    (10), 44–48.
A poor retirement plan is the most expensive kind. *Industry Week,* 1971, *170*
    (11), 48–57. September 13, 1971.
Streib, G. F., Thompson, W. C., & Schuman, E. A. The Cornell study of occupa-
    tional retirement. *Journal of Social Issues,* 1958, *14* (2), 3–17.
Wermel, M. T., & Beideman, G. M. *Retirement preparation programs: A study of
    company responsibilities.* Pasadena: California Institute of Technology, 1961.
1971 White House Conference on Aging. *Toward a national policy on aging.*
    (Final Report.) Washington: U. S. Government Printing Office, 1973. 2 vols.

Retirement Among Priests and Religious

ROSE MARY STRAIN, R.S.M.

Sister Rose Mary Strain, R.S.M., received her A.B. degree, with a major in economics, from Manhattanville College, in 1956. From 1960 to 1970 she was Provincial Treasurer for the Sisters of Mercy of the Province of New York, with headquarters at Dobbs Ferry. In 1972 she received a master's degree in education, with a major in gerontology, from Teachers College, Columbia University. Currently Sister Rose Mary is Director of Pre-retirement and Retirement for the Sisters of Mercy. She is also the organizer and President of CAR (Conference for Active Retirement of the Archdiocese of New York). Sister Rose Mary has lectured widely to religious communities throughout the United States on such topics as Pre-retirement, Retirement, Leisure, and Second Careers. Sister Rose Mary Strain is a member of the Gerontological Society, and a member of the Council on Aging, of the National Conference of Catholic Charities.

Although the theme of this Institute is "Aging: its challenge to the individual and to society," this paper will focus on retirement and its challenge to priests and religious, as well as on its impact on dioceses and religious communities. Sufficient reference has already been made in other papers to the fact that the aging process begins at birth and that none of us can escape the process. Retirement is another matter. It begins at a certain time or age in an individual's life, and that time or age is established by circumstances or policy. It is well to note that the word "retirement" is used in this paper

145

rather than "vigil" or "leisure years" or any other way of saying "retirement" without using the word. For if anyone should be able to recognize the truth and to accept it, it is the priest and the religious. Therefore, instead of adopting an ostrich-like attitude, we shall first take a good look at the meaning of retirement.

Webster says "to retire" means "to retreat; to withdraw, especially for privacy; to withdraw from one's occupation or position." In American society, retirement is viewed with fanciful dreams by the young and usually dreaded by the older adult. Until recently the more universal meaning has been to move away from a lifetime occupation to a sentence of idleness. Gerontological research into the death rate among men soon after retirement indicates that the weightiest cause is the sudden change from an active and meaningful occupation to a more or less inactive existence. In our work-oriented culture, prestige and satisfaction are the rewards of being able to "go to work"; but these rewards, familiar surroundings, and friends on the job, all are stripped away by odious retirement. Precisely for this reason, there is a movement in our country today to develop significant pre-retirement programs and worthwhile retirement activities, and in all these plans the most important concentration is on helping people to learn to "live with themselves." In most cases, because sufficient time has not been devoted to it in the past, developing the "self" fully can be the hardest task of a lifetime.

How does all of this, and retirement in particular, apply to priests and religious who have dedicated their lives to God in the service of His people? At long last, it has been recognized that they too are part of the human race and have needs and fears similar to those experienced by the rest of mankind. They too subscribe to the work theory of our society, and fear the day when they will have to leave the familiar post they have held for so many years. They too turn away from the concept of retirement because they do not fully understand its meaning or its potential. In the past, like old soldiers, priests and religious never died; they just faded away—with their boots on. Only weakness or illness forced them out of the active apostolate; but even in such cases the word "retirement" was rarely used. It was not until the 1960s, for the most part, that the need for retirement presented itself more urgently; but, like so many other changes in the Church, this new concept raised questions in the minds of both religious and laity. It is not at all unusual to hear the question "Can priests and religious really retire?"

Before answering the above question, we might do well to consider the meaning of vocation to the clerical and/or religious life. Lee says that vocation implies a divinely and ecclesiastically approbated way of life which is intended to enable the person having the vocation thereby to give greater glory to God, to spread His kingdom more efficaciously, and to achieve greater personal holiness (Lee, 1970, p. 145). Thus, it is obvious that the dedicated person, while in possession of his right senses, never retires from his vocation. Retirement does not mean the cessation of but transition from the full-time profession in which one has been actively engaged to another which permits lighter responsibilities and greater leisure.

When a lay person retires from a job, his life does not end. He becomes involved in a second career or in some leisure occupation. Indeed, some people have retired two and three times, having moved from one career to another, from one interest to another. Once a priest retires from full-time activity, he continues those functions of his priestly ministry which he is still capable of performing. His is a sacred role; and once he becomes a priest, a priest he remains—unless he puts limits on his own vocation. But he can be relieved of the heavy responsibilities of administration, meetings, and routine schedules when age presents its own limitations and stresses. In like manner, the religious who resigns from full-time activity in the profession for which he or she has been trained usually carries on the work of the apostolate either in the same occupation on a part-time basis or in other pursuits within the community or on the outside. Volunteer services, too, play a substantial part in the life of retired religious. For the wise individual, retirement provides time to "be" rather than to "do"—time to concentrate on the rich, warm, exciting, unique gifts God has given to human beings and for human appreciation. The goal of religious life is the supernatural —not the super-human. God never intended His chosen ones to become machines, but He does expect them to be the image and likeness He created them to be.

Why then is there so much confusion concerning retirement among priests and religious? Is it possible that some place along the way the hyphen in Father-administrator, Brother-teacher, Sister-nurse has been lost sight of, and that in our work-oriented culture vocation and avocation have become synonymous? Perhaps because lives and energies have been spent in a particular professional work, we have a tendency to evaluate our own worth and status in the light of that work. Thus, viewed subjectively, to cease doing *that* administrative work, or *that* teaching, or *that* nursing is to step into the unknown—to become useless. It means admitting one's age or inability to students and parishioners, to peers and superiors. It means moving away from familiar surroundings, usually for a religious to the motherhouse. For many a diocesan priest it means feeling like a sixth finger on the left hand if he stays in the rectory or facing a whole new unfamiliar lifestyle if he branches out on his own.

Leading gerontologists (Kutner, Fanshel, Togo, & Langner, 1956) have found that the decline in morale in the retired elderly is related to exclusion from activities which provide status, recognition, and achievement. This may not be the exact cause of retirement depression among priests and religious, but they do have the basic need to be needed, the need to contribute, and they too can fall victim to the conviction that unless one is producing one is useless. This is a strong conviction in America because of the prevalence of the Protestant work ethic. But the work ethic is really not so "modern" as the Protestants; its foundations can be traced back to Plato and Aristotle. Like all early Greeks, these writers believed that the purpose of work is to attain leisure, without which there can be no culture (Miller, 1970). They praised the virtue of a playful attitude toward life, but it was their particular philosophy on work which began the breakdown of God's uncomplicated gift to mankind, the unity of play and seriousness.

Miller claims that Plato was the source of the "Coca-Cola" philosophy of play; that is, that man pauses to be refreshed, so that he may better perform a life of labor. Plato contended that human affairs were hardly worth considering in earnest, but that in fact man must be in earnest about them because he is compelled by a sad necessity. At this point, seriousness and non-seriousness in the concept of play were separated. Aristotle went even further when he extolled serious things as intrinsically better than funny or amusing things, stating that it is childish to make serious business of amusement. Thus, the puritanical concept began: play is secondary to work; labor is primary. Miller states that these notions have been called serious *faux pas* on the part of Plato and Aristotle because they began a revolution in the history of ideas which made man feel he should be working constantly. Hence, his compulsion always to be doing something useful or serious.

The early writers of the Church sanctioned the work philosophy of Plato and Aristotle, as is evident from the documents which have come down to us. In the rules written for the religious life, hard work and devotion to God are always considered compatible. Leisure had no place of honor in the pursuit of perfection; it is always mere diversion. Therefore, it is understandable that, for priests and religious in general, who have nurtured a strong lifetime guilt complex about leisure, retirement (which has usually been associated with idleness and leisure) should pose such a threat.

In the Church, formal retirement planning did not take place until after the Decree on the Ministry and Life of Priests was issued during Vatican Council II (1966; pp. 532–576). At that time the Council urged that pastors who were unable to fulfill their office properly and fruitfully voluntarily submit their resignations. Later, the Holy See set up norms for the implementation of the Decree, and at that time the age of 75 was established as mandatory, with the bishop retaining the right to accept or defer the resignation. What has been the progress with respect to the retirement planning for priests? We will turn our attention to that question now.

RETIREMENT OF PRIESTS

The early part of the 1960s witnessed the formation of priests' senates and diocesan commissions throughout the United States, and during those years, there was considerable research into the matter of pension plans for priests; the results of this research appeared in 1968 in a report based on responses from 148 dioceses.* Of these, 63 dioceses indicated that they had some type of financial plan, but 85 had no plan for the formal retirement of priests. Of the 63 plans in effect, 28 had begun in 1968; 17 in 1967; and 12 between 1960 and 1966. In order to obtain an up-to-date report on progress with respect to retirement programs for priests, a questionnaire was sent by this writer to the chancellors of the 152 Roman Catholic dioceses in the United States in May, 1973. Replies were received from 103 dioceses, or from 67% of the total.

The questions on the survey pertained to the following areas:

1. Does the diocese have a retirement plan for its priests?†
2. Is retirement optional, or is there an age limit?
3. What is the general attitude of priests toward retirement?
4. Where do retired priests live?
5. What is the attitude of priests toward living in a home for retired priests?
6. What is the attitude of priests toward living in a general home for retired persons?
7. What is the amount of the monthly pension?
8. How much does the individual priest contribute to the retirement fund?
9. Besides the monthly pension, what benefits does the priest receive from the diocese?
10. What part-time activities does the priest prefer after retirement?
11. What are the priests' preferences for leisure activities after retirement?
12. Does the diocese have pre-retirement plans for priests?

Of the 103 dioceses responding to the questionnaire, 95, or 92%, replied that they do have retirement plans. But of the 95, only 4 indicated that their plans were *more than financial,* which seems to lead to the conclusion that the majority of dioceses see funding for a pension as the only retirement planning necessary. It is possible that this attitude reflects the smallness of the number of retired priests in these dioceses or perhaps the newness of the concept of retirement planning.

Of the 95 dioceses with formal plans, 43 set the optional age for retirement at 65; 18 at 70; and one each at 68, 72, 73, and 75. The mandatory retirement age in 33 dioceses is 70; in 40, 75; and in 2, 72. In the 17 dioceses in which there is no mandatory retirement age, seven have an optional age

---

* *CRUX of the News,* special report, September 27, 1968. Clarity Publishing, Inc., 75 Champlain Street, Albany, N.Y. 12204.

† It should be mentioned that no reference was made to finances in this question.

of 65, and one has an optional age of 70; nine, however, have neither an optional nor a mandatory retirement age. In 3 dioceses more specific plans are under study, and in 8, there are no retirement plans. In most cases, when the optional age of 65 is decided upon, benefits are reduced, with full retirement benefits paid at age 70.

Attitude of Priests toward Retirement

With respect to the general attitude of priests toward retirement, there is an obvious trend toward more and more acceptance. This change has occurred during the past decade for the following reasons: (1) because of the changes in the Church concerning the retirement of bishops and pastors since Vatican Council II; (2) because of the Institute on the retirement of priests held in January 1969 in New Orleans and sponsored by the National Conference of Catholic Charities, as well as subsequent follow-up sessions; (3) because of an increasing awareness of the existence of planned pension funds and a definite retirement age, both optional and mandatory, in most dioceses; and (4) because of the new freedom of being able to discuss retirement openly, knowing that the approval of authority exists and that there is an opportunity to make personal decisions.

Retirement, like aging, is individual, and the manner in which it is approached varies from person to person. Nevertheless, Table 1 contains those generalizations which could be drawn from the responses of the 103 dioceses replying to the questionnaire.

In general, living arrangements after retirement are left to the choice of the individual priest. Some can decide to live in a rectory or some other diocesan-owned institution. One diocese ruled against residence in the last parish served insofar as the rectory was concerned. Some priests arrange to live in their own apartment or move in with relatives or friends. Others have converted small summer bungalows into permanent living quarters throughout the years and are able to move in after retirement. In the light of definite retirement plans for the future, some younger priests are making arrangements with priest-friends now to pool their finances in order to purchase a home they can share later on.

The questionnaire also asked specifically about the attitude of priests upon retirement toward living in a home for retired priests or in a general home for retired persons. The attitudes expressed toward these two post-retirement possibilities are summarized in Table 2.

Retirement Benefits

The priests' monthly pensions vary from $150 to $600, depending on the diocese and on whether or not the priest chooses to remain in the rectory

TABLE 1

ATTITUDE OF PRIESTS TOWARD RETIREMENT AS
INDICATED BY 103 DIOCESES IN THE UNITED STATES

Attitude	*Number of Dioceses*
Excellent	1
Very good	2
Good; looking forward to retirement	22
Favorable	5
Welcomed	7
Fair	1
Positive	3
No objection	4
Most willing, once retirement is understood	3
Improving	5
Formerly negative, now greater acceptance	5
Fear at first; more acceptance later; need more education	4
Improving from resentment to resignation	1
Desire retirement at an earlier age—prefer 65	3
Older men not interested; younger men most interested	3
Each case individual; ambivalent; varies, some yes, some no	8
Older men afraid; prefer to continue full-time work	8
Retire only when forced through illness	5
Find retirement difficult to accept	4
Do not discuss retirement; scarcity of priests	3
Do not know what attitudes are about retirement	6

or in another diocesan institution after retirement. In summary: 15 dioceses pay a monthly pension between $150 and $250, with 4 of these indicating that the priest lives in the rectory; 51 dioceses pay a pension between $300 and $400, with one of these going to $500 very shortly; and 17 dioceses pay between $450 and $600 per month. In 31 dioceses the clergy are assessed between $30 and $300 annually for the retirement fund. In one diocese, which has a pension fund of $450 a month, the priest is expected to pay his own Social Security premiums as a contribution to the pension fund before he retires. In 3 dioceses the priest contributes 5% of his annual income to the pension fund; assessments in other dioceses are based on a graded formula depending on the number of years the priest has served the diocese.

TABLE 2

ATTITUDE OF PRIESTS IN 103 DIOCESES WITH RESPECT TO
LIVING IN A HOME FOR RETIRED PRIESTS OR IN A GENERAL HOME
FOR RETIRED PERSONS

Attitude Expressed	Home for Retired Priests	General Home for Retired Persons
No experience or knowledge in this regard	33	23
No home in diocese	25	16
Bitterly opposed	—	2
Opposed, to strongly opposed	18	22
Bad; not good	2	3
Negative	3	4
Unfavorable; very poor	5	3
Ambivalent	1	—
Varies	5	3
Not until very ill or senile	—	9
Depends on quality of home	—	1
A few accept	1	4
Accept home with private suite	1	—
Improved	1	—
Positive	1	2
Fairly good	—	1
Good to favorable	7	10

In 56 dioceses with pensions ranging from $200 to $600, the priests do not contribute.

With respect to benefits received from the diocese in addition to the pension check, 45 dioceses indicate Social Security. While some actually mention that the diocese pays the Social Security premiums, others merely indicate that it is an additional income for the priest, without stating who pays the premiums. Therefore, an evaluation of this benefit is not possible from the data available. In 62 dioceses hospitalization is paid for the priest by the diocese, six of these indicating that they also pay for major-medical benefits. Since it is possible that other dioceses also pay for major-medical benefits, but consider them part of the total hospitalization payments, a fair basis for comparison again is not available. In 3 dioceses, retreats are paid for by the diocese; in 3, workshops; in 2, automobiles; in one, automobile insurance; and in one, medical prescriptions.

Part-time and Leisure Activities

As far as part-time activities on the part of retired priests are concerned, there is great variety, with many dioceses indicating that only some of their retired priests are thus involved. A number of dioceses indicated that they were not able to answer this question. In the case of one diocese, the priests ask that everything be clearly spelled out before they get involved in a part-time activity, inasmuch as they do not care for a restricting schedule. In those dioceses in which retired priests engage in part-time activity, the picture is as follows. In 49 dioceses, retired priests are reported as taking weekend duty; in 30, they take rectory duty (but usually only a limited amount); in 13, they work in hospitals; in 12, they visit the sick; in 9, they visit the aged; in 11, they serve as chaplains in religious communities; in 5, they are involved in work in senior citizen centers; in 2, they are involved in CCD (Confraternity of Christian Doctrine) work; and finally, in one diocese, they visit prisons, and in another they are involved in a home for youth.

With respect to leisure activities, the dioceses responded as follows. In 43 dioceses, it is reported that for leisure activities the retired priests travel; in 43, they read; in 10, they play golf; in 4, they write; in 3, they paint or garden; and in 2, they fish. Other dioceses report farming, visiting friends, watching television, and resting to be pass-time activities. Many dioceses indicated that they have no idea what the retired priests do with their time.

Pre-retirement Planning for Priests

Out of the 103 dioceses reporting, only 5 actually indicated some type of pre-retirement planning by way of seminars, workshops, conferences, etc., but of the 5, 3 indicated that these were for priests over 65 years of age. In 9 other dioceses, committees and/or priests' senates are working on plans. Various surveys have been made in an effort to determine the needs as well as the wishes of the priests concerning retirement; whether they wish the diocese to build or purchase a building with apartments for retired priests; etc. In one diocese the priests' senate is working with a religious sister in organizing pre-retirement plans; in 2 dioceses, it is felt that there is no need for such plans. Other dioceses report less formal plans such as the priest serving the last years before retirement in a small parish or having reduced accountability; in many dioceses the personnel director or the bishop visits the priest beforehand to discuss retirement; in some dioceses the priests attend workshops and conferences held by the religious of the diocese. Finally, 63 dioceses report no pre-retirement plans.

Unfortunately, very few dioceses are encouraging the development of pre-retirement plans. If religious and the laity find this type of planning beneficial, it is unrealistic to contend that priests would not. How many of the clergy know about finances, about investing even their very small savings? What about health and exercise? What plans are made for medical checkups? If we are what we eat, then nutrition is no small item on the list. The diocese would reap the benefits of this kind of pre-retirement planning for the priests in more productive and healthier men.

What kind of educational opportunities are provided? It is not attractive when the individual has to pay a large fee out of a small check to attend a lecture or a course, but the diocese should be able to make arrangements for special rates with lecturers and educational institutions. There is no time or age limit in adult learning.

Before a good pre-retirement plan can be developed, one of the most important inputs must necessarily be the opinions and wishes of the priests. The overall picture, for example, of the attitude of priests about a home for priests should give second thoughts to diocesan officials who intend to build one without an explicit survey from the clergy of that particular diocese. Such a survey can portray many attitudes for a planning committee.

One diocese which has a good retirement pension and additional benefits at the present time entertained the thought of building a group retirement home for the priests. A questionnaire was sent out to all the clergy, retired and non-retired, to which they received a better-than-50% reply.* It is interesting to note how opinions vary between the retired and the non-retired as to whether they wish to live in a retirement home. The following table will give some idea of reactions to the questions asked:

TABLE 3

RETIREMENT ATTITUDES OF PRIESTS AS SURVEYED IN ONE DIOCESE

	Per cent of Retired	Per cent of Active
Are you interested in living in a group retirement home?		
Yes	21.1	44.0
No	57.9	22.5
Don't Know	21.1	33.5
Live in present or recent rectory as pastor emeritus?		
Yes	33.3	7.2
No	50.0	58.4
Don't Know	5.6	23.3
Prefer to live with family or other relatives after retirement?		
Yes	11.8	14.2

* Report received by the writer from the diocese involved, which wishes the name to be withheld. The survey was conducted in October 1972.

TABLE 3 (*Cont'd*)

RETIREMENT ATTITUDES OF PRIESTS AS SURVEYED IN ONE DIOCESE

	Per cent of Retired	Per cent of Active
No	88.2	51.4
Don't Know	0.0	24.4
Reasons for retiring (respondents asked to check more than one)		
Health	55.0	56.5
Disability	25.0	30.8
Not able to keep up with work	30.0	42.4
Desire to travel	0.0	13.0
Desire to write, study, teach	0.0	9.7
Personal reasons	10.0	29.7
Other	10.0	13.2
Opinion of present arrangement for retired priests		
Excellent	15.8	7.4
Good	31.6	36.1
Fair	56.8	28.7
Poor	0.0	16.4
Don't Know	15.8	11.5
Reasons for feeling present arrangements to be inadequate (respondents asked to check more than one)		
Not adequate pension	30.0	18.9
Not adequate housing facilities	15.0	37.0
Not adequate recreational facilities	5.0	14.9
Not adequate religious programs	0.0	14.6
Not adequate social programs	0.0	13.8
Not adequate cultural programs	0.0	8.1
Not adequate personal interest provisional facilities	5.0	17.3
Not adequate involvement in community or outside affairs	0.0	9.7
Other	5.0	10.3
What functions do you expect a retirement home to fulfill?		
A place to live leisurely with other retired clergy members	25.0	41.9
A source of continuing a similar life style, both religiously and personally as before retirement	35.0	55.4
A sense of remaining attached, in a special way, to the Catholic Church; a continuation of certain practices (saying Mass, distributing the sacraments, etc.)	75.0	75.8
No function	10.0	3.5
Other	0.0	6.2

A review of the material presented in Table 3 makes it easier to visualize the development of retirement plans tailored to suit the needs and desires of priests so that they will be able to face the ever-increasing leisure years well-informed and well-prepared. Perhaps dioceses will work toward this goal more readily now that the financial aspects have been programed.

IMPACT OF RETIREMENT IN RELIGIOUS COMMUNITIES

Faced with the post-war increase in vocations and the new Formation Program in the 1950s, religious communities throughout the United States felt compelled to borrow money to add to their capital on hand, in order to build larger novitiates and houses of studies. Candidates to the order had to be housed in new facilities, and younger religious who remained in training to finish their education required houses of studies, or juniorates as some communities labeled them. Those orders of religious women which could possibly manage the financing built infirmaries for the increasing number of sick and elderly religious. Funds were borrowed to answer the crying need for the building of new high schools, new colleges, and new wings on hospitals. The demand for highly educated religious to meet the needs of youth and the standards of the educational system also had to be met at a great price. Funds were running low, but hope was high. The cost of education would be more than justified in the well-trained, competent teachers and hospital personnel who would staff the institutions of the community.

The 1960s, however, brought many surprises and some heartaches in the form of empty novitiates and houses of studies, a number of which are still being amortized. Mortgaged high schools lost many of the well-trained religious to the larger community of the Church. State financial-aid programs moved some of the colleges out of the hands of congregations into the hands of Boards of Directors, on which fewer and fewer religious serve. Changes took place all around. Sesame Street children, the new math, computerized reporting systems, changing attitudes among the children, caused perplexing problems for men and women who were already struggling to conceal the normal burdens of aging.

The pace was moving too fast for these older religious, and they secretly desired escape while they were still able to retain the respect and maintain the discipline of the students in the class. Not until actual retirement funding was discussed and planned for at so many of the community chapters did these religious begin to let go. The knowledge that there was money set aside for each one when he or she retired, and that a check would be issued to the local house if that should be the chosen place of residence for the retiree, encouraged the voluntary retirement of the religious who had long since passed the 65th year.

Financial Burden of Retirement for Religious Personnel

Major superiors of religious orders of men and women realized that they were late in starting plans and programs to meet the needs of these pioneer retirees. In answer to their requests for assistance with this growing financial burden, bishops throughout the country responded by working out various ways of contributing to the pension funds of the religious men and women who had built the schools and institutions of their dioceses with their dedicated lives and contributed services. In one leading archdiocese, the pastors and administrators paid a thirteenth check each year to the retirement fund of the religious community for each of its members serving in the schools or other diocesan offices. Another large archdiocese increased the individual stipend paid to religious to include the premiums for a retirement fund. Studies presented to other dioceses indicated that 23% of the salary or stipend of the teaching religious is needed to cover the future retirement of the individual religious, apart from assisting the already retired religious; increases were made on the basis of this information. One diocese has set up an all-coverage pension plan for priests, religious, and lay people, and has issued two booklets, one to cover priests, the other to cover religious and laity. In this way active members of each community are covered by the diocesan plan. Other dioceses have set aside funds to cover the religious who have retired from the active apostolate. These funds have been divided proportionately among the various communities involved, enabling them to set up their own financial retirement program. These funds have also been the deciding factor in whether or not some of these orders would enter the Social Security system, since they are now in a position to pay the necessary retroactive initial cost which makes their entering the system worthwhile.

Since we are touching on the subject of Social Security, it seems in order to point out here that religious communities should consider the feasibility of entering the system if they have not already done so. Not all communities will benefit from this move at the present time. A good actuarial study, proper data fed into the computer, sound financial advice, a prudent lawyer, and a list of alternatives to choose from are all recommended before the final decision is made. The cost is high, and once a community is enrolled in the Social Security system, it cannot withdraw. Throughout the country there are experts working with the major superiors of men and women, and with CORT (Conference of Religious Treasurers) in particular. These men and women have studied the question of Social Security as it relates to religious communities and, therefore, are in a position to give assistance and sound advice. The minimum Social Security benefit is $84.50.* It is obvious

* Across-the-board benefit increases in Social Security were passed by Congress and approved by President Nixon in January 1974, with the total increase of 11% to be implemented in two stages, but completed by July 1974, making the new minimum benefit $93.80.

that this monthly pension will not be sufficient to care for the needs of retired religious, and that it can be at best merely a supplement. Thus, communities should also be in the process of building private pension funds for retirement purposes. A recent study of the basic needs of religious women (excluding rent, utilities, province support, and all other overhead) indicates that the amount per capita is in the vicinity of $165 per month. The figure for religious men is quoted at a higher rate. Therefore, in planning a private fund, this fact and the fact of continually rising costs should be kept in mind.

Difficulties Faced by Older Religious

Although financial planning is a very important factor in the retirement program for religious, it is not the most important. Men and women provincials share a deep concern for the aging members of their orders. In 1967 a study† made of 146 communities of religious women revealed the traumatic difficulties these older members were facing. Some of the findings are as follows:

64.1% suffered from loneliness
40.3% suffered from insecurity and from being out of things
34.0% suffered from inability to continue doing one's work
28.5% felt they were of no use
22.5% suffered from depression, boredom, and fear.

Building homes for retired religious, or even converting unused novitiates into living quarters suitable for the retired, will not answer the problems cited above. It is much better, psychologically, for the retired religious to remain as long as possible in the local mission house. Unless the place of retirement, whether it be a motherhouse or a separate dwelling, provides opportunities for involvement in activities, duties, and volunteer work, it will become merely a vegetation site. Abilities and talents will remain untapped and waste away, leaving the only highlights of the day the three hearty meals. Prayer has always been an important part of the entire day of a religious, and retirement does provide more time for this leisure with God. But if a person was not called to a contemplative order early in life, it is doubtful that this calling will come in the late sixties, seventies, or eighties. Meaningful activity, is important, not mere busy-work, for this is insulting to men and women who have been educators and administrators all their

† This study on Aging and the Retired Sister in America was conducted by Sister Margaret Mary, o.s.b., and was reported at the Institute on Planning for Pre-retirement and Retirement of Religious, sponsored by the National Conference of Catholic Charities and held in Chicago in 1968.

lives. The basic cry from the depth of all human beings is the "need to be needed," and meaningful activity will give the person something to look forward to in getting up each morning. There is no general directory on the nature of this activity because just as individuals differ from one another, so each community has its own personality and its own creative way of developing people.

A Director of Pre-retirement and Retirement for Religious Communities

One recommendation to religious communities is that an individual religious be given the position of coordinating pre-retirement and retirement planning and programs for the community. This is a challenging task simply because retirement is a challenge to the individual and to the community. The whole area is new to religious and there are no capsule panaceas.

There is no such thing as *a* program; there can be almost as many programs as there are individuals because retirement is so individual. The first rule of thumb is the dignity of the individual. The director will find that he or she is working with a new generation of older people with very definite needs in a changing society and a changing Church. That religious is a pioneer with a price to pay, and success will not always be the crowning reward. But, despite the fact that the older religious are atypical retirees in 1973, progress will be made if the early foundation is patiently laid. The necessary tools for the director are a position, which includes delegated responsibility and commensurate authority, a budget, and permission to proceed with projects. Higher authority should reenforce the director's authority by constantly referring the older religious back to the director and by planning team meetings with the directors of renewal, education, health, apostolates, retirement, and so on, so that a more efficient and worthwhile program can be set up for the entire community.

Too often the retirement director works in a vacuum, so to speak, simply because the members of his or her community do not understand the concepts of pre-retirement and retirement in relation to religious. The major superior, who may appreciate what the position involves, will integrate retirement planning into the network of community activities with greater ease if communication is possible across the board as in the team approach mentioned above, rather than merely between the director and the superior. Also, the director should make every effort to initiate a good working committee representing all age brackets and all apostolates of the community.

After this group is functioning, it is helpful to have a peripheral team of consultants, both lay and religious, who are experts in the fields of spiritual life (Scripture, liturgy, etc.), medicine, nutrition, mental health, arts and crafts, education, nursing, physical health, and psychology. By working with committees such as these, as well as with the above-mentioned team at periodic meetings, the director will be able to avoid duplication of effort and promote worthwhile projects and programs for the entire community. In suggesting a full-time director, it is well to mention that he or she should be a well-trained person with a deep sense of prayer and dependence upon God. In addition to having an affection for, and understanding of, the older members of the community, the director will need an ample supply of patience and a holy resiliency.

Earlier in this paper we mentioned the need for pre-retirement planning for priests. There is even a greater need for this type of planning in religious communities where so many men or so many women live together. The most important step for tomorrow's retirement program is today's pre-retirement planning, which should include the spiritual, mental, and physical needs of each individual. In religious life great stress has been put on spiritual development, but it was not until the late 1950s and 1960s that attention turned also to the psychological needs of religious. The psychiatrist found his place in the sun during those years in America, and most definitely in the consultant's corner of religious life. Provincial administrations have gone to great lengths in an effort to maintain secrecy concerning the bills and the individuals involved in receiving this help, much of which could be avoided with the assistance of good pre-retirement programs. Such programs could be introduced for religious 35-years-of-age-and-older and could pertain to career evaluation, mid-career educational opportunities, mental health conferences, and leisure workshops. No other group of people are so highly trained nor sensitized to the gifts of God, as are religious and priests. Therefore, officials in dioceses and religious orders have a serious responsibility to develop ways and means to channel this rich source of manpower and brain power so that they will continue to contribute at optimum as long as possible. Future direction of the Church will depend on the healthy minds and bodies of today's priests and religious.

RETIREMENT RESPONSIBILITY OF INDIVIDUAL PRIESTS AND RELIGIOUS

Every conceivable plan or program can be initiated to help make the life of the priest or religious richer and more meaningful, but no one can change the individual or his attitudes. That is a personal responsibility. When people retire, they usually bring with them what they have been all their lives, only more so. If a person has been holy and generous all of his or her life, then the fruits will be seen, especially in infirmaries. If selfish and complaining, that fact too, unfortunately, shines out like a beacon light.

Where, then, does one begin? The answer is with "self." The truth may hurt, but introspection will show what kind of religious people individuals have been. How many have lived under the same roof with other individuals, yet in so many ways have remained strangers? How often have they sat at table with an individual, or lived in the next room, but have absolutely no idea about the pain or distress their neighbor is suffering? How often have they asked the trite question: "How are you?" but never even waited for the reply, or been really interested? Is it really a truism to say that men or women who live in a religious community are fortunate: they will never be lonely because they have each other? Do they?

One of the surest ways to avoid loneliness in religious life is to make friends. Greeley suggests that friendship is a gift—the gift of oneself. In his book *The friendship game,* he writes:

> in order that we might persuade the other to accept our invitation, we offer him an inducement, that is to say, we offer him ourself. We say to the other, "I will give you me, I will not hold back, I will not hide, I will put myself at your service, will be willing to listen and to support, to run the risk of being hurt. I am yours to do with as you want, but my faith in you is so great that I know I have nothing to fear from you." . . . there is nothing more difficult for man to do than to make such a gift. If only he could give it once and not have to do it again. But friendship is not a single gift; it is rather a constant renewal [Greeley, 1970, pp. 27–28].

Obviously, one cannot have friends unless one is first a friend. Friendship means acceptance, but we cannot accept other people until we have accepted ourselves with all our faults and all our good points. Here leisure offers an opportunity for personal and spiritual growth. Leisure is an attitude of affirmation; it enables one to see oneself in one's limitations and in one's weakness; the attitude of leisure frees one to find the extraordinary in the ordinary things of life. Leisure is an attitude of soul which is developed through the quiet awareness of God—His creatures and His creation. Josef Pieper (1964) speaks of leisure as an attitude of the mind and a condition of the soul which fosters a capacity to perceive the reality of the world. It implies a sense of wonder—contemplative wonder about the ordinary things of the world and about the creator.

As we mentioned earlier in this paper, play (leisure) is a gift from God. Contemplation actually means playing with God. Cox (1965) writes about the close relationship between contemplation and the celebration of life— the sunsets, symphonies, and happy moments; and Neale (1969) expounds on the interchangeableness of the words "leisure" and "play" because both contain four basic elements: peace, freedom, delight, and illusion. In his theory of play, Neale (1969) writes about the two fundamental needs of all men: the need to discharge energy and the need to design experience. He defines work as a result of the conflict between these needs, and play as the result of harmony. These two fundamental needs function in conflict or in harmony to create the self of work or the self of play. Action is not the distinguishing difference between work and play.

Because of inner harmony, the play-self can find adventure in success or in failure, in work or in retirement. The play-self finds adventure in the daily occurrences around him, whereas the work-self lives in a world of conflict, deprived of delight in chance, in risk, or in striking events. Neale says that there is no room for surprise or novelty in the work-self. The playful self has resolved inner conflicts and therefore is at peace with self and with the world around him. Only because he has dealt with his inner conflicts is the playful person able to accept himself as he really is, for better or for worse.

Paul Haun (1965) describes the playful person as one who is functioning at his peak—he is able to work well, to love well, and to play well. Being free of tension, he is able to sleep well. And, we might add, that person has the best disposition to pray well. This is the true Christian, because he or she is able to celebrate life and radiate its joy because of a playful cast of mind. The true Christian knows that every human encounter is an eternal opportunity, and he can find beauty in all of God's creatures—people, time, place, events. He finds excitement and new life in the people around him. He takes the time to make new acquaintances and to share himself with others, and he can do this because he knows that one has to be relaxed and playful to experiment—to search deeply—to take a risk.

Huizinga (1970) tells us that nature could have given us many ways of discharging energies, of finding relaxation, and of meeting the demands of life with more ease, but instead she gave us play, with its tensions, its mirth, and its fun. Thomas Aquinas preached that if man does not have wholesome pleasures, he will seek unwholesome ones. How many religious and priests seek the unwholesome pleasures of despair and boredom? Yes, they are pleasures, for, strangely enough, the victims find consolation in the misery they experience.

In our world today, too many people have forgotten how to laugh; they have lost their sense of humor. Priests and religious, above all people, should never be carriers of gloom, particularly among their fellow priests and religious. Part of the trouble with many of us is that we take ourselves too seriously, without really knowing ourselves that well. Our work or our play, activity or retirement, can become a continuous celebration of life if only the true meaning of leisure can be grasped and appreciated. Instead of fearing or trying to avoid pre-retirement and retirement, we will be able to accept it as part of the adventure in life—with retirement having the definite bonus of more time to play with God and His universe. More time can be devoted to the Apostolate of the Aging as a peer, not a planner, once retirement is accepted. The "them" we refer to today are the "us" of tomorrow.

Therefore, whatever programs, and fears, and attitudes, priests and religious build or tolerate now, whatever policies and legislation they act on now, will lay the foundation for the world we live in tomorrow. The field is wide open, and there is a crying need for leaders. It is time to clear away the spider web of personal fears and the high-voltage fence which society has built around "retirement." It is time to prove to the world what dedication really means to the priest and religious. It is time to say that we truly accept the limitations of aging because as long as God grants the ability, there are ways to spread His Kingdom. Nothing is impossible for those who care. If the number of retired people is steadily increasing in America, what a tremendous service retired priests and religious can render to mankind simply by being leaders in how to retire.

REFERENCES

Cox, H. *The secular city.* New York: Macmillan, 1965.

Greeley, A. M. *The friendship game.* Garden City, N.Y.: Doubleday, 1970.

Haun, P. *Recreation: A medical viewpoint.* New York: Teachers College Press, 1965.

Huizinga, J. *Homo ludens: A study of the play element in culture.* Boston: Beacon Press, 1970.

Kutner, B., Fanshel, D., Togo, A. M., & Langner, T. S. *Five hundred over sixty: A community survey on aging.* New York: Russell Sage Foundation, 1956.

Lee, J. M. Layhood as vocation and career. In W. E. Bartlett (Ed.) *Evolving religious careers.* Washington, D.C.: Center for Applied Research in the Apostolate (CARA), 1970. Pp. 144–166.

Miller, D. *Gods and games: Toward a theology of play.* New York: World, 1970.

Neale, R. E. *In praise of play.* New York: Harper & Row, 1969.

Pieper, J. *Leisure, the basis of culture* (trans. A. Dru). New York: Pantheon, 1964.

Vatican Council II. Decree on the Ministry and Life of Priests. In W. M. Abbott (S.J.) (Ed.) *The documents of Vatican II.* New York: Herder & Herder, 1966. Pp. 532–576.

V

THE EXPERIENCE OF RETIREMENT

The Experience of Retirement

BENJAMIN L. MASSE, S.J.
SAMUEL SCHEIBER
MARIE LAURETTE LOVELY, S.C.
HARRY A. SCHWARTZ
RAE BRAGMAN

In this section five people, who were engaged in a variety of occupations during their working years, all now retired, present their varied experiences with retirement. In order of presentation: Father Benjamin L. Masse, S.J. speaks as a retired priest, who was a journalist during his professional career, and, for 30 years, an Associate Editor of the Jesuit periodical America. *Mr. Samuel Scheiber, who lives in Peekskill, retired from his own business in 1969 at the age of 67 so that, he says, "I could give more time to what I really wanted to do." Sister Marie Laurette, S.C. is a retired nun, who was a teacher, she says "of eighth grades mostly." She is now a volunteer, working with Catholic residents at the Riverdale Nursing Home near the College of Mount St. Vincent where she resides. Mr. Harry A. Schwartz is a retired business executive, residing in Mamaroneck, who has the distinction, among our "Voices of Experience," of having retired twice. Finally, Mrs. Rae Bragman, a widow, served for 25 years as Principal of the Religious School of Temple Israel, New Rochelle, New York, retiring from this post eight years ago.*

167

THE EXPERIENCE OF A RETIRED PRIEST

BENJAMIN L. MASSE, S.J.

Before reciting the short and simple annals of the retirement of Father
Senex, of the Society of Jesus, I should like to offer a few observations about
priestly senescence.

First of all, this story has only partial relevance to the retirement of
diocesan priests or religious brothers. Neither is it meant to illustrate the
experience of retirement in general, or even of early retirement. After all,
religious priests have been retiring for about 1,500 years now—roughly, I
suppose, from the time the great Saint Benedict founded his order. In any
sizable community—and more especially in novitiates and houses of study
—nothing used to be more familiar than the sight of elderly priests who,
burdened by the weight of years or laboring under physical or mental infirmities, had been relieved of their duties and were free to use their time as
nature allowed and they saw fit.

Nor is there anything new about early retirement. If the whole truth
must be told, some religious priests—a small minority, to be sure—were
retiring early long before the influence of Vatican Council II was felt in
the Church. For reasons which were not always clear to their brothers in
the Lord, these men decided that they were no longer able to do their
accustomed work and, at an age when most of their contemporaries were
still heavily engaged, simply stopped doing it.

Rather, this account is meant to describe something new in religious life:
the mandatory retirement of priests at an age when many of them are
still able to perform the work for which they were trained and in which
they have labored to the satisfaction of superiors. In this respect, religious
orders and congregations and, indeed, the Church as a whole, have now
caught up with the secular world, where mandatory retirement, generally
at age 65, has been for some time an accepted practice in business, education, and many non-elective government jobs.

Since a priest remains a man despite vows and the holy oils of ordination,
we can safely assume that much of the literature of gerontology is germane
to our subject. Precisely because Father Senex is a religious priest, however,
it would also seem likely, *a priori*, that some generalities about aging and
retirement would not apply in the same way to him, or with the same force,
as they do to others, even to other priests.

It is on those modalities that I hope the story of Father Senex may cast
a little light.

Finally, I wish to call attention to two facts which have pertinence for
every aspect of the mandatory retirement of priest-religious.

First, by virtue of his priesthood—and this he has in common with all priests—he is never fully retired, in the sense that a corporation executive, or a factory worker, or a government bureaucrat is retired. As long as a priest can go to the altar of God to offer the Holy Sacrifice of the Mass, he remains in business professionally, even if he can offer Mass only privately.

Secondly, by virtue of his vow of obedience he has, by faith, the assurance that he is doing the will of God. In imposing retirement on him, superiors may be making a mistake, humanly speaking; but in obeying their order he cannot possibly do wrong. In accepting their decision, he is, in fact, acting virtuously.

And so it happened that one day Father Provincial arrived for his annual visitation. During a conference with Father Senex, he informed him that the Fathers Provincial had recently voted to adopt a new retirement policy. As of now, the men engaged in the work of the community were to step aside at age 65. Since Father Senex was only a few weeks away from his 65th birthday, the provincials had agreed that he should be granted a year of grace to plan his retirement. Chances were that superiors would ratify any decision he made. All they expected was that he would support himself, arrange for medical and hospital insurance, and make a contribution to his province's retirement fund. If he desired, the Province Director of Retirement would assist him in making the transition.

In this low-key, matter-of-fact way there began a new and unforeseen chapter in the life of Father Senex. Mentally and emotionally, he was in no mood to start a new chapter, not after thirty years of highly professional work. He had achieved some distinction in his field. He had status and the sense of security which goes with it. By traditional practice, he could look forward to continued service until the infirmities of age or death put an end to his work.

Now, suddenly, his familiar world fell apart. He was on his own, with a mandate to choose another one. For this grant of relative independence his training had not prepared him. All through his life he had been at the disposal of superiors, going where they told him to go, doing what they told him to do. He had always been a member of a well-administered community, with few duties beyond the performance of his work. He had had no experience in the management of money. When he needed anything, from clothes to medical care, the local superior had provided it. Now he was to manage his own affairs, with only general supervision from those who held the place of God in his regard.

Father Senex began planning for the future. As he did so, he started to experience a delayed reaction to the provincials' decision. It gradually dawned on him that he was growing old; that he was, indeed, an old man. Up till that time, he had never thought much about aging. He did not feel old, or look old, or act old. He was younger than his chronological age. Yet he was old and, as he considered a new apostolate, he would have to keep that in mind. For physical reasons, he should begin pacing himself. The new work ought to be less demanding than the old. Furthermore, it should be work which he would be able to perform four or five years hence.

Father Senex also started thinking about remuneration for his work, but he did not become very excited about it. He felt financially secure, as only those who have a vow of poverty can feel secure. He had no retirement benefits coming from the Social Security system; nor did he have a private pension of any kind. He had something better: he had a religious community. He never doubted that, whatever the future held, his order would take care of him. In choosing his apostolate, then, remuneration would not have to be a major consideration. It would certainly weigh less heavily on the scales than physical health.

What should the major considerations be?

With a background of forty years in religious life, Father Senex automatically rated spiritual well-being and effectiveness at the top of the list. In which of the apostolates open to him could he best grow spiritually and make the most acceptable contribution to the expansion of Christ's Kingdom?

A second major consideration was psychological. Which apostolate would be most congenial and mentally and emotionally satisfying? Father Senex was aware of the loneliness which the aged frequently experience, and he was even more sensitive to the impatience the elderly often feel in the face of frustrations. He had no wish to become a problem in his old age.

With those considerations in mind, Father Senex posed the big question which had to be answered before he could get down to specifics. Should he seek an apostolate in his professional field? Or should he make a clean break with the past and try his hand at something new? Well aware that this was the hardest decision he would have to make, he pondered long over it. He prayed over it. He sought the counsel of others.

If he made a clean break, he would liquidate the investment of a lifetime. All he had acquired by study and experience would become largely useless to others. It would also cease to be a part of his own life. The whole rhythm of his existence would be changed.

Wasn't that what his superiors intended? In imposing retirement, were they not saying, in effect, that he had come to the end of the line? That what he had been doing was no longer of great value, or if it was of value, that it could be done more effectively by a younger man? Were not they telling him, by action if not by words, that at this stage of his life he could be more useful if he shifted to some other apostolate?

On the other hand, not only was the choice of other apostolates limited, but to none of them could Father Senex bring much experience. Almost from the time of ordination, he had been what is known nowadays as a hyphenated priest. Except for daily Mass, offered privately, and, one hopes, a higher motivation, he had been like any other professional in his field.

Could he take up residence in a rectory and live the life of a parish priest? Could he function as a chaplain in a hospital, a prison, or in some other institution? Would he miss life in a religious community? Away from his brothers in Christ, from the only family he had, would he experience loneliness?

Yet, except for minor administrative jobs in his religious order, those apostolates were just about the only ones open to him.

The idea of a spiritual apostolate, after so many years of involvement in secular subjects, was not without its attraction. It would certainly expand the dimensions of his priesthood. In a matter of months, he would hear more confessions, give more communions, make more sick calls, visit more hospitals, baptize more babies, and bury more dead than he had in all the years since his ordination. He would also deliver more homilies and read more theology. In short, for continued spiritual growth and for expanding spiritual horizons, a parish or institutional ministry could provide opportunities which he had never before had a chance to enjoy. He would have to meet new challenges and acquire new skills. This way there would be no living off accumulated capital, no coasting more or less gracefully downhill toward inevitable debility and death. The newness of the apostolate might even restore some of the fine fervor of his younger years.

Weeks went by, and still Father Senex wavered between the new and the old. One day he leaned toward the old (he had received several solid offers). The next day he leaned toward the new. Finally, in an effort to end the agony of decision-making, he polled his friends. They were of some help, but not much. They split evenly between the old and the new. At this point, Father Senex had to take refuge in his faith. The thought occurred to him, and kept occurring, that none of this anguish would have been necessary if superiors had not adopted an unprecedented retirement rule. Then it was that trust in a kindly Providence, which "shapes our ends, rough hew them as we will," together with the implications of his vow of obedience, kept him from emotional bouts of anger and vexation.

There was no point in deferring the decision any longer, hoping, as it were, for a revelation from on high. So, with all the world decidedly not standing on tiptoe in expectation, Father Senex took a deep breath and opted for the new.

Once the decision was made, the next one was relatively easy. Between an apostolate in an institution or one in a parish, Father Senex hesitated scarcely at all. He elected to start life in a parish, possibly for no weightier reason than that a pastor-friend very much wanted him and dusted off the rectory's welcome mat. At that stage in life, to be wanted is good for a man's morale.

Experts, especially the psychiatrists, may suspect that this account of Father Senex's adjustment to retirement is somewhat less than complete.

When he moved to a parish, did he really burn all his bridges behind him? Did he enter a strange world without any provision for an escape hatch? What happened to the prudence and caution which we associate with senior citizens, veterans of life's complexities and the swaying tides of battle?

To be completely candid, Father Senex did hedge his bet. Though he left for the parish with every intention of participating fully in its life, he did not break up his library or drop all his subscriptions to professional journals.

Does that mean that Father Senex never fully accepted retirement? That he did not, in fact, really retire?

Well, who except Almighty God knows the depths of the human heart and the secret, convoluted processes of the human mind? The fact is that eight months after taking up parochial duties Father Senex returned to his profession on a part-time basis. It was not that he didn't find a great measure of satisfaction in parish work—in fact the satisfactions far outweighed the irritations and frustrations—but rather that the old challenges never subsided and kept calling for a response.

When last heard of, Father Senex was playing ball in two leagues, in both cases more as a relief pitcher than a regular starter. He was complementing his part-time professional work with part-time duty in a parish. How long he would be able to continue his dual role, he did not know. Of this much he felt certain. When the time did finally come to break definitively with the past, to retire once and for all, he would do so with none of the interior anguish he felt the first time around. He would be stepping aside this time voluntarily, and stepping aside because he realized that the last out had been made and the game was over; that he was no longer able, physically or mentally, to make a contribution to the team. At last God's will in his regard would be completely clear.

THE EXPERIENCE OF A RETIRED BUSINESSMAN

SAMUEL SCHEIBER

I was born in 1902. I retired in 1969 as president of a good-sized business. It would be very dramatic if I could relate how bored and lonely I was when I retired; how I missed getting up each morning and having a place to go to work and being with people. I have *not* been bored nor at a loss about what to do with my spare time. I have been busier than when I ran my own business. In fact, I must ration my time. When one gets older one gets tired faster and recuperates more slowly.

For 40 years I was a volunteer at a settlement house in the slums of New York City. I was its boys' club leader, vice president of its board of directors, chairman of its camp, which, together with many others, I helped move to a location near where I have been living for the past 40 years. I received a lifetime dividend when I met my wife who was a girls' club leader at the same settlement house. Life was full of the most interesting activities of social service, but I am here to talk about another period of life.

In 1958 I began thinking more and more about the fact that so many were working for youth and so few for the aging. This reflection was the beginning of a new life for me. In 1959 I organized the Annual Westchester County Senior Citizens' Boat Ride. We began with 600 and later, when it grew to 3,200, we transferred from Playland to Yonkers. This was only a one-day-a-year senior citizens' program. So that same year I organized the Peekskill Senior Citizens' Club, with Catholics, Protestants, Jews, blacks, whites, and Puerto Ricans as members. This was an all-year program.

The more I became involved, the more I realized how large the need was. I spoke to other communities to encourage and induce them to organize senior citizens' clubs. Right from the beginning Peekskill was a service club, working not only for our members, but for our community and for the more than 3,000 Peekskill aging who did not belong to our club. Year after year our interests and activities grew—cancer pads, hospital jackets, visits to the homebound, Retired Senior Volunteer Plan, Foster Grandparents, public health nursing, Day-Care Center Christmas party, Harlem Valley State Hospital, Senior Information and Referral Service, health center for the poor, nutrition, bowling, arts and crafts classes, hearings at City Hall, games, trips, picnics, geriatric exercises, summer theatre, a visit to a proposed Senior-Citizens' Housing Project to make suggestions, and more. I could go on and on. Activities for senior citizens help to keep them busy and more interested in living. They are conscious of the eventuality of old age, but life is good. They are not bored and do not just listen to their arteries hardening, finally winding up in an institution, away from family, friends, and their community.

Why are people reluctant to talk about, or even think about, getting old and retiring? No one can escape it. It is an important part of Life. I am past 70. It seems that it was only a few years ago that I was 30 or 40. I could say much about how fast time moves. Too many people, if and when they are thinking about getting older and retiring, think that they must accumulate money, and that with it they will have security and happiness. Sure, money helps, but there is a lot more to a good, normal retirement than just dollars. There are satisfactions in being involved in human services which surpass mere hobbies. I wanted to spend more time in those busy, happy activities of long ago.

I didn't know it at the time, but as I grew older I thought about it more and more. I am convinced, without any reservation, that one need not worry about retiring if he starts at an early age to become involved in the many problems which are crying out for understanding and help. Begin at an early age. Don't wait until you are 50 or 60. The longer you wait the less help it will be with your future retirement. Modern senior citizens are not just sitting on their porches, rocking back and forth, waiting, just waiting. Visit a senior citizens' club. These people want to be an active part of Life. They are a large reservoir of brains and experience, and are being called upon more and more to help. It is better for them if they participate, and better for their families and for their communities.

For the conclusion of my reflections of my retirement experience I would like to emphasize a few thoughts. I have read, studied, and thought a great deal about the aging. None of these activities have taught me as much, nor have they given me as much knowledge and satisfaction, as working and living with the aged.

Older persons, despite their lifelong experience, and despite the fact that they know more about their needs and priorities than those who as yet are untouched by the experience of aging, are not adequately included in the thinking and planning about those needs and priorities.

It is said that older people are rambling and repetitious. I suppose to a degree, I think a small degree, they are. However, if one wants to get a broader viewpoint, he should be patient and listen. Instead of allowing the aging to tell "where it hurts them," too many people break in and talk when they should listen. If these people feel that they don't have much time, the aging have less.

It has been my experience, after a close relationship with many older people for the past 15 years, that most of them eventually express the thought that their greatest fear is that they will not be able to retain some semblance of dignity. The importance of a human being's dignity must never be underestimated. Everything I have said today has been the result of my own observations, but, in concluding, I would like to borrow an observation from someone else. Dr. Russell Noyes, a psychiatrist, at the University of Iowa, says: "The person who maintains his dignity and courage while dying in effect preserves it for a lifetime and for the memory of his surviving family."

THE EXPERIENCE OF A RETIRED NUN

MARIE LAURETTE LOVELY, S.C.

I like the title of our panel, "Voices of Experience."* The old adage "Experience is the best teacher" is so true. There are kinds of knowledge which cannot be transmitted by books but only through personal contact: the knowledge of life experience.

* This was a sub-title given to this panel in the printed program of the Institute.— Ed.

Stepping out of the teaching profession into the field of nursing homes was foreign to me. With a few workshops as a preliminary preparation, I learned much by observing situations on the job. There are about 55 Catholics among the 200 residents in the non-sectarian nursing home I visit.

My first responsibility is to seek out the newly admitted to help them adjust to their new surroundings. It is so rewarding to see them gradually become contented, as I count their present blessings with them. And there are blessings, when one is no longer able to do for oneself, relieved of the burden of shopping, cooking, cleaning, and so on.

My second service is to accompany the priest when he brings Holy Communion from room to room on First Fridays. Noting the frequent change of rooms, I check the room numbers and with list in hand can lead Father to the right places. On the days we have the Liturgy, it is helpful for me to lead the prayers and hymns since the residents are hesitant to do so.

Everything one does is relevant, whether lighting a cigarette or praying with a person. Walking a patient to the patio, which the aides are not always free to do, is no small favor, especially when the third floor folks would never get a change of scene or fresh air since there are no patios from the third floor.

All these little helps make dark days bright and cheery for the older folks, which they appreciate. They won't make the headlines of the daily papers, but where values count most, namely in eternity, they will rate high.

So with a Christian attitude toward the aging, one is enabled to identify better with them. To deplore is not enough; we must, if we can, contribute in some positive way, little as it may be. The losses which accompany our latter years are all too obvious. What is not obvious is the tremendous gain the years have given us in other ways. Who recognizes the later developmental stage of life as a time for deep contemplation instead of an empty stare into space or unfilled vacuum? A letting-go is a normal, natural part of the growth process. It is the stripping stage when one is confined to small spaces and bound by prohibitions, especially in an institution. The threshold to eternity is what I call nursing homes because, much as one would have it otherwise, there is no return to former living. And so we try to help the residents to self-acceptance of their present situation, which is crucial to their psychological well-being, as they realize they cannot change the elements which are sometimes unacceptable or problematic.

THE EXPERIENCE OF A RETIRED BUSINESS EXECUTIVE

HARRY A. SCHWARTZ

I have been asked to speak of my retirement experience. The fact is I am not retired, in the full sense of the word. I do have a business which I started some four or five years ago. This business, however, requires so little of my time that I am, in effect, subject to all the experiences and adjustments of full retirement. It is pertinent to mention at this point, what I suppose is obvious, that I am close to 70. Why, you may ask, did I undertake this burden so late in life?

I was forced to start this business of my own because of my age. Despite many years of experience in my field, considerable expertise, excellent health, and functioning in high gear, I was unable to obtain suitable employment.

Until about 20 years ago, I owned and operated a very successful business, employing some 50 persons. Because of changing conditions in the industry, I decided it best to liquidate the business at that time. Also, I had been considering retirement for some years, and looked forward to unscheduled leisure, away from the pressures and tyrannies of business demands. I had a variety of outside interests, and, of course, like most of us, many unfulfilled dreams. I planned to travel, to indulge in hobbies, perhaps to develop talents I always believed I had.

However, after a year or so I found myself restless, dissatisfied, and with a growing sense of disappointment. My hobbies were just that—hobbies. Travel was indeed great, and I enjoyed the experience of new lands, new sights, and new cultures. But, for me, at 50, travel lacked the excitement and adventure I had anticipated. The talents I had hoped to develop seemed inconsequential. Perhaps it was too late to nourish them; maybe they required a discipline too difficult at my age; perhaps I had been in "harness" too long. So I decided to go back into the business world.

I was disinclined to start my own business again. I preferred, at this stage in life, to look for suitable employment in the field in which I had acquired so much experience. I was utterly certain that I would have no difficulty obtaining a job at a high executive level. I was recommended to two companies looking for an executive with the qualifications I was able to offer. I soon learned that, oddly enough, my qualifications disqualified me. The reason? Obviously one cannot acquire 30 years' experience, and be much less than 50 years old. I was rejected in both instances, solely because of my age. Younger men, though less qualified, were preferred. To begin with, I would be starting at the top, so to speak. Also, the assumption was, that being in my fifties, I was at the peak of capability, and my competence and usefulness would then begin to diminish. And very importantly, the health, insurance, and retirement plans which most substantial companies provide impose extra liability and higher costs for the older employee.

Industry, in our youth-oriented society, tends to reject the older applicant and discard the older employee. This setback taught me a lesson. Fortunately, I appeared at that time much younger than my actual years. I decided to take advantage of this fact by lying about my age and applying to other companies. I arbitrarily reduced my age by 10 years, and juggled the number of years of experience, without detracting from my obvious qualifications. The age dilemma was thus solved. I received several desirable offers, and accepted a position with a comparatively new company, headed by two young men of great ability. All they lacked was the experience and the know-how I could offer.

I was with this firm about seven years. During this period the rise of the company was phenomenal, and it was still growing. Without undue modesty, I might add that I had made a considerable contribution to their success. However, they began an expansion program which required new executive personnel. I was now a veteran employee, and ostensibly approaching 50, although I was actually about 58. Soon I found myself being phased out of major decision-making and activity. As a result, I was forced to resign.

I then succeeded in obtaining another job, of equal importance, again lying about my age. This time it was necessary to lop off about 13 or 14 years, and thanks to my youngish appearance, the deception was not difficult. After three or four years, I was again confronted with the same situation, and again I was unemployed. I now was actually about 63 years old, but presumably only 53 or 54. Nevertheless, because of my qualifications, I was once more able to secure a satisfactory position, but this time only on a year-to-year basis. This lasted about three years, and again I was out of work, this time permanently. Despite the fact that I could practice some deception about my age, I was beginning to show the unmistakable signs of a fading Peter Pan.

Though under no financial pressure, I was disinclined to retire completely. I wanted to keep in the mainstream of business life, and if you will, in the mainstream of life itself. I was unwilling to assign myself to the rocking chair, or be resigned to a passive senior citizen role. Rather than be the recipient of old-age benefits and subsidies, I preferred to be a useful, productive tax-payer. It was good for my ego. The only recourse left was to resume my own business.

The experience I have just related may be unique in its details. But there must be significant numbers of senior citizens of executive stature who would prefer to remain active in their area of competence, but who are shunted aside because of age. I can cite other instances.

An acquaintance of mine, for example, had been with a major, internationally known company for 30 years, and although regarded as one of the best chemical engineers in the field, was retired at age 60. Still exceptionally competent and respected, he obtained a similar job, but as a consultant on a per diem basis. He performed so well, however, that his daily job stretched into five years and, incidentally, at a higher rate of pay than he had earned before. Again he was retired, this time permanently. He is in first-rate health, and utterly competent. His enforced retirement is a distress, and a bore. He is disaffected, with little motivation, because he truly loved his work. He receives considerable retirement benefits, which, incidentally, he does not need. He would be far happier at work in a field in which he has gained eminence and wide respect, and where there are few who are his peers in capability.

Aside from my personal experience, I should like to make some observations which I believe have relevance to the subject of aging. As we all know, the great and growing number of older persons have impelled expanding programs of aid, both by private and government agencies, an example of which is the legislation passed by the 89th Congress, with the slogan "A new day for the older American." This legislation provides jobs for the unemployed over 55 and includes, as well, a variety of other benefits. However, such good legislation, in my opinion, does not go deeply enough into the problems of the aged. It tends to lump together all persons into age categories, and to treat them accordingly. Like many other programs intended to respond to the needs of the elderly, this one, I believe, represents a serious failure to deal with the older person on the basis of varying and psychological needs.

It is true that recognition was given to this failure in the 1971 White House Conference on Aging. One of the items of planning is to include a service for all age groups, with enough flexibility to take care of the especially disadvantaged elderly—meaning, of course, the economically disadvantaged. This does indicate some awareness of the need for flexibility. Implementation is another matter. But, please note, the awareness refers to the economically disadvantaged. Apparently, no thought was given to the economically advantaged older person with deep social and psychological problems.

With greater life expectancy, a newer problem faces the older person; a problem barely recognized as yet, and hardly faced up to. Living longer inevitably increases the number of persons bereft of their marital partners, by death, separation, or divorce. I will speak of the latter because it was my own experience.

In the first stages of married life, say up to 20 years, the marital binding forces, outside of the emotional relationship, are, generally, the task of bringing up a family and the involvement with a business or profession. But when all the children have gone their separate ways, the binding forces tend to dissipate. Sometimes the couple find their paths diverging, often to such an extent that, in effect, they live separate lives. Usually, because of habit, or because of the unthinkable disruption of a real separation or divorce, they slide into a different kind of relationship. They manage an accommodation to each other, despite differing interests, activities, and outlooks. But often enough the end result is actual separation or divorce. This happened to me, after 27 years of marriage. Statistics compiled by New

York State in 1970, in population areas of 250,000 or more, show the following, for ages 55 to 85+, in round figures:

total population	3,800,000
total married	2,250,000
widowed	1,000,000
separated/divorced	250,000

For the older person, the trial of separation or divorce, even more than widowhood, is, at the least, painful, and it could be shattering to one party, and possibly to both.

Finally, let me presume to introduce a thought which has beset me. I am certain it is not original, and I make no professional claims on the subject. I merely offer my own reflections. The generation-gap, especially in our own country, is something everyone talks about, and moans about. I wonder if there has ever been a serious study of the matter with a view to doing something about it.

It is the nature of the young to feel a separateness from older people, and they find it a little incredible that they too are marching to old age. An integral part of learning, from childhood on, should perhaps include a comprehension of the transitions within all stages of life, from childhood to old age. Understanding, empathy, acceptance, and not mere tolerance for the elderly, should be part of the educative process. I do not suggest that this be merely a classroom function. I mean something broader; in the home, in the attitudes of society in all areas, in entertainment, television, movies. Each night, on one of the television stations, there is a five-second message asking: "Do you know where your children are?" Why not, "Do you know where your parents are?"

Young people look for heroes, and strive to emulate them. What greater example of heroic characters and achievers than such people as: Toscanini, Picasso, Edison, Benjamin Franklin, Oliver Wendell Holmes, Churchill, Harriman, de Gaulle, Pablo Casals, Grandma Moses, Norman Thomas, Michelangelo, Sophocles, and others too numerous to mention. All these are, or were, in their seventies, eighties, and even nineties.

These were not merely exceptionally talented people, but people with the will to make a contribution to society and civilization; to fulfill themselves, right to the end. These people were heroes. Atrophy of interests and activities can set in at any age, even with the young. Conversely, the latter years can be fruitful and creative, and give substance to Robert Browning's thesis that "The best is yet to be."

Growing to understand this must have an attitudinal effect on the young. This concept, I submit, would benefit society, socially and even economically. Certainly, the plight of the unwanted, or shunted-off, older person would be ameliorated. Such an approach might even serve to diminish, and perhaps bridge, the generation gap.

THE EXPERIENCE OF A RETIRED RELIGIOUS EDUCATOR

RAE BRAGMAN

I can present only the highlights of my experience of retirement, which must, of necessity, be personal.

Since the term "Women's Lib" was not in vogue in my younger days, it is relevant for me to show how and why I became a retiree. My husband was one of the early psychiatrists whose interests I shared, and my life was enriched. He died at a very early age. I moved from Binghamton to New York City with my nine- and ten-year-old daughters to be near family. As soon as I was physically able, I looked for work as the family breadwinner, and because of my past experience in public-school and religious education, I was able to find a part-time position as principal of the Temple Israel School in New Rochelle. It was a small school at that time, but it mushroomed; my position soon became full time, and I found myself in charge of 1,300 students and a faculty of more than 60.

There was no contract stating that I was to leave at the end of a specific period or at a specified age. But I had given so completely of myself to my work and to rearing my daughters until they acquired their bachelor degrees that there had been little time left to indulge my own whims and fancies. So when, after 25 years of dedication, I was asked to continue, my resolve was firm to experience the feeling of release from pressure and the joy of having free time. If it were necessary, to supplement my income, I would apply for substitute teaching.

Retirement implies previous employment and some financial income. It has a different connotation and status from aging—which is not a popular word with those involved in the process, although everybody ages from the day of birth. Particularly today, when we live in a cult of youth, we like to feel that old age is happening to someone else, not to us. The alternative to old age is not pleasant to contemplate, and there are many people who proclaim their age proudly and publicly. I am not one of them. I feel that it is the spirit of youth and enthusiasm for life which determine one's age. I do concede that I move at a slower pace, that I walk instead of run.

Retirement is an extension of one's previous life. I think that only a small minority of retirees experience a complete reversal of old habits, characteristics, and personality—the "how to retire happily" articles and books notwithstanding.

Number one on my list of priorities after retirement was truly an extension of my life in the past. My husband's love of psychiatry had been matched by his love of literature and of writing. A few days after I retired, I took down from the cupboard shelves the many medical journals and magazines which had been gathering dust for 25 years. In each one, there was an article or essay which my husband had written. I felt that they were all relevant to the present, since they dealt with the relationship of psychiatry to literature, with human-interest material, medical wisdom, and the history of medicine. I had hoped that they could be published in a single volume which I would entitle "A Psychiatrist Looks at Life and Literature."

A series on "Case Studies of Troubled Writers," such as Ruskin and Swinburne, were as interesting in the re-reading as they had been in the past. One of the troubled writers was Arthur Symons (1865–1945), a leading English author and critic. His friend Havelock Ellis, at that time world-famous, read the study in a British psychiatric journal and wrote a lengthy letter to my husband.

The letter was missing, and my effort to find a copy was an absorbing and time-consuming process. An English cousin discovered that the woman who had lived with Ellis for many years without benefit of clergy was still alive in England, though very old. She had written a biography of Ellis, in which she highlighted her own relationship and which I read with great interest. It was she who directed me to a French professor who had written a critical biography of Arthur Symons, and to whom she had given a copy of the letter. The book appeared as late as 1963 with the letter quoted in full, long after Symon's death and 40 years after Ellis had written it.

I continued to do considerable reading; researched in the library of the New York Academy of Medicine; had extensive correspondence; and contacted publishers. "Publishing is a matter of profit," said one of them, adding, "If only your husband's name had been Jung or Freud, there would be no problem."

A more important objective was to provide for each of my daughters a compilation of their father's writings, so that in the future they could share with their children the thoughts and ideals of the grandfather they never knew.

To me, family continuity and unity, a knowledge of and a pride in their roots, are a wonderful legacy to bequeath to your descendants. With priority number one finished, I gathered together from members of the family, photographs of grandparents, great- and great-great grandparents. All these found their way into two family-tree albums as gifts to my daughters and their families. I recommend this project to all retirees who are grandparents as a way to give to their children and grandchildren a sense of personal identity with and pride in their own past. My mother did this for me orally. She would have loved seeing the visual record.

One cannot just close the door on 25 years of living with a job or profession; it is natural to feel that one still has something to contribute. I had a great interest in the techniques of teaching through the use of audio-visual materials, and, after our school had become known in this area of education through a book which my staff and I had had published as a joint venture, I was invited to serve on two audio-visual committees. The objective of the first committee was to produce filmstrips for Jewish education which are used in non-Jewish schools as well; and of the second, to view films, filmstrips, and slides and to offer critiques, discussions, and evaluations of the materials. The evaluations were collected and published annually in an attempt to assist schools and organizations to select audio-visual materials discriminately. Continuing to serve on both committees for several years afforded me a pleasant transition to retirement.

Teaching the Jewish tradition of obligatory sharing with others had been an integral part of the curriculum in our religious school. There was a weekly collection called "Tzedakah," a Hebrew word meaning "righteousness." It was *never* called charity. The funds were allocated to Jewish and non-Jewish causes alike by the student council, but there were also special collections with which the students were closely identified. One of these was for the Leo Baeck School in Haifa. Our children's contributions to the Baeck Scholarship Fund helped many needy students receive a high school education beyond the ninth grade. I served for seven years as the chairman of the Leo Baeck School Scholarship Fund for the National Association of Temple Educators, after our school's program had been extended to Reform religious schools throughout the United States and Canada. I continued as chairman for three years after my retirement, another pleasant transition.

I belong to several organizations to which I have given of my time, but currently my most active organizational effort is with the Brandeis National Women's Committee, which is solely responsible for supporting the library of Brandeis University. It is intellectually satisfying, with many study groups on various subjects.

But my great pleasure has been to travel. Now I make plans to go at any season without the urgency of future tasks needing attention. I travel mostly with groups since group travel is much less expensive and relieves one of the bothersome details connected with traveling. My most thrilling adventure was in 1966, a 45-day trip "Around the World." In addition to the excitement of seeing the sights and sounds of strange, exotic countries, this trip had a special significance. Because this was a group sponsored by Americans for Democratic Action, we met with ambassadors or their representatives in each country and were briefed extensively. In India, for example, we met with Chester Bowles, informal and gracious in the lovely residence built as part of the American embassy, and in Tokyo with Ambassador Edwin Reischauer, the brilliant expert on Japan, who gave generously of his time. Another highlight in all my travels has been to seek out the Jewish community, and in the Middle East and the Orient, there has always been that special feeling of kinship with my people in far-flung places of the world.

Since organizations are always on the alert to discover people who will provide programs for their meetings, I have often been drafted to give talks based on my travel experiences. One series, in which I used slides and film-strips, dealt with "Jews in Distant Lands"; another, with Israel, a subject with which I feel very much at home. My first visit to Israel was in the summer of 1949, one year after that nation's independence. I went as part of an exchange-student group from New York University, in connection with a course—the first of its kind—called "Israel Workshop." It was my first flight in a plane and, considering the plane's antiquity, I am fortunate that it was not my last. My most recent trip to Israel took place in the spring of 1969, after my retirement and after the Six-Day War. Remembering vividly how primitive Israel had been in 1949 and how we had been barred from the Old City, I found this trip, by contrast, especially moving as I witnessed the fulfillment of Israel's "impossible dream."

And so, by participating in these community and overseas endeavors, I hope I am following the precepts of Hillel, a famous rabbi of ancient times, who said:

If I am not for myself, who will be for me?
Yet if I am for myself *only*, what am I?
And if not now, when?

In many communities, avenues are being opened to enrich the lives of senior citizens culturally and intellectually. My leisure time has given me the opportunity in New Rochelle, for instance, to attend special classes in art, honors-program lectures, and a film series at Iona College, open to the public. Last year the college extended to senior citizens the privilege of enrolling in any course free of charge. I took advantage of Iona's generosity, without having a sense of guilt when it was necessary to "cut" a class. The College of New Rochelle is following Iona's example in the fall. They are both Catholic colleges, and I, for one, am most appreciative.

Many people are flocking to retirement villages which stress adult to-getherness. I prefer to spend most of my year at home. I like to socialize with my contemporaries, but I also enjoy the company of many younger friends.

I cherish my own independence and the privacy of my own apartment. I cherish equally that I have more time to spend with my family. It is a special joy to go to school programs in which the grandchildren participate, to bask in their accomplishments, to listen to their ideas and ideals as they mature. It is an opportunity to keep in touch with young people, to know what the present generation thinks and feels. If retirement is an extension of our previous lives, this, then, is its ultimate expression.

VI
THE CHALLENGE FOR THE
AGING INDIVIDUAL

The Challenge of Aging
for Marriage Partners

SEYMOUR B. JACOBSON

Seymour B. Jacobson, M.D., received his A.B. degree from Columbia College in 1939, and his M.D. from New York University in 1943. He is a diplomate, American Board of Psychiatry and Neurology, and a Fellow, of both the American Psychiatric Association and the New York Academy of Medicine. Dr. Jacobson has had an extensive and long-continued involvement with the psychiatric problems of the aged. He is corresponding editor, Journal of Geriatric Psychiatry, *and Secretary, Group for Geriatric Psychiatry of New York. He is a member of the Committee on Aging, Community Service Society of New York; and of the Citizens' Committee on Aging, Community Council of Greater New York. Currently, he is attending psychiatrist, the Jewish Home and Hospital for the Aged, New York City.*

Previous contributors have addressed themselves to the question of aging and the challenge it presents for society and for the church. We are now to consider the challenge of aging for the individual in the context of marriage and the mutual relationship which marriage defines.

Through its complex of customs, marriage provides for activities necessary to the existence of society, of culture, and of life itself. Basically, these are procreation, the physical care and social upbringing of children, and economic cooperation. Individuals find in marriage the means of satisfying their biologically and culturally determined needs. It provides affection, companionship, sexual gratification, the opportunity to establish a family, and mutual support. Through what Ackerman has called complementarity, or reciprocal role-relations, marriage partners seek not only to satisfy their needs but also to "find avenues for the solution of conflict, support for needed self-esteem, and the bolstering of crucial forms of defense against anxiety" (Ackerman, 1966, p. 72). To put it simply: marriage partners look for a haven in which they are free to walk around in their underwear and where their fur can occasionally be rubbed the right way.

But marriages, despite the auspices of this Institute, are not made in heaven. Each partner brings into the marriage different endowments and life experiences; different personalities and adaptive patterns; different conscious and unconscious expectations. In the intimacy of marriage, the partners share many experiences, some of which inevitably lead to conflicts. If these conflicts are resolved, they can provide better understanding, increased personal growth, and greater stability of the relationship. If they cannot be resolved, there are several possible consequences. One is that the marriage itself may not be tolerated and will end in divorce. Less dramatically, conflicts may be openly expressed in irritability, resentment, and hostility. A third consequence is that the feelings aroused by the conflicts may lie dormant, only to be brought to the surface by stress.

Divorce rarely occurs among the aged, although its incidence is seen to be increasing. A severely conflicting couple will be kept together by a number of considerations. The elderly are influenced by two additional age-related factors. One is that they have an increased need for the narcissistic supplies provided by the possession of a husband or wife. The other is that they are fearful of the anticipated calamities of old age and are reluctant to face them alone. Marital discord, however, is not uncommon in aged couples. Goldfarb offers an interesting explanation for this. He posits that in many marriages there are lifelong patterns of emotional dependency in one or both partners. The choice of a spouse in such marriages is based on the expectation that the other party will serve as a protective parent-surrogate. Goldfarb says:

> marriage and parenthood represent culturally defined modes of self-fulfillment and opportunities for developing gratifying interpersonal relationships. Hence the incentive to marry and raise a family is exceptionally strong in the dependent person. . . . The dependency may be mutual, each of the marital partners deriving satisfaction from a relationship of reciprocal bondage. In that case, dependency is a cohesive force in marriage. But it may also be a disruptive force [Goldfarb, 1969, p. 7].

Speaking of old-age dependency, Goldfarb goes on to say:

> In the dependent person, changes with age in personal appearance, health, sexual vigor, and earning capacity evoke fears of diminishing ability to attract and hold a "loving" person, or to perform in such ways as to gain one [Goldfarb, 1969, p. 8].

Similar changes in a spouse can be equally threatening to a
person. Loss of mastery, feelings of helplessness, and the emot
and anger follow. In either case, maladaptive efforts to regain se
severe stress in the marital relationship. This is especially so in the vulnerable period of old age.

Old age is, by definition, the period of declining function which follows
maturity and leads to death. The challenge of aging for the individual is
three-fold: to deal with the losses of physical, mental, social, and economic
resources which accompany old age; to complete the other developmental
tasks of late life; and to live out the years remaining with dignity and
reasonable contentment. The challenge of aging for aged couples is to do
all this and more. It is also to redefine constantly their mutual relationship
so as to maintain it in the face of inner change and changes in the world
around them. Husbands and wives who have survived together into late
life have already arrived at some workable accommodation to each other
and achieved a more or less harmonious balance. They have met the challenge of aging for marriage partners many times.

How effectively they will continue to meet this challenge depends on
three variables: the kind and magnitude of their losses of physical, mental,
social, and economic resources; the nature and amount of the resources
remaining to them; the emotional health of their marriage. All these variables interact, each strengthening or weakening the partners' overall ability
to respond to changing circumstances. Even severe impairments of certain
functions can be offset. The presence of compensating resources or of a
healthy capacity to shift reciprocal role-relations can help maintain the
equilibrium of the marriage remarkably well. Sooner or later, however, the
capacity of the marital unit to function will fail. The practical consequences
of this are many; the ultimate one is separation through death. There are
many changes in the lives of older marriage partners before this end is
reached. We will touch on only a few of them: retirement, decrease of sexual
activity, chronic physical illness with disability, and mental illness.

RETIREMENT

Retirement is a relatively early happening in the lives of the aged couple.
According to Bromley, it

> presents both men and women with serious problems of adjustment—altera-
> tions in their daily schedule of activities, less financial security, changes in the
> social roles and status, reductions in responsibility and authority, changes in
> social and family relations, and poorer physical health [Bromley, 1966, p.
> 103].

The changes in the relations between elderly marriage partners are usually
precipitated by the termination of the husband's employment.

Cavan has studied what happens to the couple in old age upon the retirement of the husband, analyzing it in terms of the changes which occur in social role and self-concept. She describes an individual's occupation as an important aspect of his social role and a significant means through which he expresses his self-concept. For the man, this self-concept is that of a competent, decisive, successful person who is usefully productive in some kind of work and is capable of providing for his family (Cavan, 1965, p. 388). The woman's self-concept is not very different, and it relates to her social role of wife, mother, and homemaker. With retirement, the man is excluded from his former place of work; he is separated from his associations with his group of co-workers; and he is looked upon differently by other people. His social role is changed, and he is no longer in a position to carry out its functions. This is difficult to accept, and he remains largely motivated by his old self-concept. Unfortunately, there is no place where he can express this old self-concept except at home. Without a regular 9-to-5 schedule to maintain, he hangs around and is constantly underfoot. As a self-appointed expert, he interferes with his wife's activities and household responsibilities. This situation has led more than one woman to complain that while she had married her husband for love, she had not married him for lunch.

The threat which all of this poses to a wife's security can lead to much marital conflict. One way in which this conflict can be lessened is through the retiree's participation in programs such as SERVE* or Foster Grandparents,† which benefit both the community and the individual. Another is through membership in a senior citizens' center—as was demonstrated during a recent field trip I made with a group of medical students to the Hodson Center. An elderly gentleman was in the poolroom about to drop a ball in a corner pocket. We interrupted the game to ask him how he had come to join the center. His story was not at all unusual. He had retired from his job eight years ago, at 70. He spent the next weeks at home getting on his wife's nerves. She finally complained to their family doctor in desperation. This wise physician quickly grasped the problem, had his nurse locate the nearest senior center, and urged the husband to go there. He did, found new friends and new interests, and has happily stayed out of his wife's hair— at least for five days of the week.

---

*SERVE is an acronym for Serve and Enrich Retirement by Volunteer Experiences. It started as a program for the aged on Staten Island under the sponsorship of the Community Service Society of New York, and is still operated by the Society, which is located at 105 East 22nd St., New York, N.Y. 10010. This program served as a model for the development of RSVP—Retired Senior Volunteer Program—which now has 600 local chapters, with its national office c/o ACTION, 806 Connecticut Ave., N.W., Washington, D.C. 20525.

† Foster Grandparents is a program also sponsored by ACTION, which provides for paid services to children by the elderly poor.

DECREASE OF SEXUAL ACTIVITY

Sex plays a vital part in the relationship of marriage partners. Sexual attraction usually brings them together; sexual intercourse is the mechanism for having children; and pleasurable sex provides them with constant opportunities to renew their emotional and physical intimacy.

Sexual dysfunction is certainly not unknown in early and middle marriages. Until recently, such dysfunction was taken for granted in older marriages, and it was generally accepted that sexual activity ended with old age. It is now known that many aged marriage-partners are capable of enjoying sexual intercourse, as the studies of Kinsey (Kinsey, Pomeroy, & Martin, 1948; Kinsey, Pomeroy, Martin, & Gebhard, 1953), of Masters and Johnson (1970), and of Pfeiffer (1969) and his co-workers at Duke have documented. Pfeiffer's ten-year longitudinal study of persons aged 60 to 90, including 31 intact couples, gives substantial data confirming the fact that both interest in sex and sexual activity go on well into late married life (Pfeiffer, Verwoerdt, & Wang, 1968).

There is no doubt that there is a decline in sexual activity between marriage partners with advanced years. One obvious reason is that sexual vigor decreases as a part of the natural reduction of all physiological capacities with aging. Butler and Lewis (1973) have suggested a number of other possible causes including physical illness, which either directly or indirectly affects the aged person's ability to perform sexually; the side-effects of certain medications; illness and resultant unavailability of a spouse; and loss of interest in the spouse because of unattractiveness or boredom.

All these issues can affect the amount of intercourse between aged couples and the quality of the pleasure it provides. One consideration, however, is of particular dynamic significance. That is the prior sexual adjustment of the individual partners. A person who is sexually inhibited will often participate in marital sexual relations reluctantly and with little satisfaction. Aging will then be utilized as a pretext for withdrawing from unwanted sexual contact with the spouse. This point is illustrated by the following:

> An elderly couple, in their mid-70s, were admitted to a home for the aged. They were given a room together in accordance with the policy of the institution. Shortly after admission, the wife demanded that she be separated from her husband because of his sexual overtures. She had been able to avoid them in their prior living arrangement.

It is apparent that sexual intercourse can be a cohesive force in older marriages, and its continuation is desirable. When it no longer occurs, the reasons should be as thoroughly examined as they are with younger couples. Some forms of sexual dysfunction in the aged are responsive to counseling and treatment; the elderly can benefit from both. A gratifying number can be restored to some level of sexual activity, and others can be helped to adjust to their limitations.

CHRONIC PHYSICAL ILLNESS WITH DISABILITY

Chronic physical illness with disability is a not infrequent accompaniment of old age. It affects not only the ill marriage-partner but also his spouse, who herself may be frail or in poor health. The care of a severely sick person can exhaust his mate emotionally and physically. The effort involved can literally be killing, as is evidenced by the fact that a substantial number of husbands and wives die within a year of the death of the spouse for whom they had been responsible.

Financial means is a prime resource when chronic illness strikes the aged. Savings are rapidly depleted, and even those with apparently adequate funds will eventually exhaust them. Institutional placement will then have to be considered. The decision to place a spouse is usually agonizing to make and extremely difficult to carry out. The arrangements which are finally made are rarely satisfactory to all concerned. Here is an example of a situation which required institutionalization.

A 64-year-old man suffered a severe stroke and required almost total physical care. His somewhat younger wife was determined to have him remain at home. Since his daytime needs were beyond her, she took a job and used her salary to hire a daytime attendant. She took care of him at night. Several years later she was forced to retire. Since she could no longer afford the attendant, she took on the responsibility the full 24 hours. She steadfastly refused to consider placing her husband in an institution until she could no longer carry on. His admission to a nursing home was arranged, and she visited him every day. Her guilt at her "desertion" was overwhelming and was compounded by his death six months later.

The well partner may sometimes be unwilling to separate from the companion of a lifetime when institutionalization is unavoidable. They may then enter the institution together. Here is one such instance.

A 76-year-old man was afflicted by a number of chronic diseases. His frail wife had for some years kept up their home and had lovingly tended to her husband. When he became legally blind, she could no longer continue her efforts. The problem was resolved by their joint admission to a home for the aged. The needs of both could be met there, and she could continue to provide him with personal attention and the emotional support of her presence.

MENTAL ILLNESS

Mental illness at any stage of life is a devastating event both for the sick person and for his family; it is possibly more so in old age. Earlier contributors have already given consideration to the particular forms of mental disorder seen in late life. I should like to elaborate on two of them: chronic organic brain syndrome and late paraphrenia.

Chronic organic brain syndrome is the psychological reflection of brain damage resulting either from senile change in the brain or from cerebro-vascular arteriosclerosis. The impaired orientation, memory, and general intellectual function which are the hallmarks of this disease are trouble-some enough. The frequently associated disturbances of feeling, thought, and behavior can be even more distressing. They require psychiatric inter-vention and can often be modified by appropriate medication. The manage-ment of a disturbed senile person calls on all the strengths of the family and all the resources of the community; it often requires hospitalization. The dis-astrous effect this condition can have on a marriage is impossible to grasp unless one has had personal or professional experience with it.

Late paraphrenia is a somewhat rare but extremely troublesome mental disorder. It is a paranoid state occurring in the elderly which is most re-sistant to treatment and most difficult to manage. The following case illus-trates this well.

A 72-year-old man was referred for treatment by the judge before whom he had been arraigned on complaint of his wife. He had developed the de-lusion that she was trying to poison him, and he had threatened her with a gun. She called the police, and the judge placed him on probation on the condition that he have treatment. Medication was prescribed but refused; his threats against his wife continued, and he was ultimately committed to a state hospital.

The tendency for unpleasant character-traits to become more pronounced in old age produces other problems for aged marriage-partners. Other overt disturbances which occur in late life may be manifestations of unsuccessful attempts to deal with the emotional response to aging. The form which these disturbances take is determined by the individual's personality, his view of his circumstances, and his expectation of relief. Treatment is often very help-ful in lessening the underlying emotional state and in thus reducing the marital stress.

CONCLUSION

The challenge of aging for marriage partners is difficult, indeed. Marriage is complex, constantly changing, and frequently precarious. The altered circumstances and increased stresses associated with old age make it more so. The distress of an elderly person, in most instances, is made less acute by the presence of a husband or wife with whom declining years can be shared. The death of a spouse creates tremendous problems for the survivor.

Both men and women are beset by loneliness and suffer from it regardless of what the quality of their marriage had been. Replacement of a lost spouse by remarriage is quite common among men, less so among women. Common law relationships are not unusual between the aged because of the financial penalties imposed for marriage by Social Security regulations. This injustice, let us hope, will be remedied by more considerate legislation.

Those of us who are professionally concerned with the elderly face our own special challenge. We must not only continue to use our special skills in the service of all the aged; we must also become aware of the needs of those elderly whose marriages need our help. These troubled marriages are remarkably responsive, and our efforts will reward us as well as them.

REFERENCES

Ackerman, N. W. *Treating the troubled family*. New York: Basic Books, 1966.

Bromley, D. B. *The psychology of human ageing*. Baltimore: Penguin, 1966.

Butler, R. N., & Lewis, M. I. *Aging and mental health*. St. Louis: Mosby, 1973.

Cavan, R. S. The couple in old age. In R. S. Cavan (Ed.) *Marriage and family in the modern world: A book of readings*. (2nd ed.) New York: Crowell, 1965. Pp. 387–394.

Goldfarb, A. I. The psychodynamics of dependency and the search for aid. In R. A. Kalish (Ed.) *The dependencies of old people*. (Occasional papers in gerontology, No. 6) Ann Arbor: Institute of Gerontology, University of Michigan, 1969. Pp. 1–15.

Kinsey, A. C., Pomeroy, W. B., & Martin, C. E. *Sexual behavior in the human male*. Philadelphia: Saunders, 1948.

Kinsey, A. C., Pomeroy, W. B., Martin, C. E., & Gebhard, P. H. *Sexual behavior in the human female*. Philadelphia: Saunders, 1953.

Masters, W. H., & Johnson, V. E. *Human sexual inadequacy*. Boston: Little, Brown, 1970.

Pfeiffer, E. Geriatric sex behavior. *Medical Aspects of Human Sexuality*, 1969, *3* (7), 19–28.

Pfeiffer, E., Verwoerdt, A., & Wang, H. S. Sexual behavior in aged men and women. I. Observations on 254 community volunteers. *Archives of General Psychiatry*, 1968, *19*, 753–758.

Aging and Career Development

TOM HICKEY

Tom Hickey received an A.B. degree with honors from Gonzaga University in Spokane, Washington, in 1963, and an M.A., in developmental psychology, from California State University, Los Angeles, in 1967. At that point he began to focus specifically on the latter part of the adult life span, and earned an M.P.H. (1968), and Dr.P.H. (1970) at U.C.L.A. emphasizing social gerontology. Dr. Hickey's academic work has included positions in the psychology departments at California State University, Occidental College, and now in The College of Human Development at The Pennsylvania State University, where he teaches life span development, social gerontology, and grief management. He is also the academic coordinator of Continuing Education programs for the providers of social and health services to the elderly of Pennsylvania. Dr. Hickey has published attitudinal and intergenerational research, and is currently working on a methodological study of evaluative models for short-term training. In addition to consultation on career development and retirement preparation, he serves in a number of advisory capacities in gerontology on a national level.

Nos ignoremus, quid sit matura senectus.
Scire aevi meritum, non numerare decet.
Let us never know what old age is.
Let us know the happiness time brings, not count the years.
                    DECIMUS MAGNUS AUSONIUS (*c.* A.D. 350)

It may seem to us somewhat of a paradox that the fears of old age were present to the early Romans when we consider that their life expectancy at

195

birth was little more than half the number of years projected at birth in America today. Yet, there must have been elderly people living in the era of Ausonius; and his dictum bespeaks, perhaps, a much earlier historical beginning of the negative perceptions of old age than one would typically imagine. The emphasis of this paper is on *career development* rather than on the process of aging. Nevertheless, the theme of this Institute is the challenge of aging to the individual and to society. The term "challenge" here seems to imply a struggle or a confrontation, with a potential for both positive and negative outcomes. Thus, when speaking of career development over the life span, one is aware of a continuing confrontation between what is termed "career," and both the aging process and society's perceptions of chronological age.

The outcomes of this continuing confrontation are measured at a series of choice points in adult life. It is commonly accepted, for example, that in his early twenties, a man has a wide range of choices, and that his work role at that point may be more life-supporting than career-related; whereas in the late twenties there should be some distinguishable relationship between previous college or professional training and current occupation, and by the mid-thirties this relationship should show stability and progression. Thus, the latter are a result of socially correct career choices made at various points along the way—choices which presumably provide personal satisfaction and social status. Simultaneously, however, each successive choice delimits the options available at the next choice point. Therefore, the challenge of career development at mid-life continues to be an age-related one in terms of one's personal perspective or subjective aging, as well as in terms of society's expectations (i.e., a 45-year-old lawyer would not typically turn to the practice of medicine as a second career). In fact, the challenge may increase for an individual with time.

Career has been defined as "a profession affording opportunities of advancement" (*Oxford Universal Dictionary*, 1964). Given the foregoing description of a typical career development and the reduction with age in available options, this definition seems to be far from accurate—at least as it relates to mid-life career development. The implication from this definition is that the notion of a viable career gradually becomes non-existent as advancement opportunities decrease. Although this paper challenges the social ethic or value underlying that assumption, its prevalence in American society requires that it not be dismissed too lightly. However, a secondary definition describes career as "one's course or progress through life" (*Oxford Universal Dictionary,* 1964). This statement more accurately portrays the theme of this paper, which focuses on the development of career over time —especially when viewed from the perspective of mid-life choice points. The meanings ascribed here to the term "aging," or the aging process, are subjective and societal. They are subjective in that they reflect personal capabilities, attitudes, motivations, and life goals (or subjective perceptions thereof). The societal—or other-than-self—perspectives are important in that they portray and delimit the choice points at various chronological ages.

CAREER DEVELOPMENT AND THE WORK CONCEPT

To study career development—at any point in the adult life span—one must begin historically with the concept of work. As a matter of fact, had this Institute been held a decade or so ago, this treatise would probably have been entitled "Occupational Choice and Life Satisfaction," or "Participation and Adaptation in the Work Force." The emphasis on *career* is a relatively new one, with its origins clearly emanating from society's concept of work.

Work, then, has played a critical role in our society, not only in satisfying our nation's material needs, but also in the less often acknowledged effect it has on the individual's psychological and social functioning. This emphasis on work is, in a large part, a function of our culture. We are told, for instance, that for the early Greeks and Romans, work was a bane, and that leisure was the basis for a fulfilling life (Hearnshaw, 1966). There is further evidence that our concept of a proper work week is built upon norms established during the Industrial Revolution, a period of highly inflated work standards (Wilensky, 1961). Some observers state that the almost sacred quality attached to work is now declining (Friedman & Havighurst, 1954; Santayana, 1950); others feel it has changed little (Morse & Weiss, 1955); and still others feel that this is an irrelevant point (Gerontological Society, 1969). Regardless of one's perspective, it is clear that the topic remains one of vital concern in our society today, and that it is at the basis of understanding career patterns. Variations in attitudes toward work between older and younger age-cohorts, for example, clearly reflect differentiated meanings ascribed to the traditional work ethic.

Reflecting this impact of work on our society is the degree of attention it has received from social scientists over the years. Extremes or aberrations in normal career patterns have received particular attention: unemployment, marginal employment, occupational mobility, early retirement, etc. Until recently, however, relatively little work has been done on the established worker during middle- and late-career periods, and on the changing meanings of work and career for him. Consequently, policymakers have tended to ignore this group, focusing instead on those particular problem areas about which so much has already been written.

Perhaps there has been too much complacency in assuming that all the needs of middle-aged or older workers are being met under present circumstances, or that they are similar to those of younger workers. On the other hand, more mature workers may have generally been satisfied in the past, with more recent developments in society having invalidated this continuing assumption. In any case, it seems imperative at the present time to examine the status of the worker in middle- and late-career periods. Just as the adult personality continues to change over time, so, too, should one expect that work will have different subjective meanings at different stages in the life span. The benefits would be clearly evident if it were possible to match personality needs at various stages of the life cycle with societal and economic needs external to the individual.

METHODOLOGY

The literature on work has been primarily of three kinds: theoretical (Form & Miller, 1949; Wilensky, 1960, 1968); non-empirical (Davidson, 1966; McFarland & Philbrook, 1958; Weber, 1969); and a variety of research studies based largely on questionnaires or survey methodologies. The meaning of work for the individual and for society has been a particularly attractive topic to sociologists and social psychologists, while questions concerning middle and late career have been more characteristically within the domain of gerontologists and, in a few cases, economists.

The questionnaire represents by far the most popular method for obtaining data in all areas related to work during and following middle age (Davidson & Kunze, 1965; Morse & Weiss, 1955; Rusalem, 1963; Sofer, 1970). However, Wilensky noted in 1961 that many of these studies failed to control for common SES* variables (e.g., sex and educational level); and a review of recent literature suggests his observation continues to remain a valid one. Other methods have occasionally been employed, a notable exception being the study of Friedman & Havighurst (1954), who also used the interview. However, the goals of such studies have been tangential to the main concern of this review. Given the general lack of methodological sophistication which has characterized the area, the findings summarized herein must be interpreted with some caution. Moreover, one would hope that as a society, when we progress from the level of understanding to policy or action for mid-life career development, our creative solutions in this area at least, will be based more on the generation of new ideas and creative alternatives than solely on this earlier body of literature on work and occupational choice.

THE MEANING OF WORK

Initially it might be beneficial to turn to the general meaning of work, ignoring the age variable for the moment. Social scientists studying this question have variously posited a number of non-economic derivatives from

---

* Socioeconomic Status. For explanation, see footnote on page 126.—Ed.

work: it fulfills identity and status needs, and provides necessary social and activity outlets; it can establish a sense of accomplishment and secure a sense of family role; and it can structure time (Gross, 1958; Morse & Weiss, 1955; Mumford, 1970; Rusalem, 1963; Sofer, 1970). In turn, it has long been noted that work serves to anchor the individual to society; the dangers to society of a high unemployment rate are well known (Morse & Weiss, 1955; Wilensky, 1960). Work is so important that one's occupation has been considered to be a critical sociological variable, and perhaps the most important one (Parker, 1971). Further, the absence of work in just about any form (unemployment, leisure, retirement) is often accompanied by negative connotations in that social relationships are frequently established and maintained in the context of role and position.

It has also been observed that, not only are psychological and social rewards an important part of work, they are frequently seen as being more important than economic rewards. Morse and Weiss (1955) and Sofer (1970) agree that identity and status needs are paramount, although their relative importance has been observed to vary somewhat according to occupational level. Rusalem (1963) found in a large sample of old and disabled unemployed that there was strong determination to find work, despite the difficulties involved, and that of those who were hired, only 8% considered the main benefit to be financial. Morse and Weiss (1955), employing a different approach, asked a sample of workers if they would continue working if they suddenly received a large inheritance; 80% maintained that they would. The Gerontological Society Report (1969) found that, of a sample of those earning over $10,000 yearly, only 4% mentioned income as a reason for working as much as they did. Finally, any kind of career disappointment generally has negative ramifications which far exceed economic concerns, often leading to a profoundly disturbing effect on identity (Goffman, 1952; Sofer, 1970).

MEANING OF WORK IN MIDDLE AGE AND ITS RELATIONSHIP TO CAREER DEVELOPMENT

Since it is apparent that the effects of working (or not working) are generally quite important to the individual psychologically and socially, it would be helpful to examine these effects in the particular context of mid-career. Once again, it is necessary to look at the meaning of work, but within the framework of a developmental theory of careers. What have they contributed to an understanding of the meaning of work and career, specifically at mid-life?

The earliest theoretical approach in this area was the study of *trait-factors* (as reported by Williamson, 1965), in which a direct matching of interests and abilities with the real world of work presumably led to job productivity and individual satisfaction. This model also resulted in the development of a series of vocational interests and occupational-preference inventories, as well as to counseling procedures for entering and remaining in the labor force. Unfortunately—for our purposes here—this theoretical model has not been effectively utilized for mid-life career change or for labor-force re-entry. The failure to consider the age variable completely—especially in terms of motivational experiential differences between older and younger adults—may account for this.

A related career-development theory blends the trait-factor model with the study of personality. The emphasis here has been on the personality needs, types, and factors involved in occupational choice and career satisfaction (Holland, 1959; Roe, 1957; and Small, 1953). Some theorists have attempted empirically to link occupational satisfaction with personal requirements for the fulfillment of various needs—many of apparently genetic or childhood origins; while others have matched the personality characteristics of individuals choosing a career with the lifestyles of persons who are successfully pursuing specific occupations.

In the rapidly paced technological society of the 1970s, where a constantly changing environment has a swift and significant impact on lifestyle, it becomes almost an academic exercise to postulate a consistency model matching childhood needs with those at mid-life. It is fairly obvious that the environmental and experiential effects of 20 years of adult working and living play a large part in mid-life choices. At the same time, any theory of career development with life-span implications must take into consideration an individual's needs (as in Roe's postulates) and lifestyle preferences. For the most part, this has not occurred. As a matter of fact, a frequently reported cause for disillusionment in second careers and retirement emerges from dissatisfaction or disappointment in pursuing activities which one had never tried and "always thought he wanted to do," but which have little relationship to those things in his lifestyle which have provided satisfaction in the past.

A sociological model of career development has its central point in the effects of environmental or outside influences on man in the choices of, and adaptations to, career. This position is a somewhat deterministic one, and has been espoused by a number of writers (Caplow, 1954; Hollingshead, 1949; Miller & Form, 1951). This is the view which is frequently expressed as "being in the right place at the right time," or, conversely, "*you* were always lucky, while *I* was given a rough time by life." Of interest to those concerned with the study of mid-life career change is some modification of this model, combining it with a theory of personality. Some individuals, for instance, are more adaptive, more prone to risk-taking, and, therefore, more likely to cope with changes imposed by external forces. Thus, for these individuals, career dissatisfaction and the "locked-in" feeling give way fairly quickly to the motivation to change one's occupation in a way which better suits personality and lifestyle needs at a different stage in adult life.

Perhaps the most relevant theoretical framework from a developmental perspective could be called the *self-concept* theory. This approach emerges from the writings of two giants in this field: Charlotte Bühler (1933) and Donald Super (1957). The application of this theory in the counseling context was developed in the early writings of Carl Rogers (1951). This approach was effectively summarized by Osipow when he wrote that:

> (1) individuals develop more clearly defined self-concepts as they grow older, although these vary to conform with the changes in one's view of reality as correlated with aging; (2) people develop images of the occupational world which they compare with their self-image in trying to make career decisions; and (3) the adequacy of the eventual career decision is based on the similarity between an individual's self-concept and the vocational concept of the career he eventually chooses [Osipow, 1968, p. 11].

In these schemes, the period of mid-career is labeled the "stable" or "indulgency" stage; in each successive stage it is implied that the concept of work is particularly critical at this age. There is supporting evidence that work is generally more rewarding during one's fifties than at any other time in one's career. Two explanations have been offered for such findings. Wilensky (1960) hypothesizes that job satisfaction is a function of aspirations and needs *vs.* rewards, and that these come together in the most beneficial relationship during the fifties (i.e., needs are declining and rewards increasing). Davidson and Kunze (1965), on the other hand, propose that the answer may lie in longitudinal selectivity: those in their fifties who did not enjoy their work might have quit working by this age. Although each explanation has some merit, there is reason to believe that other, perhaps more salient, factors are operating. While Wilensky asserted that aspirations and needs decline in the fifties, it is probably more accurate to state that they are changing. In fact, Davis (1967) has produced evidence to the effect that aspiration levels are just as high for older workers as for younger ones. Students of adult personality similarly refer to the increasing emphasis on mastery and control of the environment. Neugarten (1968) called this the "executive process of middle age"; while Erikson (1968) labeled it "generativity," which included the concepts of productivity and creativity. Although working with a narrowly circumscribed sample, Miner (1962) observed that at age 40, or soon thereafter, work behavior tends to become less conforming and more independent—which seems to support the above notions.

With such changes in mid-life—the tendency to put more into and get more out of work—the role of career choice assumes a heightened meaning. Such questions as: "How much should I work? How much leisure do I want?

Should I change careers? When should I retire?" can take on highly emotional overtones. One study (Gerontological Society, 1969) views the mid-career crisis, which affects some workers at about age 50, as both a challenge and an opportunity. Such a situation can force the worker to make decisions which "may be a source of new growth."

At the present time it is impossible to trace past trends or predict future ones concerning such work–leisure decisions. Research on the role of leisure as it relates to this topic has been equivocal, and perhaps reflects the ambivalence with which it is still treated in our society. There are contradictory reports on the value of leisure for the successful worker (Davidson, 1966; Parker, 1971); disagreement as to whether or not general economic growth increases the propensity to leisure (reviewed by Wilensky, 1961); and completely opposite assessments of the status of leisure for the middle-aged worker in contemporary society (Kreps, 1968; Parker, 1971). In the previously-mentioned survey of individuals earning over $10,000 yearly, only 13% of the respondents mentioned the benefits of leisure as a reason for not working more (Gerontological Society, 1969). Perhaps the only conclusion to be drawn from all this is that the relationship of work and leisure at this stage of life is a complex one with nothing to be gained by viewing the two concepts as dichotomous ones.

Similarly, we know very little about an individual's propensity to change careers in middle age; it is a topic which has drawn little attention from social scientists. Perhaps, as a result, it does not appear coincidental that our country lags far behind Western Europe in offering opportunities for job retraining at this stage of life (Belbin & Belbin, 1968). It has been stressed repeatedly, however, that a mid-career job change (whether seen as a downward, lateral, or upward move) can be particularly stressful (Goffman, 1952; Gross, 1958; Sofer, 1970).

Nevertheless, the Committee of the Gerontological Society (1969) asserted that there is an increasing interest in changing careers in the forties and fifties. Some large firms are responding to such pressures by offering sabbaticals and mid-career clinics. One can readily see the related benefits of establishing new job opportunities for older workers on a far wider scale. It is perhaps regrettable that this idea has evolved so slowly in the United States, since it has such wide appeal in other countries.

CONTINUING ABILITY TO WORK

The previous discussion would be of relatively limited value if the once-widely-held impression were accurate that mental and physical skills deteriorate rapidly beginning in middle age. The fact that work is important to a man in mid-career would not be of particular interest to an employer if the worker could no longer do his job. Fortunately past injustices and misconceptions in this area are being reversed, with contributions coming from cognitive studies and research in industrial psychology. There is convincing evidence that many workers make their greatest contributions in mid-career; that general abilities decline at a much slower rate than was previously suspected; and that such losses as do occur may be more than compensated for in other ways (such as performance accuracy).

According to the U. S. Bureau of Labor Statistics, for example, there is no measurable decline in the efficiency of office-workers as age increases; in factory work, the decline in efficiency is slight until age 55, but the older worker remains generally more consistent than his younger counterpart (Greenberg, 1961). Kreps (1967) asserts that a key to reduced productivity with age is to be found in inadequate working conditions. Given the proper environment, work output for ages 60–69 is just as high as that at the 15–24 age range. Others report that behavioral and attitudinal changes which occur with age tend to make the worker increasingly more valuable to his employer.

Several variables appear to be involved in the question of the continuing ability to work, and perhaps it is the complex nature of their interrelationships which is responsible for the controversy which has surrounded the issue. Three central variables of particular relevance are intelligence, rate of physical decline, and self-esteem. Intelligence, in particular, has received extensive attention for several decades, the results of which have recently been ably reviewed by Horn (1970). Essentially, the concept of intelligence has been dichotomized: one component improves with age, the other declines. Horn and Cattell (1967) have defined the former, *crystallized intelligence,* as those abilities (such as verbal skill) on which cumulative experience would have a positive effect. *Fluid intelligence,* which declines with age, consists of those reasoning abilities which appear to be more related to genetic or biological heritage than to culture or environment. Given these findings, it is no surprise to encounter claims that those in occupations which stress cognitive activity of a reasonably predictable kind, as opposed to workers whose jobs require only physical skills, tend to work longer before retirement (Friedman & Havighurst, 1954).

The question of declining physical skills as they relate to work has also come under reconsideration. Although many physical skills undoubtedly decline more rapidly than overall cognitive ability, the belief that older workers are retrained with more difficulty has been justifiably attacked from many quarters (Belbin, 1964; Gerontological Society, 1969; and Hearnshaw, 1966). Convincing evidence has accumulated which indicates that older workers learn new skills just as rapidly as younger workers, as long as appropriate teaching techniques are adopted to compensate for reduced rates of response, short-term memory loss, etc. Furthermore, it appears that sensory and perceptual processes decline more slowly than was previously supposed (Gerontological Society, 1969). Just as speed was an important determiner of skill retraining, so Szafran (1968) has reported that practice is critical in maintaining perception and eye-hand coordination. In a study of commercial pilots, Szafran found that such skills in many cases will not decline from age 20 to 67. The Committee of the Gerontological Society (1969) recommended that similar studies be conducted in other occupations, with the aim of developing criteria to operationalize functional age, rather than relying principally on chronological age to determine time of retirement.

Finally, an older worker's ability to work might remain at a high level despite a decline in physical and cognitive abilities. It has already been seen that work can have heightened meaning for older adults, so that increased motivation might more than compensate for such deficits. This is somewhat of an idealistic recommendation, given the prevalence of working environments which encourage the disengagement and gradual withdrawal of the older worker, eventually resulting in a reduction of the all-important identification with the job. Hearnshaw (1966), for instance, sees the primary problems of occupational adjustment among older people as an exaggerated "loss of confidence in the capacity to learn and to adjust." It is the position of this writer that such alterations in confidence—often precipitated by external prejudices—are the primary cause for the frequently noted declines in working ability. There are obvious implications here for the education of society, and for the continuing education of the middle-aged worker.

SOME ECONOMIC AND SOCIAL RECOMMENDATIONS

Our age-stratified society has traditionally locked the worker into a career pattern from which escape is discouraged. The common stereotype is that he pursues one line of work, in a position which gradually decreases in value beginning at mid-life, until he retires at the earliest economically practicable time. This pattern is perpetuated in our society without regard for individual desires. There are recent indications, however, of an increasing dissatisfaction with the status of lifetime career-patterns, second careers, leisure, and retirement as they have existed in the past. Similarly, much of what has been reported here tends to dispose of commonly held myths and/or stereotypes about the older worker. In view of this, it would seem timely now to re-analyze the position of the middle-aged and older worker in our society, and the extent to which recommendations might be made toward the development of a more beneficial social policy in this area.

Flexibility in Work and Leisure

A flexible retirement plan involves complex economic and social interrelationships, but it is one which has had strong supporters for a number of years (Breckinridge, 1953). Traditionally, the mandatory retirement age has been a tool for countering high unemployment at the expense of older individuals able and eager to work (Busse & Kreps, 1964; Kreps, 1968). In general, flexible retirement is more sensitive to the needs of the worker, while a mandatory retirement policy reduces administrative problems. An extensive list of the advantages and the disadvantages of each has been presented elsewhere (Poorman, 1962).

Among the most compelling advantages of flexible retirement are benefits both to the individual's self-esteem and to the economy as a whole. Juanita Kreps, who has been a primary advocate of such a policy, asserts that flexible retirement, which would allow many older people to continue working, coupled with a reduced work week for all age groups, would have the effect of creating part-time unemployment for all rather than total unemployment for older workers (Kreps, 1968). The benefits would be many: (*a*) all of society could share in the increased leisure time; (*b*) the consumption of goods and services would go up with the increased leisure, stimulating the economy in general and raising the demand for labor; (*c*) given the choice of working or not working at a time when one's employment might continue to have elements central to a sense of identity, the older person's self-esteem would be likely to increase; and (*d*) spreading one's earnings over a longer period of years would decrease financial strains and feelings of economic dependency in later life. The most important of these is the element of choice: every individual, regardless of age, would have an increased option as to whether to pursue increased work or increased leisure, based increasingly on the respective value of each for him.

Such a solution might well answer the observation on retirement made by Friedman and Havighurst to the effect that: "The young man's dream becomes the old man's reality. But is it a fair exchange?" (Friedman & Havighurst, 1954, p. 2). With flexible retirement and a shortened work week, the exchange would not have to be postponed for the length of a career— the young worker could have additional leisure, the older person could continue to pursue a career.

The idea of continuing work, but at a reduced rate, is another idea worthy of exploration. The Committee of the Gerontological Society (1969) has recommended that pilot programs be developed for older workers along three lines: shorter work weeks, longer vacations, and part-time jobs. Once again, it would appear that there could be mutual benefits for both the older worker and the employer.

New Jobs

A related issue is the need for the development of new jobs for older workers, a concept which has been explored more extensively outside the United States (Belbin & Belbin, 1968). Perhaps government incentives will therefore be necessary to encourage employers to develop such programs (Gerontological Society, 1969). In addition, there would appear to be numerous possibilities for older workers in areas in which government could have direct influence: health care, education, and social programs. Most of the job opportunities which have opened up for older people evolved from an economic rationale, or became available specifically for older people almost by chance. Very few occupational roles have been determined by known psychosocial needs of the middle and older years of adulthood.

Continuing Adult Education

It has been said that "If a man has a working life of 40 years, he may need to be re-educated four or five times if he is to fit himself for different positions in society as he ages" (Bowden, 1964, p. 920). This observation increases in validity with the rapidly increasing rate of technological change (Toffler, 1970). The need for updating specific skills and refreshing the general knowledge of adults will similarly increase. Unfortunately, however, it has been noted that adult education programs have not been reaching those people who are most in need, and that, in fact, very few people over the age of 50 participate (Gerontological Society, 1969).

The disadvantaged educational position of many older workers appears to be both the primary cause of loss of ability with age, and the source of the solution to the problem of occupational adjustment in the later work-years. Just as loss of confidence is more central to declining productivity than either mental or physical changes, so a lack of education—or the obsolescence of one's knowledge base—is primarily responsible for the development of these self-doubts. In light of this, it would seem that occupational adjustment of the older person has a strong relationship to adult education.

The challenge is clear. Although opportunities for the continuing education of older people have been available, for a variety of reasons the response has been discouraging. Such programs as already exist should be made more attractive to such people by shifting the focus from a competitive undergraduate model to one which more effectively utilizes the experiential wisdom and skill of the middle-aged and older adult, his known performance-accuracy, and, above all, the differing motivational levels between older and younger adults approaching the educational process. Moreover, the content and substance of such programs should be planned more rationally and systematically. While it is clear that adult education in this context does not refer to training for recreation skills or crafts, nevertheless, the substantive areas which should be included are not well-delineated. At the College for Older Americans in Erie, Pennsylvania, for example, there was a surprisingly large registration for courses in philosophy and the humanities at their inaugural session in 1972. This type of response would usually not be anticipated.

Finally, the question of economic support for adult education must be addressed. Until very recently, when these programs were greatly constricted, the federal government provided subsidies, in the form of traineeships, for post-graduate education. Similarly, there was much talk (until last year) of a new form of welfare assistance called the *guaranteed annual income*. Without support for or criticism of either of these programs, it must be pointed out that both contain the basis of a support model for adult education. If the middle-aged worker had the economic support for a temporary period during which time he could pursue education or retraining for a second career, the degree of his freedom at that choice point in life would be greatly increased. Simultaneously, the whole issue of vested interests in retirement programs, portable pensions, etc., would need to be re-examined.

Since this paper is not presented from the economist's viewpoint, these issues will not be dealt with. However, it is fair to say, in a marketing economy, that even if opportunities were provided for second careers, and if the appropriate adult education programs for such careers were available, these alone would not guarantee a large participant, or consumer, group. In order to be workable, an economic support system would have to be developed simultaneously which would encompass previous lifestyle and occupational or career investments, as well as the specialized needs of a more limited or finite future.

The Role of Research

At this point, the research issues are eminently clear. Moreover, when considered in the context of many other ideas presented at this Institute, the challenge of second careers is a confrontation between an individual who has made a working investment in a social system, and the expectations of that system as perceived by the individual or a large segment of society. Such perceptions and expectations need to be understood and, in some cases, modified. Many of the following ideas and recommendations for research evolve from earlier statements in this paper about the confrontation between the aging process and career development. Others are summarized from a national conference on flexible careers which was held three years ago, with participation by labor, management, government, and research (Havighurst, 1971).

(a) *Work-orientation.* The assumption that ours is a work-oriented society is undoubtedly a valid one, but is the validity of this assumption decreasing with each succeeding generation? Are young people less oriented toward work than their parents? Are there differences in the work-orientations of men *vs.* women, college-educated *vs.* skill-trained people, self-employed *vs.* employees, etc.? These and similar questions have never been fully answered. It would seem that there is need for extensive attitudinal research focused on the degree of man's interest in work per se, and its value to him.

(b) *Work–leisure*. Related to the work-orientation is the question raised frequently by Juanita Kreps regarding the balance between work and leisure. What are the time-dollar trade-offs? How much income is an individual willing to forgo in favor of more leisure time? How do these trade-offs potentially differ by age, sex, class, status, occupation, etc.? What is management's view? What are the cost-benefit issues, and what economic alternatives would need to be devised for bartering length of workdays, work weeks, and vacations for or against retirement credits? This is a very important area of research for industrial gerontologists and economists.

(c) *Alternative models*. Psychosocial and economic research is needed to compare and contrast the various prototype programs which have evolved in recent years to provide alternatives to the traditional work-retirement sequence. There have been a few programs with various retirement options developed in industry and the trade unions. While some of these have been reported individually, there has been no comprehensive analysis of their overall effectiveness, or a follow-up of individuals who participated.

(d) *Career shifts*. Another retrospective analysis could be directed at people who have changed careers at mid-life. This group would include those who had a planned or systematic career change (e.g., athletes, career military, etc.), and those who are forced out of work at mid-life by the obsolescence of their skills. This analysis would focus not only on the intermediary steps between two careers, but also on the adjustment patterns in planned and forced career change. This would be quite timely, given the current supply and demand shifts in some professional fields.

(e) *Career predictors*. It is evident from the career-development theories summarized in this paper, as well as from the fact that this topic is so relevant today, that longitudinal studies must be undertaken to develop reliable predictors of career development which would more carefully include work functions and individual differences, as opposed to existing (and somewhat outdated) generic occupational categories.

(f) *Leisure culture*. In line with earlier recommendations regarding the development of new jobs and second-career opportunities more specifically targeted for older adults, sociologists must tell us more about leisure as a quasi-permanent lifestyle in society. If we are indeed moving more toward a developmental view which sees man spending equal thirds of his lifetime in preparing, working, and retiring, what then are the emerging dimensions (i.e., needs, interests, activities) of that final period? Of significant interest here is something which could be labeled the "leisure industry." Prior to the solidification or institutionalization of that industry, what kinds of interventions can occur now which would assure a role for older adults? In the evolution of an entirely new leisure culture, how can we plan for the participation of the active people who wish to pursue second careers, part-time retirement jobs, etc.? This is an especially important issue if we believe the biologists who say that we are on the verge of extending the life span.

(*g*) *Service roles.* A final addition to this list, which is by no means an exhaustive one, is the recommendation for initiating research into the area of humanistic and service roles as second careers. It is frequently noted that older adults are concerned with their personal legacy which extends beyond their lifetimes. For the most part, this is to be found in the family context where adult children's success, respect, and love have a direct impact on parental satisfaction in late life. But it is also evident that for many people a wider degree of satisfaction can be derived from making a positive contribution to the solution of social needs and problems. The more affluent accomplish this with money, while others do it with their time in a voluntary role. A third opportunity could be added which would provide both second careers and the requisite satisfaction to be derived from a role which contributes to the human good.

CONCLUSION

The challenge of second careers to the aging individual is a monumental one with the potential risk of highly significant and different outcomes. On the one hand, it represents a critical choice point in an individual's life, where he must carefully assess his total lifestyle, projecting (as accurately as possible) future interests, needs, and desires. Moreover, it forces recognition—howsoever momentary—of man's finiteness and the aging process itself. It demands of an individual careful thought and response to some fairly basic questions: How much life is left to me? What do I want to do with it? What am I doing now which could be eliminated as incidental, given the shortness of time? How much strength, energy, interest do I have for daily working? How much financial and social dependency am I willing to experience if I break away from the independent security of a lifelong career? How do I want to spend my free time?

On the other hand, the challenge of second careers to society is one which requires significant shifts in social attitudes and policies toward work and leisure. The fact that this topic appears on the program of this Institute and many others with increasing frequency is evidence that this challenge will not disappear nor permit itself to be overlooked. The lock-step work-career ladders from youth to old age which are so prevalent in today's society must give way to more flexibility. Second careers and career change must become terms associated with adulthood in general, rather than with old age and obsolescence. This challenge, then, is fundamental to the economic and social values of our culture, as well as to the philosophical beliefs and the psychological attitudes of the individual who interacts daily as a member of that society.

REFERENCES

Becker, H. S., & Strauss, A. L. Careers, personality and adult socialization. In B. L. Neugarten (Ed.) *Middle age and aging.* Chicago: University of Chicago Press, 1968. Pp. 311–320.

Belbin, E. Retraining the middle aged. *New Society,* 1964, *77,* 6–8.

Belbin, E., & Belbin, R. M. New careers in middle age. In B. L. Neugarten (Ed.) *Middle age and aging.* Chicago: University of Chicago Press, 1968. Pp. 341–346.

Bowden, L. Education and administration. *Listener,* 1964, *71,* 920–921.

Breckinridge, E. *Effective use of older workers.* Chicago: Wilcox & Follett, 1953.

Bühler, C. *Der menschliche Lebenslauf als psychologisches Problem.* Leipzig: Hirzel, 1933.

Busse, E. W., & Kreps, J. Criteria for retirement: A re-examination. *The Gerontologist,* 1964, *4* (Pt. I), 115–120.

Caplow, T. *The sociology of work.* Minneapolis: University of Minnesota Press, 1954.

Davidson, W. R. Some observations about early retirement in industry. *Industrial Gerontology,* 1966, *2,* 26–30.

Davidson, W. R., & Kunze, K. R. Psychological, social and economic meanings of work in modern society: Their effects on the worker facing retirement. *The Gerontologist,* 1965, *5* (Pt. I), 129–133, 159.

Davis, R. W. Social influences on the aspiration tendency of older people. *Journal of Gerontology,* 1967, *22,* 510–516.

Erikson, E. H. Generativity and ego integrity. In B. L. Neugarten (Ed.) *Middle age and aging.* Chicago: University of Chicago Press, 1968. Pp. 85–87.

Form, W. H., & Miller, D. C. Occupational career pattern as a sociological instrument. *American Journal of Sociology,* 1949, *54,* 317–329.

Friedman, E. A., & Havighurst, R. J. *The meaning of work and retirement.* Chicago: University of Chicago Press, 1954.

Gerontological Society, Committee on Research and Developmental Goals in Social Gerontology. Work, leisure and education: Toward the goal of creating flexible life styles. *The Gerontologist,* 1969, *9* (4, Pt. 11), 17–36.

Goffman, E. On cooling the mark out: Some aspects of adaptation to failure. *Psychiatry,* 1952, *15,* 451–463.

Greenberg, L. Productivity of older workers. *The Gerontologist,* 1961, *1,* 38–51.

Gross, E. *Work and society.* New York: Crowell, 1958.

Havighurst, R. J. Report of a conference on flexible careers. *The Gerontologist.* 1971, *11* (1, Pt. 11), 21–25.

Hearnshaw, L. S. The role of work environment. *The Gerontologist,* 1966, *6,* 95–96, 127.

Holland, J. L. A theory of vocational choice. *Journal of Counseling Psychology,* 1959, *6,* 35–45.

Hollingshead, A. B. *Elmstown's youth.* New York: Wiley, 1949.

Horn, J. L. Organization of data on life-span development of human abilities. In L. R. Goulet & P. R. Baltes (Eds.) *Life span developmental psychology: Research and theory.* New York: Academic Press, 1970. Pp. 423–466.

Horn, J. L., & Cattell, R. B. Age differences in fluid and crystallized intelligence. *Acta Psychologica,* 1967, *26,* 107–129.

Kreps, J. M. Job performance and job opportunity: A note. *The Gerontologist,* 1967, *7,* 24–27.

Kreps, J. M. Economic policy and the nation's aged. *The Gerontologist,* 1968, *8* (Pt. II), 37–43.

McFarland, R. A., & Philbrook, F. R. Job placement and adjustment for older workers. *Geriatrics,* 1958, *13,* 802–807.

Miller, D. C., & Form, W. H. *Industrial sociology.* New York: Harper & Row, 1951.

Miner, J. B. Conformity among university professors and business executives. *Administrative Science Quarterly,* 1962, *7,* 96–109.

Morse, N. C., & Weiss, R. W. The function and meaning of work and the job. *American Sociological Review,* 1955, *20,* 191–198.

Mumford, E. Job satisfaction—a new approach derived from an old theory. *Sociological Review,* 1970, *18,* 71–101.

Neugarten, B. L. The awareness of middle age. In B. L. Neugarten (Ed.) *Middle age and aging.* Chicago: University of Chicago Press, 1968. Pp. 93–98.

Osipow, S. H. *Theories of career development.* New York: Appleton-Century-Crofts. 1968.

Oxford Universal Dictionary. C. T. Onions (Ed.) Oxford: Clarendon Press, 1964.

Parker, S. R. A sociological portrait: Occupation. *New Society,* 1971, *18,* 766–768.

Poorman, W. F. Senior citizens in the labor market. *The Gerontologist,* 1962, *2,* 23–27.

Roe, A. Early determinants of vocational choice. *Journal of Counseling Psychology,* 1957, *5,* 212–217.

Rogers, C. R. *Client-centered therapy.* Boston: Houghton Mifflin, 1951.

Rusalem, H. Deterrents to vocational disengagement among older disabled workers. *The Gerontologist,* 1963, *3,* 64–68.

Santayana, G. *Atoms of thought.* New York: Philosophical Library, 1950.

Small, L. Personality determinants of vocational choice. *Psychological Monographs,* 1953, *67* (1, Whole No. 351).

Sofer, C. *Men in mid-career.* Cambridge: Cambridge University Press, 1970.

Super, D. E. *The psychology of careers.* New York: Harper & Row, 1957.

Szafran, J. Psychophysiological studies of aging in pilots. In G. A. Talland (Ed.) *Human aging and behavior.* New York: Academic Press, 1968. Pp. 37–74.

Toffler, A. *Future shock.* New York: Random House, 1970.

Weber, A. R. A second career for older workers. *Manpower,* 1969, *1,* 19–21.

Wilensky, H. L. Work, careers and social integration. *International Social Science Journal,* 1960, *12,* 543–560.

Wilensky, H. L. Life cycle, work situation, and participation in formal associations. In R. W. Kleemeier (Ed.) *Aging and leisure: A research perspective on the meaningful use of time.* New York: Oxford University Press, 1961. Pp. 213–242.

Wilensky, H. L. Orderly careers and social participation: The impact of work history on social integration in the middle mass. In B. L. Neugarten (Ed.) *Middle age and aging.* Chicago: University of Chicago Press, 1968. Pp. 321–340.

Williamson, E. G. *Vocational counseling: Some historical, philosophical, and theoretical perspectives.* New York: McGraw-Hill, 1965.

The Prospect of Death

LEO J. O'DONOVAN, S.J.

Father Leo J. O'Donovan, S.J., earned an A.B. degree from Georgetown University in 1956, a Ph.L. from Fordham University in 1961, an S.T.L. from Woodstock College in 1967, and the Dr. theol. degree from the University of Münster in 1971. He has been both a Fulbright Scholar and a Danforth Fellow, and was Assistant Professor of Systematic Theology at Woodstock College in New York City. He is currently on the faculty at Weston College, Cambridge, Massachusetts. Father O'Donovan is a member of the Society for Religion in Higher Education and of the American Academy of Religion. He is a contributor of philosophical and theological articles to such journals as Theological Studies, Religion in Life, Continuum, American Ecclesiastical Review, The Personalist, *and* Philosophical Studies. *He is also an associate editor of* Theological Studies.

Unfortunately we speak about the prospect of death for the aging much as we do, so very imperfectly, about death for every man. It is the great equalizer, the final appearance of the cancellation imminent in the most vigorous life, the last organic collapse intimated by every sickness. Together with the possibility of lasting fidelity and commitment, it is the great challenge to true seriousness in human existence. In the face of it, men have averted their eyes, let them fall despairingly to earth, or raised them in the hope that this experience at least might reveal some truer solution to our questions: What does life finally mean? Does it have any final direction?

Of all human experiences, death seems the most ambivalent. It can be regarded with the *horror vacui* or with stoic resignation. Sometimes it is masked and cosmeticized beyond recognition, as Jessica Mitford (1963) so vividly reminded us. But in other times it has been a constant preoccupation of daily life, imaged forth in death dances and scenes of final judgment. For the expiring Middle Ages, wrote Johan Huizinga, "An everlasting call of *memento mori* resounds through life" (Huizinga, 1924, p. 124). Death can be seen as a release from a world of imprisonment or as a return to the chaos from which life first emerged. It can be accepted heroically for the sake of a people's cause, as perhaps in Salvador Allende's death, or it can be the heartless fate of a doomed people, as many Americans increasingly view the treatment of their Indian predecessors in this land of plenty. Death can be an experience of quiet, hopeful summation or of desperate, radical negation. Is it even, properly speaking, an experience at all? Who could tell us?

These questions among many others confront every man who knows his life will end. But for the aging person, and for a society increasingly aware of its responsibilities and indebtedness to the aging, there are special dimensions to the questions which demand our attention. Much of the recent discussion of death, especially in theology, has all but completely ignored the particular challenge which the prospect of death presents for the older person. An insufficiently historical and Biblically too literal theology has even suggested that there is no Christian view of old age. But it was to a people that God's reign was announced, and it is a people which longs for its coming. Whether that reign is postponed, delayed, or achieved in every man's death is a question which should intimately affect his fellow-Christians. Is there not perhaps a far richer harvest of experience and wisdom to be learned from older people who have faced the prospect of death far longer than most of us? These reflections on just a few aspects of death are written in an effort to learn from the experience of the aging, and also it is hoped, to say a few true words of comfort to them.

"I AM NOT THE LEAST AFRAID TO DIE"

It is becoming more and more common to teach men in general and to counsel the aging in particular that an unholy fear of death has masked its true reality for us and needlessly terrorized our hearts. Were we rather to view the final event in our lives as precisely that, their determined ending, the closing of the gift which time had to offer us, then we might learn once again to face death and to deal with it as we deal with life—as best we can. It is suggested that just as the mature adult accepts the tensions and contradictions of life as inescapable, so also he can learn to accept this final contradiction. It is well known that great men have gone resolutely to their end. Dying after 73 years of prodigious activity, Charles Darwin stated simply: "I am not the least afraid to die." Nor should we too easily consider such attitudes as a new stoicism easily revived. It is only with patient struggle that hospital staffs are learning to confront death realistically with their patients, and their increasing clinical success has deservedly met with public sympathy.

And yet death somewhere strikes fear in every man alive. Try as we may to consider it calmly, it remains not just one contradiction among others, but the unadorned contradiction of our lives as a whole, the end of hopes as well as of plans, the cancellation both of achievement and of its memory as well. Can we not only affirm life but truly love it—and yet come finally to terms with losing it? If true acceptance is a fostering and a love as well as an admission, can we truly accept life *and* death? Who is really able to add together the gift of life and its irrevocable loss? Do we truly wish to learn such impermanence and still be fearless? What else in life would then be left to fear? Hate? injustice? pride? But why else are these human failures finally fearful except that they cripple life instead of fostering it?

Dylan Thomas could not accept death calmly. Looking upon his own father's death, he gave us terrible advice:

> Do not go gentle into that good night,
> Old age should burn and rave at close of day;
> Rage, rage against the dying of the light [*The collected poems of Dylan Thomas*, 1953, p. 128].

Reflecting on the contradiction of death, the Swiss theologian Hans Urs von Balthasar seems almost to provide an excuse for men who cannot follow Thomas' advice:

> The only reason that hearts do not constantly rebel against the dark omnipotence of death is that its fateful wind has always bent the trees of the soul toward it, that the powers of infidelity, of injustice, of betrayal, of spiritual debility and physical illness and infirmity are familiar to us from childhood in all their destructive strength [Balthasar, 1967, p. 49].

The negativity of death is simply too much for us, and we choose so readily to compromise with its many expressions. "They are forces," continues Balthasar, "that are not only above us, but in us, with whom we seem inexplicably to have made a compact, voluntarily, yet against our will, at a time and place we can no longer remember" (Balthasar, 1967, p. 49). A number of studies have shown, in fact, a relatively low incidence of the fear of death among both young and old. Even after reporting these studies, however, David Hendin still concludes: "It is clear that facing up to death . . . and dying is something to be feared" (Hendin, 1973, p. 103).

If death were "as it should be," perhaps then we could approve it wholly. But *is* it as it should be? Is it not rather both natural and un-natural, both acceptable and unacceptable, radically ambivalent and hence radically fearful? The dissolution of the organism is a natural event with which biology may perhaps reckon calmly. But personal life is always in search of its own integration, and it necessarily sees in death not only a final testing but a disintegration as well. For any of us, accordingly, young or old, who cannot be finally satisfied with the present integration of our lives, the depth of our dissatisfaction measures the degree to which we continue to fear death as well as learn to accept it.

The New Testament, indeed, warns us of complacency before the prospect of death. It is not merely the natural conclusion to a life shared with other living beings. It also embodies the misuse of life of which man alone is capable and thus becomes "the wages of sin" (Rm 6:23; cf. 6:16, 21). By faithlessness in response to God's love in our lives and in the lives of our neighbors, we do in fact earn death. "Sin when it is full-grown," says the Letter of James, "brings forth death" (Jm 1:15). In this view, death is not merely the final expression of our natural state but, still more strikingly, the expression of our sinful state.

Is it too much to expect that older people among us will have a deeper appreciation not only of the range of human failure and sinfulness but also of the way death summarizes and completes it? From whom can we expect to learn this lesson, whether spoken or simply lived before us, if not from men and women whose experience of life is longer and more tried? Surely it requires experience and not merely insight to know what the human heart is capable of, and just as surely it requires many years to know the endless ways in which our hearts' designs can end in death. The disintegration of life into death is what every act of lovelessness intends, but the full import of this truth can be plumbed only through time, and the aging person who actively lives his life to the end comes to know it, I think, more and more profoundly. Death is seen more often and expected more intimately as the years advance, and a Christian realism suggests that there is in the last analysis no simple answer to the question whether death approaches as friend or foe. As the possible summation of everything inimical to life, it will always be in part at least our enemy.

Christian faith also confesses death, however, as a part of God's plan. Each of the Gospels quotes Jesus as saying that it is the man who loses his life who will save it (Mt 10:39; Mk 8:35; Lk 17:33; Jn 12:25). In John's version of Jesus' saying, we find the same imagery Paul uses in 1 Corinthians 15 to suggest what resurrection means: "Unless a grain of wheat falls into the earth and dies, it remains alone; but if it dies, it bears much fruit" (Jn 12:24)—a verse which appears on the title page of Dostoevski's masterwork. "For if many died through one man's trespass, much more have the grace of God, and the free gift by the grace of that one man Jesus Christ abounded for many . . . so that, as sin reigned in death, grace also might reign through righteousness to eternal life through Jesus Christ our Lord" (Rm 5:15, 21). The covenant of God with man engenders the hope that we may truly respond to this invitation to final communion—among ourselves, but through and in our Creator. It is a hope, through Him, of overcoming hate with love and death with life (cf. Rm 12:21).

Death, then, is to be feared to the degree that it expresses disunity and sinfulness in our lives. It is fearful inasmuch as we approach it lovelessly, but hopeful inasmuch as we can meet it with generous and converted hearts. Who knows, finally, the balance of generosity and selfishness which is in him? Will anyone who has not lived long even know the depth of the question? Still we may all hope, and with increasing age increasingly hope, that where sin has increased, grace may abound all the more, and that perfect love may yet cast out fear (cf. Rm 6:20; 1 Jn 4:18).

"WE DIE ALONE"

Our hope is grounded, historically, in a community of faith called the Church and having at its center a man who faced death as all the rest of us do—and yet differently. For Jesus of Nazareth, confessed as Lord by the Christian Church, death, like life, was accepted *as* a mission and *for* a people. He is described repeatedly in the New Testament as sent by God, revealing in His life God as His Father, and calling men together under the reign of that one Father (cf. Mk 2:17; Mt 11:25ff; Jn 3:16, 10:10; Ga 3:28; Col 3:11). The reconciliation of man with God and thus with himself, an essentially renewing conversion of mankind to the truest source and goal of its life—this comes as close, I think, to summarizing the Gospel as any theme can, if it is not foolish even to try.* To be a new people, re-created where there was no people: this is the core of the Church's hope when it confesses that its Lord "makes all things new" (Rv 21:5). Indeed with such a vocation, as Edward Schillebeeckx so tersely puts it, "humanity is possible" (Schillebeeckx, 1968, p. 193).

But if this solidarity is at the root of our calling together, what then of death, which remains the most isolated act, if it is an act, in human existence? Is it not true, as Pascal wrote, that "we die alone"? Can any man follow us there, accompany us, share that burden, observe its actual occurrence?

---

* It is worth noting in this regard that the social dimensions of the Roman Catholic Church's liturgical prayer for the sick has been most fortunately re-emphasized in the new rite for the Sacrament of the Anointing of the Sick which became effective in 1973. The Bishops' Committee on the Liturgy comments: "The revised rite thus represents a movement away from a quasi-private to a preferred communal celebration. Anointing of the sick, perhaps the most liturgically deprived of all the sacramental ministrations of the Church, is never administered in a quasi-magical, mechanistic manner but rather as a sacrament of the community of faith" (Bishops' Committee on the Liturgy, 1973, p. 12).

And who knows the problem so well as the aging, for whom loneliness is the harshest harvest of their advancing years? More than any other diminishment whether mental or physical, political or economic, it is loneliness which can impoverish life for a man or woman who year by year survives old friends and acquaintances, accustomed styles of life and social expectations, even the former shape of a city and its services. Is it not the old who are most often left in our society to die apart, away, alone? In a city like New York, where approximately 13% of its population is 65 or older, the isolation of living alone with restricted means can be cruel indeed. "Though you may live in town," comments one of Jacques Brel's songs, "you live so far away, when you've lived too long."

And yet the central conviction of Christian life does remain the reconciliation of man with God and thus with himself—a life, consequently, not of separation but of communion. Can the situation be otherwise for death? Or do we hope in communion for a time, reconciliation with a limit? Would that really be "a new heaven and a new earth" (Rv 21:1; cf. 2 P 3:13)? Would it be worth making any final sacrifice for?

Paul's view is unmistakable. Preaching ever and again Christ crucified (1 Co 1:23), he tells us that every man who has been converted to God and baptized into Christ Jesus has been baptized "into His death" (Rm 6:3). A solidarity of life is at issue which carries through to the last moment, to the moment which lies hidden in every other, when we must either return despairingly into dust or fall with hope into the hands of God. It is not as though Christian life is assimilated to Christ's in discrete and successive stages which lie outside each other. That view misunderstands both the character of human time and also the interpretative role which Jesus' life has for our own. It is to Jesus as a man who was true to His Father's calling throughout His life and even in its final agony that the Christian is related, and thus to Jesus in His life *and* in His death.

It startles that residual individualism of ours which is strangely supported by the functionalist society in which we live so desperately in search of intimacy. But the New Testament nonetheless insists on the realism of our share together in Christ's life and death. "You have died," the Epistle to the Colossians says, addressing not just individuals but a Church, "and your life is hid with Christ in God. When Christ who is our life appears, then you also will appear with Him in glory" (Col 3:3–4). He who was innocently condemned and cruelly crucified lives transfigured with His Father as the irrevocable revelation of man's true calling. We must search out that meaning for our lives, but we seek it appropriately only when we seek it in all Jesus did and suffered, in His death as well as in His life.

This assimilation to the person of Christ in His life and death is for each of us, and for all of us together, a lifelong challenge, the challenge which most intimately shapes our lives and realizes their value. Perhaps we

speak more hesitantly than Paul, but like him we all confess in some way
a personal center outside ourselves in terms of which we hope finally to
understand ourselves: "None of us lives to himself, and none of us dies to
himself. If we live, we live to the Lord, and if we die, we die to the Lord;
so then, whether we live or whether we die, we are the Lord's" (Rm 14:7–8).
It is of course the hope of Christians to share the risen, transfigured life
of the Lord—"if we have died with Christ, we believe that we shall also
live with him" (Rm 6:8)—but there is no way to that glory except
through the cross on which the life of Jesus reached its term. "Unless the
resurrected Jesus is confessed as the crucified Lord," writes Ernst Käsemann, "the resurrection becomes only an ideogram for the glorification of
the world, a term expressing a cosmological and anthropological ideology"
(Käsemann, 1970, p. 175).

It may be true, then, that no one immediately follows us at the moment
of our death, that no one from our visible company can accompany us
there. But it is truer still that in death the Christian does follow his Lord,
does, at the Lord's invitation, join *His* company. It is a following we dare
not risk uninvited, but it is still more certainly an invitation which will not
be withdrawn. It is a lifelong invitation, to be true to this calling finally,
and we seek the faithfulness of our end at every moment before it. In
moments of success and of failure, we seek like Paul "to show that the
transcendent power belongs to God and not to us" (2 Co 4:7), and with
him we realize in our own ways that it is only if we are "always carrying
in the body the death of Jesus, that the life of Jesus may also be manifested
in our bodies" (2 Co 4:10). Without any contempt for the values of history and of nature, but rather with the hope that their final truth may be
fulfilled by God, the Christian says with Paul that one thing alone suffices
in the end: "That I may know [Christ] and the power of His resurrection,
and may share His sufferings, becoming like Him in His death, that if possible I may attain the resurrection from the dead" (Ph 3:10–11).

No one is so unavoidably called to choose clearly between the death of
Adam and the death of Christ as the aging person who has progressively
fewer and fewer close friends and relatives to stand by him at death.
Death's terror may be less by reason of its more accustomed intrusions
into the experience of older people, but its loneliness can be all the greater,
and so also the profound realization of the difference between dying utterly
alone, a creature of wind-blown dust, or dying alone in the company of
Christ.

In the diminishment of old age, the presence of death in life is not only
acknowledged and realized, as for every realistic person it must be, but
daily expressed, as only a conscious but waning life can do. For the aging
man or woman there is daily experience and witness that though we may
believe wholeheartedly in our union with God and with one another through

His Son, still "we have this treasure in earthen vessels" (2 Co 4:7). This is a different experience, in continuity with the possibility of death at every moment of life, but nevertheless lived out through longer years, generally reduced outside activity, and quieter modes of perception. When such people view death not with stoic resignation but with Christian faith, then surely they themselves live and give to others an invaluable, particular testimony of patient strength and tested hope. Accepting death both as an expression of sinfulness and as the beginning of eternity, older people add to the witness of their faith patient years the rest of us cannot call upon. Surely it can be said of them, then, that through their longer experience of the prospect of death they "complete what is lacking in Christ's afflictions for the sake of His body, that is, the Church" (Col 1:124). Surely, too, they themselves live and give to the rest of us a new perspective on that confidence with which the faithful man asks and answers:

> Who shall separate us from the love of Christ? . . . For I am convinced that there is nothing in death or life, in the realm of spirits or superhuman powers, in the world as it is or the world as it shall be, in the forces of the universe, in heights or depths—nothing in all creation that can separate us from the love of God in Christ Jesus our Lord [Rm 8:35, 38–39].

Older Christians, then, do indeed die alone—and yet with the Lord. They can approach and accept death for His sake and the sake of His Church, trusting God's power to become fully evident in that point without dimension where our individual resources appear to vanish and yet where their relations to other men and women strain also toward an event of final revelation. Called by the Lord to a meeting face to face, the dying person ineluctably calls us, too, after him. And if he is old, he calls with the weight of all his years.

"I DON'T UNDERSTAND WHAT I'M SUPPOSED TO DO"

Recognizing that we may approach death with either hope or fear (and generally with a measure of both), and seeing that it is possible to die utterly alone or alone with Christ, we may still ask whether we know *how* to die, or can even imagine ourselves knowing how when the time comes. Dying at the age of 82, and after having given us in *The death of Ivan Ilyich* one of literature's finest portrayals of an approaching death, Leo Tolstoy still said on his deathbed: "I don't understand what I'm supposed to do." It might be expected that older persons, having lived longer with the prospect of death, would know better not only what death is but also how to die. And yet in many ways it seems that at this crucial time, as at many others in life, personal time somehow transcends the time of psychological development, and we find the question posed in a purity of form which meets each of us with almost equal bluntness: How to die?

Increasingly the discussion of death in our society is emphasizing the need to make dignity once again possible for our dying. Repugnance is growing, Dr. Frank J. Ayd, Jr. reports, "to the obscenity of modern dying— a ritual sacrifice on the altar of technology" (Hendin, 1973, p. 77). More and more people are alarmed at the contrast between the humane conditions of preparing to die at home, in the company of family and younger neighbors, and the scientistic exaggerations of life not promoted but simply prolonged amid voiceless machines and charts without feeling.* According to Dr. Elisabeth Kübler-Ross (1973, p. 159), 80% of our population die in institutions. Many of us are finally awakening to what this imposes on our dying people and how it deprives the living as well of invaluable human experience. Children see death less and less in a truly human way, with whatever dignity it is managed. Bombarded as they are by the distant, violent death of media "entertainment," our children can scarcely be expected to learn that life and death might go together. One of the clear reasons, I think, for the inordinate success of Ingmar Bergman's *Cries and Whispers* both in New York and at Cannes in 1972 was the vivid portrayal of death in a family circle, in a home which had known both happiness and sorrow, youth and age, together, a challenge both to the dying and to the living.

In her compassionate and immensely practical book *On death and dying,* Elisabeth Kübler-Ross (1970) has provided us with invaluable suggestions on typical stages through which terminally ill patients are likely to pass. These moments include initial denial and anger, after which the patient generally moves on through phases of bargaining and depression, coming then to preparatory grief, and lastly to the possibility of final acceptance. None of the phases, of course, is a pure type, and each one may include aspects of the other four. The stages "do not replace each other but can exist next to each other and overlap at times" (Kübler-Ross, 1970, p. 263). Along with many other researchers, Kübler-Ross generally encourages an understanding discussion with the dying about their suffering and approaching death. A terrible chord of recognition is struck in many of us, I suspect, when we recall how quickly, and how often perhaps, we have fled this basic task of human solidarity.† And yet Robert E. Neale wisely warns us that here in particular, "there is no general answer" (Neale, 1973, p. 22). Dis-

---

* Much of the terminological difficulty in current discussions of euthanasia may very well be due to the "technological isolation" of the question in recent years.

† In a similar vein, Wolfhart Pannenberg says of the time after the resurrection of Jesus that "God can henceforth no longer be present in any other way than as he was proclaimed by Jesus, namely, as the Father who wants all men to be his children and who makes them his children by his forgiving love, and moves them to community among each other" (Pannenberg, 1970, p. 235).

cussing Glaser and Strauss's (1966, pp. 132ff.) typology of "awareness contexts" in dying patients, Neale points out that while it is surely an extreme never to discuss death with the dying, it may also be another unbearable extreme for some patients to discuss it too openly. In this respect, death scarcely admits of more clarity than life does.

But supposing that we restore a more personal atmosphere to the suffering at life's end and even that we perhaps make progress in understanding the modes of death not only physiologically but psychologically, can we then imagine that we will better understand how to die? There is something in us which refuses to accept an "answer" to this question. Preparation for the event, yes; but an answer to be given when it comes, no. It is somehow similar to our instinctive knowledge that we will have more to say to a friend when next we see him than we could ever imagine in advance.

In addition, and still more important, there is an irreducibly new conjunction in human death of the elements of acting and being acted upon, of doing and being done to, which are basic to all our experience. Nothing we do as men has effect merely outside ourselves; all our actions reflect on us in some way and change us as well as our environment. Nothing our environment does to us leaves it unchanged either. This is an inescapable consequence of activity in a material creation, and we all recognize it when we recognize that a certain amount of pain and suffering must always be involved in being human in this world. Perhaps we recognize it less when we are acting successfully. But then too we are not only changing but being changed—whether we are grasping for power and alienating our own lives or struggling for justice and ourselves becoming just.

In death this conjunction of action and passion appears at its starkest. It is indeed something which happens *to* us, an irruption from without, a term imposed. And yet if it is to be human in any final sense, it must also be done *by* us; it must somehow be our embodied choice. In fear and yet with hope, alone and yet with Christ, we may acknowledge the lonely threat of death, which we might well wish ourselves dispensed from, at least for a time, and yet affirm that threat as the appropriate conclusion to lives which have been, from the start, undeserved gifts and unmerited grace.

Through this dialectic of being active and being passive, there is a simultaneity of fulfillment and emptiness in death which is, as Karl Rahner has pointed out, its deepest secret (Rahner, 1965, pp. 39–41). We cannot predict the measure of each which awaits us. The paradox does remind us, however, that there is a trusting surrender at the heart of life without which it all too easily becomes a mockery of autonomous self-assertion; there is a passion of obedience to a greater good without which any action of love can quickly become self-serving and empty. The prospect of death becomes, then, the greatest challenge to the true obedience which is required of us through all of life: doing what it is given us to do—in this case returning life itself to the creator and falling without security into His hands. If we can believe this, we can indeed hope to be responsible and free men also with respect to our deaths. Dr. Cicely Saunders has said she believes "that to talk of accepting death when its approach is inevitable is not mere resignation or submission on the part of the patient, nor defeat or neglect on the part of the doctor; for each of them accepting death's coming is the very opposite of doing nothing" (Hendin, 1973, p. 114). When both theoretically and practically we realize the intersection of acting and suffering which is characteristic of life as well as of death, then I think Dr. Saunders' words speak accurately for all of us.

At death, accordingly, we need a final obedience which actively summarizes the obedient responsibility of our whole lives. Can we learn something particular about this obedience from older people? I think the answer is certain. For age brings with it time to prepare for death, not by dwelling morbidly on its fascination nor merely in terms of grossly quantified experience. Age brings with it most often a further experience of human suffering in the broadest sense; of having things done to and perhaps for one more often than one can do them oneself; of having more memories and images of an active life than present experience of it; of accepting security, where it is found, rather than creating it. Surely the opportunity in peace to compose these elements of activity and passivity in life and then finally in death comprises a human challenge of incalculable dignity. Where else, in an age of anxiety, is our society so likely to be provided with images of an acceptance springing not from resignation but from hope? How much longer can we afford not to let our older people tell us how it is that death not only happens to them but that it is *they* who die?

YES AND NO

If there is any question from which we turn away deeply unsettled by even our most provisional answers, then surely it is the question of death. I have tried to reflect on only a few of its aspects here, asking about the fear of death, the loneliness which accompanies it, the awesome enigma of its manner. In each respect, a special experience and insight on death seem suggested to us from the viewpoint of the aging. There is a wisdom and an integrity to be sought from our older members, as Erik Erikson has once again emphasized for our time (Erikson, 1968, p. 140), and it bears quite acutely on the final issue we face in fact every day of our lives.

Are we afraid of death? Do we die alone? Do we know how to die? I have tried to answer these questions both "Yes" and "No," and I want to add in closing how important it is that we not oversimplify our answers. It does not seem to me any progress whatsoever, whether for the dying or for the living who stand near them, to eliminate any of the real fear or solitude or obscurity of death—and certainly least of all for the sake of human dignity. As we search to regain an appropriately human acquaintance and even intimacy with death, as we become clinically more frank and also more feeling about it, as we confront the many valid modes of the right to die, still we must recognize that it is too fundamentally a personal reality for us to approach it at a merely functional level and thus to try to solve it like any other "problem." "All the endeavors of technology, though useful in the extreme, cannot calm [man's] anxiety" before death, as Vatican II has insisted in the Pastoral Constitution on the Church in the Modern World (Vatican Council II, 1966, n. 18, p. 215). It is too finally serious a question for that, and even "a solidly established faith" in the mystery of Christ as an answer to our anxiety does not alter what the Council, with writers like Marcel (1950, 1951), Boros (1965), and Rahner (1965), expressly called "the mystery of death" (Vatican Council II, 1966, n. 18, p. 215).

Biblically speaking, we need to meditate all through our lives on how the central figure in our community apparently refused to simplify death (O'Donovan, 1974). For the Gospels of Matthew and Mark will always continue to startle their hearers with their quotation of Jesus' words on the cross: "My God, my God, why hast thou forsaken me?" (Mt 27:46; Mk 15:34). And yet there is lasting comfort to be drawn for ourselves and our deceased from that other aspect of Christ's death which is quoted by St. Luke: "Father, into thy hands I commit my spirit!" (Lk 23:46). In this man, I believe, fear is integrated into trust, solitude into communion, and suffering into redeeming action. As the rest of us, young and old, face the irreducible aspects of death's question to us, we can hope to join Him and to be allowed to bring to our deaths gracefully more of what we shall need to meet them: not a terrorized but a holy fear, not a blind but a final obedience, not loneliness but a dying with Christ for His sake and His Body's.

REFERENCES

Balthasar, H. U. v. *A theological anthropology.* New York: Sheed & Ward, 1967.
Bishops' Committee on the Liturgy. *Anointing and pastoral care of the sick: Commentary on the rite for the anointing and pastoral care of the sick.* Washington: United States Catholic Conference, 1973.
Boros, L. *The mystery of death.* New York: Herder & Herder, 1965.
The collected poems of Dylan Thomas. New York: New Directions, 1953.
Erikson, E. H. *Identity, youth, and crisis.* New York: Norton, 1968.
Glaser, B. G., & Strauss, A. L. *Awareness of dying.* Chicago: Aldine, 1966.
Hendin, D. *Death as a fact of life.* New York: Norton, 1973.
Huizinga, J. *The waning of the middle ages.* London: Arnold, 1924.
Käsemann, E. The Pauline theology of the cross. *Interpretation,* 1970, *24,* 151–177.
Kübler-Ross, E. *On death and dying.* New York: Macmillan, 1970.
Kübler-Ross, E. Life and death: Lessons from the dying. In R. H. Williams, (Ed.)

To live and to die: When, why, and how. New York: Springer-Verlag, 1973. Pp. 150–159.

Marcel, G. *The mystery of being* (2 vols.). Chicago: Regnery, 1950, 1951.

Mitford, J. *The American way of death.* New York: Simon & Schuster, 1963.

Neale, R. E. *The art of dying.* New York: Harper & Row, 1973.

O'Donovan, L. J. (s.j.) Approaches to the passion. *Worship,* 1974, *48,* 130–142.

Pannenberg, W. *Basic questions in theology.* Vol. I. Philadelphia: Fortress, 1970.

Rahner, K. (s.j.) *On the theology of death* (2nd Eng. ed.). New York: Herder & Herder, 1965.

Schillebeeckx, E. (o.p.) *God the future of man.* New York: Sheed & Ward, 1968.

Vatican Council II. Pastoral Constitution on the Church in the Modern World. In W. M. Abbott (s.j.) (Ed.) *The documents of Vatican II.* New York: Herder & Herder, 1966. Pp. 199–308.

VII
THE CHALLENGE FOR SOCIETY

The Older Person and his Family

MARY SCHOLASTICA HANDREN, R.S.M.

Sister Mary Scholastica Handren, R.S.M., received her B.S. in nursing from Mount St. Agnes College, Baltimore, in 1947, and her M.S.W. degree from St. Louis University in 1951. Sister Mary Scholastica's work experience, in keeping with her degrees, has spanned the two fields of nursing and social work. From 1951 to 1959 she was Director, Department of Social Work, Mercy Hospital, Baltimore, and from 1959 to 1963 she was Administrator of Mercy Hospital. From 1967 through the time of the Institute, Sister Mary Scholastica was Director, Division on Aging, Associated Catholic Charities, Baltimore. Currently, she is at the Provincialate of the Sisters of Mercy in Baltimore. Sister Mary Scholastica serves as a member of a number of different boards, among them the Maryland Board of Examiners for Licensure of Nursing-Home Administrators, the Baltimore Metropolitan Senior Citizens Center Board, and the Over-60 Counseling and Employment Service Board.

> We people do not fall as trees
> when they are old.
> We have our sons and daughters—
> a future human life
>
> [Osterhuis, 1972, p. 70].

Family life today suffers from too much attention and too little attention. There are those who emphasize traditional relationships to the destruction of the people forming the relationships. Others move to a total rejection of

227

the family as a value, as a structure. Present in this picture of differing opinion and active confusion is the struggle of the generations. To say that this creates a challenge is a masterpiece of understatement.

In this paper, we shall define the family as the familiar extended family, which includes aging members, parents, and children. This definition lends itself more appropriately to our discussion of intergenerational relationships rather than the very circumscribed nuclear family. In addressing our topic, we shall briefly consider the older person and his family from a social and cultural perspective and note the influence of various misconceptions and stereotypes. We shall then review the challenge facing today's family and its older members.

A SOCIAL AND CULTURAL PERSPECTIVE

When one undertakes a discussion of social and cultural change in the family today, the scope could be limitless. There are some specifics, however, which may be reviewed.

Brody has noted that:

> Our culture has prescribed an etiquette of attitudes and behavior toward the aged. The social conventions call upon adult children to act out their concern in certain socially prescribed ritual behavior. These acceptable forms of help include introducing an old parent into the adult child's household, or providing financial support when doing so severely disadvantages the younger generations, and so on [Brody, 1966, p. 205].

These attitudes are frequently seen by those working with aging family members in parishes. The worker must understand and deal with the guilt and the hostility which may develop because of the social pressure, and he needs to be aware of the love between the adult son or daughter and the aged parent which can be severely tested by such pressure. Similarly, he must recognize and support the anguish of the aged parent as he or she struggles to protect children from excessive burdens. Many times those of us who represent the Church or the helping professions among these families have added to the complexity of the problem because of our own limited cultural perspectives.

Furthermore, the economy of our country, the fast growth of communication systems, and the mobility of our people all are vital forces in shaping our human relationships and in influencing our day-to-day behavior. The demands of work situations, for example, and the availability of rapid transportation cause many adult sons and daughters to be separated for long or frequent periods not only from aging parents but even from spouses and children. Faced with such pressures, many middle-aged persons are physically and psychically drained and thus unable to find time or energy to share with the elderly members of the family when they are nearby.

The movement to the urban center as society became increasingly industrialized broke down the very familiar multi-generational rural family. Results of this breakdown continue to be felt in our urban families.

Weinberg, in discussing the history of the immigration of people into the United States and its influence on today's family, notes:

> The patterns of family life which they established precluded the transition common to multi-generational families and undoubtedly have had significant effects on American family life. However, even in this century the vast majority of families were and are in transition from ethnic, national, or class values favoring extended family grouping to the mode represented by the ever increasing small, middle class, nuclear, urban family. Values clash; traditions are discarded; and conflict ensues between generations [Weinberg, 1969, p. 56].

Although we recognize the accuracy of Dr. Weinberg's statement, we must admit it is unfortunate that families have received little help in understanding why the conflicts have developed and how it is possible to cope with them.

The age of retirement has created numerous problems, too, within the family setting. It is one thing to have a 64-year-old father living with his married daughter and her family if the father is at work all day. It becomes another issue when the father reaches 65, remains home all day, and has his income drastically reduced. The change in this aging person has not created the problem; the change in his employment status has produced the difference. His intellectual, social, and emotional capacity could continue unimpaired for many years. How these capacities remain involved in life-producing activity becomes the central concern.

In recent years, increasing longevity is also becoming a problem within the extended family circle. Many sons and daughters willingly and lovingly caring for aged parents are faced with the necessity of planning for and adjusting to their own retirements. The complexity of this experience cannot be underestimated and will be considered again.

FALLACIES, MISCONCEPTIONS, AND STEREOTYPES

Frequently, in conversations about older persons one hears dogmatic statements indicating that the speaker has adopted popular misconceptions or even fallacies as his confirmed belief about the whole problem.

How many of us have heard the comment that a good son or daughter always takes care of poor old parents? There are two issues involved here: the moral judgment, and the question: What do we mean by taking care of parents? The moral judgment may not or possibly should not be a part of the issue. The second point is one to which we should give some attention.

What does taking care of parents mean? First, it does not mean resolving parents' problems in order to solve children's problems. This may happen as children institutionalize aging parents because they, the children, worry about parents' falling down steps, not eating properly, or harming themselves in various ways. Those who are involved with admissions to institutions are very aware of this experience. Nor does taking care necessarily mean moving parents into one's already crowded home, creating conflicts, and developing pressures impossible to resolve. Taking care should mean a loving concern which is related to the reality of the needs of the parents involved and the solutions available to the children. These evaluations must take place in as non-emotional an environment as possible, and many times persons not related either to parents or to children must create such an environment. We cannot make generalizations about caring for aging people as they continue throughout life to maintain their own individuality and must be assisted accordingly.

A very serious and, apparently, quite common misconception is the belief that senility is a part of the aging process, and that all aged persons become senile if they live long enough. Such thinking is found among many middle-aged sons and daughters, and may possibly be an explanation of their absolute rejection of their own aging processes and of the whole idea of anyone's growing old. This belief is partly understandable if we realize that many middle-aged persons today were students during the years when cross-sectional intelligence tests were coming into vogue, and the theory that one's intelligence deteriorates after the age of 50 was supported by numerous studies. Those of us working in the field of aging know that additional longitudinal studies in recent years have indicated that the capacity of the individual to learn and to grow continues throughout most of the life span. Unquestionably, we have a responsibility to share this kind of information with the elderly and with their families.

There are also many people who do not know that only 5% of senility in older people today is caused by physical deterioration. Many people may become senile because of lack of interest, or isolation, or boredom. The need for continuing education becomes very apparent as one notes this widespread lack of information.

Many times one hears that certain religious, racial, or ethnic groups never have any problems with the aged because they take care of their own. Bertha Simos conducted an interesting study in 1969 in a West Coast Jewish family agency. She notes:

> From the literature and from popular belief it was anticipated that in this sample of Jewish people one would find close-knit, warm family relationships [Simos, 1970, p. 137].

One of her concluding remarks states:

> Where parents had been relatively stable emotionally and able to respond spontaneously and adequately to the needs of the growing child out of the fullness of life and the richness of their own experience, that child might indeed have been reared in a warm nurturing environment. Positive feelings could continue into the old age of the parents despite physical and personality changes which the years might bring. Relationships with parents in some cases improved as the years brought understanding, acceptance and even affection [Simos, 1970, p. 137].

In a further statement it was noted, however:

> Where there had been personal pathology, gross social and economic deprivation, the trauma of culture change, or a combination of these and other factors leaving their mark on the individual, the Jewish parent, like any other, was unable to bestow upon his child an abundance he did not possess [Simos, 1970, p. 137].

This study, although conducted with a relatively small sample, certainly underlines the need of recognizing that individual differences do make an impact on relationships and that generalizations can be at best inappropriate and frequently quite inaccurate.

Another common fallacy with which we live is the idea that the old and the young are in competition for the time and attention of middle-aged children or parents. Duvall reports a study conducted in 1961 with 47,000 PTA leaders across the country. One question was: To your knowledge, with whom else do your children talk over personal concerns?

When parents' responses to this question were tabulated:

> It was the grandparent who led all other adults as those to whom school-age and adolescent children went with their intimate concerns. Six times as many parents said grandparents were their children's confidants as mentioned pastors, Sunday school teachers, and other Church leaders [Duvall, 1970, p. 141].

Again in Duvall's study, we receive an indication of the danger and the inaccuracy of a superficial evaluation of these human relationships.

THE CHALLENGE FOR TODAY'S FAMILY

What is the challenge of today's family as it relates to its aged members? There are six areas which should be considered, although this list is by no means all-inclusive.

Aging Parents Remain Capable of Responsibility

The family is challenged to allow parents and other aging members to be, to continue to grow, to learn, to be involved, to participate in life. Children must develop ways to make it possible for this to happen. They must be helped to understand that, simply because the aging person reaches age 65, 75, or 85, it does not mean that everyone in the family must begin to wait on this person, to center one's life on him, or to conclude that now there is an invalid in the house. Children need to know that the more normal the environment, and the more normal the relationships, the more adequately the aging person will live.

Those who are ministering to the aging must help families recognize that although the aging person reaches an advanced age he or she continues to be an adult, able to take responsibility, able to continue to serve, able to participate in life. This is a very real challenge to our family today because there seem to be two very common attitudes about families. One group adopt the attitude that children are responsible for parents, must provide for them, and care for them entirely. This attitude at first glance seems to be a good one, a truly Christian one. The fallacy hidden here is that parents are seen as incapable of being responsible for themselves. As this is underlined, the aging person has more and more of his personal freedom removed and, hence, more and more of his humanity stifled.

The second group adopt the attitude that over-concern for parents is one of the "hang-ups" of middle class, middle-aged children, and should be abolished. Parents should plan for their own needs. Adult children have their own problems and are unable to give attention to the needs of aging parents. The fallacy here, of course, is the extremely reactionary point of view adopted to protect the inadequacies of those holding this vision. The real challenge is to develop a mature, well-balanced point of view which avoids both extremes.

Social Criticism when Children Allow their Aging Parents Independence

The second challenge develops when adult children begin to allow their aging parents to be, to grow, and to become involved. Many persons who do not understand what aging is about do not understand this relationship between children and their parents and tend to become critical. The challenge here is no small one. To continue to free the elderly so that they may participate in life throughout life while one responds to the social pressures of sharp criticism requires a deep conviction of the value of one's position in this issue. It is in this area that clergy and religious as well as other professionals can give their greatest support. The family which has accepted this challenge needs continued reassurance and encouragement from those of us who understand the importance of the family's effort.

Learning Remains Possible into Old Age

Another challenge for the family is to become more and more knowledgeable about what it means to age and how to make the most of the opportunities of aging for one's parents and for oneself. There is continuing research exploring the many facets of the aging process. The discoveries of this research should be available not only to those aging but also to those who live and work with them. Information on adult learning-capacity, mentioned above, is only one small part of the data available, but how different life for the elderly becomes when they understand that the learning process continues for most of the life span and how different the relationship of children with parents becomes when both are aware of this one fact.

McClusky notes in his studies of the adult learner that it is the intent of his theory that

A sense of frontiersmanship can be cultivated and restored, that the adventure and wonder of life can be renewed, if not increased. If to his self-expectation as a continuing learner, an adult could add a picture of himself as one continuing to discover, he could heighten his ability to learn and inquire, . . . and the thrust of his inquiry would be reinforced by the cumulative satisfactions resulting from his constant probe of the edge of the unknown [McClusky, 1972, p. 12].

The stimulation of this approach to life needs to be made available not only to the aging person and his family but, perhaps more importantly, to our many communications media which do so much to maintain and encourage an attitude of tolerance and condescension toward the aging.

In another area of research, much is currently being learned about the need for environmental adaptation to provide for the sensory deprivation and spatial needs of aging persons. Pastalan recommends:

an approach that will enhance the relevance of design by organizing spatial requirements around certain psychosocial and physiological facts of life . . . sensory deterioration can be compensated for with properly intensified and orchestrated stimuli; . . . greater attention should be given to using sensory modalities other than vision and audition in more effectively cuing design spaces [Pastalan, 1971, pp. 8–9].

Children with aging family members living in their homes could secure many helpful suggestions from such data.

Aging Children Caring for Aged Parents

Another challenge to the family is to deal with the reality of the extended life span and all that it involves. What does this mean? We mentioned above the increased longevity of aging and also the problems created by retirees attempting to care for aging parents. Until families accept this possibility as a reality and become objective in dealing with the resulting pressures, it will be impossible to resolve the many conflicts which develop. Aging children must be able to free themselves from the emotional burden of aging parents, and yet maintain warm supporting relationships. Plans for one's parents should be completed rationally and objectively long before one retires. Our middle-aged adults must meet the challenge of the reality that their parents may be around as they themselves age, and that these parents need to live their lives independently and freely as they, the middle-aged, have a right to live their lives in the same way. Again, here is an area in which ministry to aging must extend itself beyond the immediate need of the aged person to reach the adult children, help them understand their own responsibilities, and help them understand how these may be interpreted as they relate to the needs of aging parents.

Responsibility for Changing Attitudes toward Aging in the Community

A fifth challenge to the family of the aging person is to accept responsibility for changing the attitudes of other people in the community: the neighborhood, the parish, the civic group. We have talked a good bit in our country about establishing a national policy on aging. I believe this policy will never be developed until the family is convinced of the values of the older person and of aging as a part of life. This may seem a rather simplistic approach, but we recognize that after the process of involvement of the White House Conference for three years, the existence of a national policy on aging remains questionable. Again, we must emphasize the importance of participation in this responsibility by clergy, religious, and other professionals.

Protecting the Value of Life in the Aged

A final challenge to the family is to accept and develop a position of leadership in supporting and protecting the value of life at any age. Certainly we see in the world today a growing disregard for the human person. We know the aged as a group have suffered much from this disregard. Many have argued the need for leadership in many areas of concern today. Should not the family, the protector of life, become the defender of life as it is lived to its completion?

CONCLUSION

It may seem that we have over drawn the relationship of the family with its aging members. Yet this is where our society is today. Its middle-aged adults are stretching from the generation ahead to the generation following them. Our society asks an adult group to cope with three generations at one time. With the rate of social change with which we live, it may be that this coping is the greatest challenge of all. Yet, a continuing look at specific issues involved in changing understandings, in changing values, must go on.

The need for clarification of the meaning of the roles of family members is apparent. The need for growth in understanding of the potential of the individual is urgent. The need for increased awareness in our society of these clarifications and understandings is critical. My comments have touched only the surface of these needs. It is hoped that our educational institutions will continue to search out solutions to these needs and share them through all possible communication media.

REFERENCES

Brody, E. M. The aging family. *The Gerontologist*, 1966, *6*, 201–206.

Duvall, E. M. *Faith in families*. Chicago: Rand McNally, 1970.

McClusky, H. Y. An approach to a differential psychology of the adult potential. Ann Arbor: University of Michigan, Institute of Gerontology, 1972. Mimeographed.

Osterhuis, T. H. A song about people. In B. Huijbers (Ed.) *A God of men: New hymns and psalms for congregations*. Cincinnati: North American Liturgy Resources, 1972. Pp. 69–70.

Pastalan, L. A. How the elderly negotiate their environment. Paper presented at Environment for the aged: A working conference on behavioral research, utilization, and environmental policy. San Juan, P.R.: December 17–20, 1971.

Simos, B. G. Relations of adults with aging parents. *The Gerontologist*, 1970, *10*, 135–139.

Weinberg, J. Interpersonal relationships in multi-generational families. In W. Donahue, J. L. Kornbluh, & L. Powers (Eds.) *Living in the multi-generational family*. Ann Arbor: University of Michigan Press, 1969. Pp. 52–59.

Community Services to the Aging

CLARE J. KAGEL

After receiving her early training in music and a B.S. degree from the Juilliard School of Music, Clare J. Kagel gradually moved into work with the aged. She earned a master's degree in Therapeutic Recreation: Service to the Aging from Teachers College, Columbia University, in 1970. From 1961 to 1967 and again from 1971 on, Mrs. Kagel has been Director of Recreation at the Jewish Home and Hospital for the Aged. Since 1967 she has been instructor in Service to the Aging in the Program in Leisure Education at Teachers College. During the summers of 1969 and 1970, Mrs. Kagel led two international seminars for Columbia University students which visited services to the aging and disabled in Norway, Sweden, Denmark, Holland, England, and Ireland.

A serious study of the problems of aging cannot afford to limit itself to writings of a professionally oriented gerontological nature, to the neglect of popular literature. Journals reflect not only valuable statistical data, but current public attitude. The choice of the problems of aging as the subject of several journalistic studies in recent years indicates the concern of the general public with these problems (*Time*, 1970; Phillips, 1970; Deeken, 1971; Goro, 1972).

As an illustration of this public concern, we might consider the article in *Time* magazine entitled "Growing old in America: The unwanted generation" (*Time*, 1970), which points up the marginality of position experienced by many older Americans. Such separatism, source of much suffering for the aging American, is very difficult to reverse once it has reached the stage of public acknowledgment.

This sense of exclusion is addressed by a community approach to the problems of aging, which is concerned not only with the problems in themselves, but with the sense of belonging included by definition in the word community.

The Oxford dictionary indicates that the sense of belonging which is part of community includes a sense of equality of right and rank, mutual responsibility and life, in association with others (*Oxford English dictionary,* 1971).

EARLIEST COMMUNITY EFFORTS FOR THE AGING

Historically, we find that the earliest traditions of community services for the aged grew out of religious or denominational groups which, in many situations, took on the role of the extended family for those who had none. In the seventeenth and eighteenth centuries, the Friendly Societies of England began to grow and thrive; they were organizations originally formed to provide burial services for their members, but they went on to perform functions for those who were still living, again much like a family unit. Governmental organizations certainly existed and played a role historically in caring for the aged person who was without other resources: yes, the elderly were cared for just as were debtors, criminals, orphans, and the insane—frequently in the same facilities. This traditional kind of care has extended well into our day, with the difference that now the prisons are generally reserved for the criminal, the states have built hospitals for the mentally ill, orphans have found a form of housing in foster homes (probably one of the more civilized developments of modern times), and the aged are left in many areas with the "poor farm." It has now frequently been renamed the county home, but it retains much of its former stigma, although this type of institution has strong competition from the growing numbers of proprietary nursing homes across the country.

In much of the community approach, we find an emphasis on the illness and disability which frequently accompany old age. The general model of care has been based on a medical model, stressing ill health, the need for the physician, and, frequently, the preferability of institutionalization as a means of simplifying care and at the same time removing the unpleasant sight of ill elderly persons from the view of the general public.

We are now moving away from this attitude, although it will take many years to develop appropriate alternatives to meet the needs of the ever-increasing aging population. The continued lag on the part of the traditional community and social agencies in attuning their services to the needs of the time is one of the most unfortunate and difficult-to-deal-with factors in this move; it might suggest, however, the need for new, less traditional, and more creative approaches to serving the aging.

DEVELOPMENTS IN EUROPE

It would be to our advantage in the United States to examine developments which have taken place in the "old world" in the area of community service to the aging. Commencing with the kinds of social insurance initiated in Germany at the time of Bismarck, a movement began in northern Europe toward the provision of comprehensive services for older persons. The results, in the Scandinavian countries and in the Netherlands, for example, are fascinating to observe.

While these nations cannot lay claim to having solved all the problems of older persons, innovative approaches in care were started there decades before we began slowly to follow in their footsteps. One might cite as an example the freedom and wisdom the Scandinavian nations have shown in providing denominational groups and voluntary organizations (such as the Red Cross) with funds to provide services and facilities for the older population, removing the projects from the realm of politics and the red tape of governmental superbureaucracies. We must note in this connection the vast demographic differences between a population of 7 million—Sweden's, for instance—and our own of 180 million, and we must realize that it is impossible to copy the models of these countries exactly. Yet we can find, in the type of planning which has been done there, the germ of many good ideas. The really outstanding feature is the emphasis on the importance of maintaining the dignity and the individuality of the human being, the aging human being as well as the younger human being. We could well follow some of these approaches.

OLDER AMERICANS ACT OF 1965

It should be noted that since the passage of the Older Americans Act in 1965, a real movement has begun on the part of both the federal and state governments to develop a wider range of services for our older population, both separately and in partnership, and through cooperation with voluntary agencies. We have not yet developed a true national policy on aging, but we have a beginning; in a nation of this size, with such disparity of populations and attitudes, it will probably be some time before we arrive at complete consistency in programming. Through the fund-granting programs originated under Titles 3 and 4 of the Act in the first years of implementation, the beginnings of a number of useful and innovative programs were made possible, at least for the duration of the funding period.

In some instances the difficulties start when local communities do not make appropriate plans for picking up the slack after federal funding ends. Still—on the positive side—there are a number of programs begun formerly under Title 3 which have been able to continue, sometimes through creatively devious means, and which have brought real credit to their communities. Certainly the former Titles 3 and 4 were conceived as spurs for moving states and local communities forward in improving and initiating services for the aging. We could probably, at this point, refer quite honestly to the "community" in our "community services" title as a marriage of federal, state, local, and voluntary agencies, with funding coming from both tax revenues and voluntary funds. In a nation of our size, with the growing proportion of aging persons, this is the only way community programs seem likely to survive.

We have spoken of community from the standpoint of those who are doing the supporting; we also have to speak of the community which is being served. But first we should briefly emphasize that a community to be served cannot be thought of strictly in terms of political subdivisions, geographical location, or population size, but should be flexibly defined to adapt boundaries to local circumstances. Natural socioeconomic districts such as a sparsely populated rural area and a heavily populated metropolitan area present different problems in defining a community, all of which need to be taken into account; it might be three rural counties or it might be one church parish in the metropolitan area which form a community to be served.

CONTRIBUTIONS OF THE COMMUNITY

Turning now to consider the "services" specifically, we find that the Oxford Dictionary pinpoints, among other elements of service, the action of serving, helping or benefiting; conduct tending to the welfare or advantage of another; provision for the carrying out of some work for which there is a constant public demand (*Oxford English dictionary*, 1971).

In considering the provision of such helping work, we might speak of a three-pronged program, the first goal of which would be the prevention of the arbitrary segregation of active older adults from society. This segregation is destructive of the self-respect of the individual as a member of society; it tends to create dependencies inappropriate to age or capacity, which result in undesirable demands from the older persons upon the general population for special supportive programs; and in the end it deprives society of the contributions or potential contributions of older persons to the general welfare.

The second goal would be the development of services, as necessary, for those active older persons already segregated by current social and economic forces (some of whom are, as a result, already dependent to some degree upon society for some kind of support). Such services would then have as a major purpose the maintaining of these older persons in, or the returning of them to, the degree of social, physical, economic, and psychological independence commensurate with their individual capacities.

Finally, the third goal would be the developing and refining of services for the older adults who are now permanently unable to be active normally because of actual social, economic, physical, mental, or psychological handicaps.

In attempting to develop these services, we must deal with three kinds of plans: to meet the first goal, we need preventive services of a wide variety; to assist the second group, we must provide or coordinate maintenance plans; and, finally, for the third group we must provide protective and supportive services for the sake of those who will always be dependent.

None of these goals or plans is solely age related, since we might apply such goals for service to persons in any age group who have some sort of disability; the major difference in the population we are discussing is that in most cases we are dealing with a societally built-in disability, that of being older in a youth-oriented society. We are referring also to a society in which a proper balance of appropriate resources is still lacking. One result is the overloading of general hospitals and the unnecessary institutionalization of the chronically ill because of the lack of proper balance in other services.

NEEDS OF THE AGING WHICH CALL FOR COMMUNITY ASSISTANCE

Let us briefly consider some of the needs of the aging person which we may find it necessary to provide through community services.

Food

At the most basic level we have the needs of food, clothing, and shelter; if we break these down more specifically, we can say, regarding food, that it is not just food we need but an understanding of appropriate nutrition. Along with this understanding, there must be ways and means of purchasing foods of maximal nutritive value at minimal cost. In many urban areas, as food prices have skyrocketed, families have been banding into food-buying cooperatives. There is no reason why older persons cannot form such organizations, and indeed such activities have been a feature of some of the food and nutrition programs funded through the Older Americans Act. In any attempt to develop comprehensive services for the aging within a community framework, this type of program is certainly an important one.

Clothing

Clothing as a need would seem to be self-evident. Yet, taking for granted the idea that because of budgetary considerations many older persons have difficulty in obtaining clothing, we must also consider the manner in which wearing apparel is designed and styled and the types of fabric used. The aged population needs a good lobby with the clothing industry to see that attractive, reasonably priced clothing is available in fabrics and styles which make the act of dressing easier for the not-so-flexible hand and the act of caring for the clothing simple and inexpensive. Handsome wash-and-wear clothing is available in all-seasons apparel for children; why should this not be so for older persons?

Shelter

Shelter is a broad question, depending on the condition of the particular aging person whom we are serving, and ranging from the most independent form of living in the old family-homestead (which may be collapsing over the person's head) to the most sheltered form of nursing-home or hospital care. In this area, as in that of clothing, the issue of consumerism should be prominent. There should be more freedom of choice for the individual to select, within reasonable regard for health needs, a style of living which supports him as a dignified member of society. In some cases that might mean finding more extensive ways of making deteriorating housing livable; in others, it might mean the provision of special housing suited to the needs of the aging person, whether it be specially equipped apartments in public housing or a really well-thought-out and well-designed nursing home for the person who requires that kind of care. But in either case consideration should be given to the tastes and needs of the individuals who will be using the facilities, rather than merely to the creative brainstorms of architects who have not really thought through the issues to be considered in such design. One would expect that accommodations provided by a specific community or local organization such as a denominational group would have a maximum of opportunity for development along thoughtful and appropriate lines; this is an area in which the private sector can play a highly important role.

Environmental Safety

Another set of needs which follow very logically after shelter, we might entitle "environmental safety." While this area relates to the avoidance of accidents, it should also pertain to recent research on reinterpreting environment for use by those of other than just normal vision and hearing. It indicates the need for planning environments which take into account the normal changes in sensorimotor capacity which occur in aging. But the entire question of environment is again something which is not limited to the aging person; environmental planning should concern people of all ages since persons with various disabilities are found in every age group. One example of ways in which environments have been altered to aid those with disabilities can be seen in New York City in the policy of the past several years of replacing high curbs at street corners with ramps to make it possible for baby carriages, wheelchairs, and persons with difficulty in ambulation, to cross with relative ease. This is one of the types of adaptation which should surely be built more into city planning. To be sure, there has been federal legislation to improve planning of public buildings in recent years to allow for better accessibility for disabled persons, but more input from social scientists knowledgeable in these areas is called for, and, again, more input should be sought from the consumers.

Transportation

Another area of need is for transportation and mobility. Transportation is a very popular topic at every meeting on aging, with complaints ranging from cities where bus service is too expensive, too infrequent, or the steps to the bus too high, to the rural areas where we so frequently have large numbers of isolated older persons, in the farmlands of Iowa or the "hollows" of Appalachia. Whether the setting is urban or rural, the problem is basically the same: people need to get to services or have services brought to them. In some cases individual agencies have provided partial solutions; in many cases older persons are still waiting for means to get about. But, in addition to the equipment for moving persons about, mobility means rehabilitative services within medical and community facilities which make it possible for a person who was once able to move about to be restored at least partially to a means of contact and interaction with the wider world.

Leisure Activities

For the aging person, the most important need—after the very basic ones we have just described—is for appropriate leisure pursuits of a satisfying nature. These pursuits could fall into several categories. Recreation is one; adult education another, and an increasingly important one. Yet another is volunteer service, which is as important as any other leisure pursuit and helps the older person feel that he is still a contributing part of the community. If we were to make an analysis of the way a person's day is divided as he proceeds through life, we would see that the time given to leisure forms a much larger proportion for the older adult; provision of appropriate leisure activities is thus a very important service to the older person.

Legal Protection

The elderly also have a need for many kinds of legal protection, the first of which is, simply, fair legislation for older people, which would include a revision of certain aspects of Social Security and the setting of a national policy on pension plans. Such reform is being dealt with by a number of legal organizations, some of which grew out of the original OEO programs. The future of some of these programs is rather indefinite as sources of funding fluctuates, but there is a growing group of young attorneys who are concerned about inequities in areas which affect our aging population. All of this comes under the heading of legal protection for the elderly, as does protection against crime, white-collar crime as well as violent crime, of which so many of our older people in urban areas are victims.

Security and Support

A major area for community concern lies in the need for services which provide security and support. This might include counseling, health-care services (both at home and in clinical settings), and economic assistance. In this broad general category we must also include pressure for such programs as home-care services of a wide variety, which would make it possible for more persons to remain in their homes for longer periods; and the development of the day-hospital type of program through which the older person might receive supportive services at a central location on a regular basis and return to his home for sleeping and many of the normal activities of daily living. Within this area we must also be concerned for persons with special needs, such as the blind and the deaf, where particular programs tailored to meet their specific needs must be developed. And within this particular framework, too, we must include work with families, immediate communities, and those "significant others" who play such an important role in the lives of the aging persons we are trying to serve.

Finally there is the need for religion and the important role of religion in attitudes toward death and dying which become so much more significant as one grows older and begins to lose relatives and peers. If the community we are examining is based on a religious structure, this feature becomes all the more important when we speak of "community services."

MECHANICS OF PROVIDING THESE SERVICES

We need now to consider the mechanics of providing all these services. In order to have an organized approach to fill these many and disparate needs, we must start with an interested and knowledgeable community, a community which has a perspective of concern for the aged and an understanding of what aging means in terms of a total life span. We must have trained professionals to work both with the older adults and with other age groups in the community to prepare them to give service. We need something which could be described as a neighborhood information center—it has been called an Information and Referral Service—but what it actually would be would vary from one area to another. In some communities a family service agency might fulfill this type of function; in areas where there is a large aging population there might be an information service specifically for older persons. In any case, through this information center there must develop an awareness of where the gaps in service are, so that the community can take steps to fill these gaps.

Patterns of inter-professional and inter-agency cooperation (Estes, 1973) are also extremely important in providing service to older persons. This is something which we lack at present, and we suffer greatly from the lack. A case in point: it was claimed that in a certain area of a large city there was a desperate need for a meals-on-wheels service so that older persons could be discharged from the hospitals. This service was funded and begun, and suddenly the many hospital social workers who had recognized this need became too busy to do the paper work for referrals. For many months there was an existing meals-on-wheels service, many older persons in the hospitals, and no one in between to coordinate a program enabling the services to be reached by the people who needed them. We need the ability to coordinate existing services, to make use of existing agencies, and to avoid duplication of facilities. Much can be done by using community facilities for different age groups. Some wonderful examples of this can be seen in Scandinavian countries where a community facility serves different groups at different times of the day, where schools with large kitchens provide meal services both for outgoing meals-on-wheels programs and for older people coming in. Similar programs exist in some parts of our country too, where schools are opening their cafeterias at times when they are not being used by students so that older people can get an inexpensive hot meal.

We need also a willingness to change when necessary. This is so important in reference to the serious problem of getting organized institutions to change their directions when this is called for (Estes, 1973).

Finally, we need to be ready and able to make use of the political system and the clout of clusters of voters. For if we are to have a well-defined national policy on the aging and their problems as well as governmental involvement in a rational provision of services, legislators must be made aware of our programs and our needs. If persons who are truly interested in working with and serving the aging are not willing to stick their necks out to inform the politicians of their concern, who in the general population will do it?

This paper has attempted to outline broadly some of the major areas of need to be considered in planning community services for the aging, and some of the steps which need to be followed in order to develop coherent, cohesive plans for the community. The topic is a mammoth one, and the surface has merely been brushed, but the presentation is made in the hopes of stirring up interest in further exploration of the subject by the audience to which it is directed.

SERVICES PROVIDED BY THE RELIGIOUS COMMUNITY

In view of the religious nature of the group being addressed in this paper, we should give some thought as to whether the traditional approach to meeting the needs of the older person by the clergy—be they Catholic, Protestant, or Jewish—is adequate in the light of contemporary needs. Certain primary responsibilities of the clergy, such as pastoral counseling at crisis periods such as bereavement, and emphasis on sermon preparation, and church worship remain important. But, as with other traditional community agencies, we must question not only whether the church should be increasingly concerned with the aging, but whether old patterns of service are sufficient and realistic in regard to the changing situation of older persons. We must determine those responsibilities which are specific to the church in regard to older persons, but we must also review and define those responsibilities in which the church is conjointly responsible with the other institutions and agencies of the community.

Certain points should be emphasized in this connection: (1) the role of the pastor in providing overall leadership is essential; (2) lay persons involved in the development of programs should be related to the decision-making groups in the congregation, and such groups should include representatives of the older population, the consumers of the services; (3) the church should be aware of existing community services for the aging, of gaps in that service, and the means by which the church itself can help to fill the gaps; (4) the church should see to it that the community is made aware of the church's interest in and efforts on behalf of the community aged.

But perhaps the most essential contribution the leadership of all religious groups can make is the promotion, among all age groups, of constructive attitudes toward the aging, and this promotion should include programs of education *for* aging as part of basic religious and humanistic instruction.

The religious organization which is aware of the scriptural traditions which lie at its foundation will remember the phrase from the Psalms:

Forget me not, O Lord, in mine old age, when I am old and grey-headed, until I have shown thy strength to this generation and thy power to all those who are yet to come [Ps 71:18].

Through a wide variety of community services providing encouragement, maintenance, and support for our aging population, we can help more and more persons reach this goal and attain a more satisfying and comfortable old age.

REFERENCES

Deeken, A. (s.j.) Growing old—and how to cope with it. *America,* 1971, *124,* 315–318. March 27, 1971.

Estes, C. L. Barriers to effective community planning for the elderly. *The Gerontologist,* 1973, *13,* 178–184.

Goro, H. The old man in the Bronx. *New York Magazine,* 1972, *5* (2), 31–49. January 10, 1972.

Oxford English dictionary. Oxford: Clarendon Press, 1971.

Phillips, M. Aged wait in stony solitude. *The New York Times,* May 18, 1970. P. 31.

Time. Growing old in America—the unwanted generation. *Time,* 1970, *96* (5), 49–54. August 3, 1970.

Creating Homes for the Aged

JOHN B. AHERN

Monsignor John B. Ahern received his A.B. degree from St. Joseph's Seminary, Yonkers, New York, in 1950, and was ordained to the priesthood in 1954. He came to Catholic Charities directly after ordination, and he has remained there during the intervening 20 years. Currently, he is Director of Family and Community Services of Catholic Charities of the Archdiocese of New York. Monsignor Ahern serves as a member of a number of professional committees, among them the Standing Committee of Directors, National Conference of Catholic Charities; the Long-Term Care Committee of the Health and Hospitals Planning Council of Southern New York; and the New York State Advisory Committee to the Commissioner of Social Services.

There is a persistent legend about the hypersophistication of the average New Yorker. One morning several years ago, I followed a remarkable young man for several blocks as he walked among the subway-bound, early risers. From his shaved head to his bare feet, his body was painted a vivid red. A flimsy cloth scarcely draped him. An eye-opener? Yes, but in a perverse way. Scarcely one person in five seemed to take notice of him. As a life-time New Yorker, I am as prone as the next to say I've seen it all. Yet, that is myth—the blasé flipness which covers a modern taboo. In the complex, fractured social structure of this time and place, the first commandment seems to be: "Don't get involved."

Our relationships with each other have become enormously structured and subdivided, like the buildings we live in and the organizations we work

247

for. We have so organized our responsibilities toward one another that we can almost always refer a situation to someone else who has been appointed our surrogate for that need. Anyone who wears a uniform or distinctive garb can testify to the frequency with which our fellow-citizens pass on a problem.

One might conclude from such experience that our values have become non-social and personally insulating. To an extent this may be true. But one must also consider the sense of helplessness which most of us experience when confronted with the needs of our neighbor. Really, we may not be saying, "Don't get involved." It is quite possible that we are saying that solutions are so involved that one hardly knows where to begin. We have had some solutions fail badly in the last few decades. The public-welfare system, before it was thirty years old, was being denounced as degrading and productive only of dependence.

What saved the generation of the '30s is seen by many as dooming generations since. The inhuman slums were replaced by dehumanizing housing projects. The war on poverty became fratricidal, community guerrilla warfare. Compulsory public education must now answer to Johnny's lack of reading achievement. A booming economy, the dream of planners forty years ago, found us with 5% of our work force unemployed.

BASIC BACKGROUND FACTORS

Would that we could truly create homes for elderly people. It is very tempting to approach such a task simply and as though there were nothing to deal with. But we must relate to a very complex reality. There is an economic universe embracing the level of Social Security payments to retired persons and the effect of exports to Japan on the price of lumber. What of the social impact of post-World War II veterans' benefits on the move of young, middle-class families to the suburbs, and the abandonment of the old inner city to the racial minorities and the aging? Is early retirement to be encouraged in order to provide employment for young heads of families who can, in turn, support climbing Social Security payment rates for the increasing number of retired beneficiaries? The "shopping-bag lady," sleeping in a doorway in the East 50s, may represent one result of decisions made by medical economists and by judges deciding civil-rights cases. The success of our educational and job-creation efforts determine whether old Mrs. Smith can go shopping without fear of being mugged.

It might be well to establish some general picture of the aged in this country. A Report of the Special Committee on Aging, United States Senate, May 10, 1973, describes the aged, statistically as "every tenth American" (Special Senate Committee on Aging, 1973b). New York State can claim every tenth aged American, almost two million elderly of the 21 million

Americans over 65 years of age. Since 1900, the proportion of older Americans to the total population has increased more rapidly than that of other age groups. Each day, approximately 4,000 persons celebrate their 65th birthday, and about 3,000 persons over 65 die. Remarkably, 81% of the elderly are in sufficiently good health to manage on their own, though their per capita annual expenditures for health services are 350% higher than similar costs for the younger population. The advent of public-health programs has provided funds for 68% of such medical expenses. A person reaching 65 years of age today has a life expectancy of almost 15 years.

The statistical picture varies significantly for men and women, with obvious consequences for shelter planning. Older women live longer. Most are widows. They outnumber men by 50% and are far more likely to live by themselves. Six of ten older people live in metropolitan areas, and more than half of those people live in the older central city.

The income picture, though improving, still shows 3.1 million elderly people living in poverty. Social Security benefits have increased by more than 71% since the beginning of 1968. An automatic cost-of-living adjustment comes into effect in 1975. A long-hoped-for, federally guaranteed, minimum income becomes effective in 1974.

COMPLEXITY OF THE HOUSING PROBLEM

Whether we speak of homeowners or renters, elderly persons spend more than one-third of their income on housing; it is their largest single expense item. In New York City, the vulnerability of the aged to disproportionate housing costs had led to a further convolution of the tortured politics of rent control, maximum base rent, housing subsidies, low-income projects, and community resistance. Given the deterioration (physical and social) of the central-city housing stock and the disproportionate share of income paid for shelter by both homeowners and tenants among the elderly population, it seems ludicrous to add a complicating dimension; however, the need for and benefit of supportive services for elderly people must be part of the examination of creating a home which is dignified and humane. At the present moment, planning for the provision of basic shelter for the elderly is in chaos. The principal hope for new housing, at the lowest cost levels, rests on a variety of federal programs. Effective the first week of January 1973, the Administration halted all new commitments for the three most important subsidized housing programs for the elderly. Subsidies for the low-interest program, the low-cost public-housing program, and the rent supplement program are not to be committed for new programs, pending a thorough reassessment, by the Administration and congress, of the basic involvement of the federal government as the prime mover in these areas. This action has been particularly devastating in its impact on projects for housing the elderly. Many of these projects have only lately moved to the planning stage. Now they are halted in mid-flight. A working paper of the Special Senate Committee on Aging (1973a) notes that, by the end of 1972, all forms of federal subsidy of housing for the elderly had produced only 452,414 housing units in the country. Fewer than 50,000 additional units had been produced under a program of mortgage insurance.

The productive result of federal aids which heretofore have been available has been very modest in comparison with the need. What action will follow the present freeze is unknown. One of the possible alternatives is an application of the revenue-sharing concept to housing. Such an approach would leave to local communities the design of housing programs with federal funds. In this area particularly, the aged have not had good experience. The level of recognition given the needs of the elderly in similar efforts to engage local decisionmaking has not been high.

HOUSING IN NEW YORK CITY

In our area, the electorate has consistently voted down housing matters offered for referendum. The least expensive subsidized housing for the aged, other than public housing, falls in the classification of middle-income housing. Except for a small percentage of units, rents are disproportionate to the ability of low-income elderly to pay: $50 per room in state-aided projects and $77 per room in city-aided projects.

The New York City Rand Institute confronted the crisis in its report *Rental housing in New York City* (Lowry, 1970). The report notes that New York City has experienced a net loss of 7,000 housing units each year since 1965. The housing we had was losing ground to decay; dilapidated housing increased by 44%, and deteriorating housing by 37% in the seven-year period following 1960. In the middle 1960s, 38,000 housing units were being abandoned annually. You can be deceived by the apparent prevalence of towering public-housing projects. Slightly more than 10% of the dwelling units in the City in 1970 were publicly aided rental housing units.

A special pointedness and poignancy for the aged is found in what has been happening to one of the housing advantages they held. The aged were, more likely than not, living in rent-controlled housing. But rent-controlled housing was deteriorating at almost four times the rate of uncontrolled units. Eighty per cent of the abandoned housing in the last years of the 1960s had been classified as sound, or only deteriorating, but not dilapidated, in 1965.

On our doorstep here today, just to the west, is an example of the classic urban change. About twenty years ago, the bells began to toll, but no one heard. A middle-class, largely blue-collar, family neighborhood rejoiced as its offspring married in the parish church; got a small apartment a few subway stops north or across Fordham Road; wondered when suburbanitis struck after the second baby; clucked gleefully as the former stoop ballplayer learned about lawns; and came home from a Sunday visit to New City or Merrick and did not know the youngsters congregating on the stoop.

A host of things had converged unnoticed. College education; job mobility; the automobile; the Federal Highway Act; a more casual attitude toward credit and mortgages; and the baby boom stripped many once-stable neighborhoods of the next generation. Hundreds of miles away, other events and pressures were felt in the South and in Puerto Rico. Gradually at first, and then pell-mell, the next generation arrived—black or Spanish-speaking. The neighborhood had changed. At first, nothing much else changed. Then the level of maintenance began to slip in the hard wear of overcrowded, young families, unused to urban culture. Fear of the exuberant, sometimes boisterous, teenagers made the street less attractive. The language or lilt was strange to the ear. Even the cooking smelled different. The corner grocery became a *bodega*. Old friends moved or died; the school-centered sociability belonged to others. They realized that they were alone in their own neighborhood.

> To the elderly person in search of shelter, the question of "bricks and mortar" is secondary to the question of total living environment. . . . The atmosphere of activity and interchange is more important than square footage or closet space [Special Senate Committee on Aging, 1973a, p. 1].

THE PROBLEM OF FINANCING

I have said that public-fund support for basic shelter is in chaos, at least temporarily. The same may be said—at least temporarily—of the financial support for that range of services which enhance the total living environment of older persons. Budget ceilings and an attempt to reorder federal and local relationships appear to have slowed the enlightened developments of the last decade.

There is no private organization with the resources to make a significant contribution to the creation by construction of new housing units or medical facilities for the aged. Our elderly population, especially those who rely solely on Social Security benefits, pension payments, and public assistance for income, can expect housing adequate in quantity and type only from public subsidy or mortgage programs. Though subject to improvement in detail and flexibility, the various public programs and readily available literature provide the basic, contemporary view of suitable physical planning, accommodated to the special circumstances of the elderly. There is a certain awe which surrounds the sponsor of such a facility who has successfully untangled the tape and navigated the bureaucratic corridors. In truth, all you need is nerve, patience, a good architect, a resourceful attorney, an inventive accountant, and good timing.

The same may be said, in a more limited way, of the supportive services which help make housing a home. The community services for the aged which will enhance their self-sufficiency and support their infirmities are fairly well-known. Many are already provided for in publicly funded programs, at least theoretically. Many other such programs are privately supported on a small scale.

We cannot create the right kind of housing or congregate facilities. We must start with two necessary ingredients: interested people and money. The more crucial factor is the awareness and genuine concern of large numbers of people. Economic resources will follow this awareness and concern.

Just a few days ago, a proposed, church-sponsored housing project for the elderly was described by its prospective neighbors as a rusty spike in the heart of Bay Ridge. Two years ago, a church-sponsored nursing home was finally accepted by protesting neighbors, possibly because the alternate use was a large junior high school. On a grander scale, the political viability of subsidized housing and of publicly supported human services, in the amount needed, is so weak that many fear entrusting these responsibilities to local governmental units, which are so sensitive to taxpayer pressure. The final report of the 1971 White House Conference on Aging (1973) laid out an agenda for the decade. The current debate on the federal budget, on the concept of returning decisions and tax funds to local units of government, and on the proportion of our national expenditures to support human services are a call to meet on that agenda.

INDIVIDUAL INVOLVEMENT

What is lacking is involvement. Involvement is the challenge to the individual to put himself in contact with the needful person, the challenge to put himself in contact with the forces which shape our social policy. We may have been titillated by the scandal of Watergate because we were not involved. We may be tortured by scandalous neglect in our old age because we are not involved now. I wonder how many 27-year-olds were active in supporting the Social Security Act as it moved through Congress in 1934 and 1935. The survivors of that age group became eligible for full benefits in 1973.

Would you create decent homes for the aged? Seek out a needful older person; serve her needs to the extent that you are able; seek the help of others for what is beyond your ability. You and all of us need to experience at firsthand the effects of poverty, of infirmity, of loneliness, of uselessness.

We cannot humanly deal with policies, issues, legislation, programs, and priorities until we have translated them into living terms. Enough of us urgently clamoring for answers will force response. But today there are not enough of us. You represent unique leadership potential for a large segment of the middle class. Though there is sensitivity to moral suasion in the group, our preaching and teaching is sterile without practice and exemplary application. I suggest that we will be creative if we

1. Personally expose ourselves and others to the needs of older people.
2. Enlarge our view and that of others to understand that the needs we see are shared by many and the solutions must involve many.
3. Commit ourselves to action with others.

In 1994 I shall be 65 years old. We are creating now the society which will shelter me then. That shelter may be an urn on a shelf. I would be more secure if the current interest were in life with dignity rather than in death with dignity.

REFERENCES

Lowry, I. S. (Ed.) *Rental housing in New York City*. Vol. 1. New York: New York City Rand Institute, 1970.

Special Senate Committee on Aging. *Housing for elderly, a status report, working paper*. Washington, D.C.: Government Printing Office, 1973. (a)

Special Senate Committee on Aging. *Developments in aging*. (Senate Report No. 147—93rd Congress.) Washington, D.C.: Government Printing Office, 1973. (b)

1971 White House Conference on Aging. *Toward a national policy on aging*. (Final Report). Washington, D.C.: Government Printing Office, 1973. (2 vols.).

VIII
SUCCESSFUL AGING:
THE ULTIMATE CHALLENGE

Successful Aging:
A Sociological Viewpoint

Maria Mercedes Hartmann, s.s.n.d.

Sister Maria Mercedes Hartmann, S.S.N.D., received her A.B. degree from the College of Notre Dame of Maryland, and her M.S.W. degree from Loyola University (Chicago). She entered the School Sisters of Notre Dame in 1941, and in 1943 was assigned to the College of Notre Dame of Maryland where she continued in the Sociology Department for almost twenty-five consecutive years. From 1966 to 1969 she was Director of Information and Research at the National Conference of Catholic Charities. Since 1971, Sister Maria Mercedes has been Director of Health and Retirement for the Baltimore Province of the School Sisters of Notre Dame. Through the years Sister Maria Mercedes has participated in a number of summer workshops in Human Relations and Group Guidance, and in both 1971 and 1972 she was the Director of a summer workshop on Religious and Retirement at Georgetown University. She is a member of professional organizations in sociology and social work, and a member of the Archdiocese of Baltimore Commission on Aging.

As I studied the content and format of the Institute, I became somewhat aghast at the enormity of the task left to us in the concluding portion of the program. All through the Institute men and women known for their

257

expertise have explored the many facets of aging, the problems surrounding the elderly, and the factors impinging upon their lives. Now at the end, three of us are really presented with the ultimate challenge—to offer new insights by addressing ourselves to the subject of Successful Aging: the Ultimate Challenge!

How is it to be done? There are various ways, of course. We can present a kind of summary of the problems which have been examined during the Institute. We can present a type of positive conclusion—a conclusion with an up-beat note, so to speak—by offering the problems as challenges. This in turn would permit the three of us to enumerate quickly the problems-now-turned-challenges, leave them in your hands, and depart.

The task, though, just is not that simple. There is no doubt that part of the challenge for all of us is to recognize the problems. That is a beginning. However, the real challenge comes with the determination to root out the causes of the problems, to create that which will counteract or remove the difficulty.

SUCCESSFUL AGING, SOCIOLOGICALLY

What I have attempted to do in this paper is to put together some very basic ideas from a sociological point of view, relate them to what is happening to older people, and offer an illustration or two of how the problem can be attacked. This is the summarization step mentioned above. It delineates for us a few specifics which we can attempt to modify, prevent, or eliminate.

For me, however, one of the difficulties encountered is determining the criteria for "successful" aging. My own concept is a broad one. Sociologically speaking, I suggest it is the process of being able to grow older and at the same time continue to have a meaningful life within the function and structure of society. From the viewpoint of sociology, a person, no matter what his age, is successful when he receives from and at the same time gives to society and the social groups around him those things which he and society expect, in a mutually acceptable manner.

Throughout the Institute, attention has been focused on several discrepancies in this area. You have heard of loss of role, loss of social identity, stereotyping of the elderly, lack of continuity in their lives. New, perhaps unwanted, roles are thrust upon the elderly. They experience a loss of status, an enforced isolation in the areas of both interpersonal relationships and participation in civic and community affairs.

Dr. Irving Rosow (1973) has summarized much of this. Just as roles are established by society or social groups, so too many of the consequences of role loss are created by societal or group norms and values. In other words, while role loss may result from other than societal factors, frequently the impact of the loss is created by society, which places high value on the role, and sanctions or non-value on the lack of role possession.

For instance, the role of breadwinner has great meaning for many people, bringing with it independence, satisfaction in caring for the dependents, proof of one's abilities—all of which reflect the values of American society. Health, rather than a social factor, may require the termination of work for an individual. However, he loses not only a job; he loses prestige and status in the family, control of at least part of his life, something of his sense of worth—all because of what society has taught him, and most of us, about the values attached to working.

The older person is devalued because of and to the degree that he is excluded from meaningful social groups and activities. As roles are removed from him—earner, parent, spouse, friend—no new positive roles are assigned, and so he has a lessened social identity, and he lives an unstructured life, without specific functions, responsibilities, and, frequently it seems, rights. Social contacts diminish as work relationships are broken and friends die, because his interpersonal relationships are expected to be within his own age grade.

Because of social and cultural factors the aged, as a group, suffer status loss. Compulsory retirement, our youth-centered and youth-valued emphasis, our system of age stratification—all serve to increase the isolation of the aged and make their position in society one of increasing unimportance. Furthermore, society has done little to prepare them for this change. The process of socialization has given them values associated with independence, work, and social participation. Yet, as Lowry and Rankin (1969) indicate, the processes of resocialization (learning, developing new skills, etc.) and desocialization (the dropping of old values if these conflict with the new) have not been established to the degree that older persons, as a group, have benefited. From the point of view of the individual, society has not taught him how to "redefine the act and his own self conception" (Lowry & Rankin, 1969, pp. 83–84). Socialization, you will recall, is the internalization of society's goals and values (Inkeles, 1964). All this leads to an inevitable conclusion: the problem rests in and with the society.

SOCIETY'S RESPONSE BY MEANS OF AMELIORATION

Part two of this paper will attempt to suggest a positive tone by turning or converting problems into challenges. Let them be so changed! We now present role loss, status loss, isolation, age stratification, resocialization, desocialization, lack of social identity, personal devaluation, as all of these apply to older people in our society, as challenges.

The challenges here, however, are not to the older person—that is the psychologist's area—but to society and to us. If we are willing to accept them, what must we do?

At least two thrusts are necessary. One concern is with those who are already among the elderly, to reduce to the greatest extent possible the debilitating and unfortunate aspects of our present societal structure and value system. A second concern is for those who are even now moving out of youth and middle age into that category we refer to as the elderly. One thrust is ameliorative; the other, preventive.

The challenge of assisting the already elderly is of an ameliorative nature. We must find, then put into action, ways to lessen these societal pressures. If there is role loss, new and meaningful roles must be created. If there is status loss, this must be changed. Social identity must be restored.

Actually the task may not be as difficult, at least in specific instances, as it may seem at first glance. Over the past decade considerable research and experience have made available the kinds of information we need. One factor in successful aging, for instance, seems to be the presence of continuity in lifestyle especially when moving from the fifties into the sixties and beyond (Rosow, 1973; Kuypers, 1972; Seguin, 1973).

This knowledge has implications for those who are working with older persons, for programs, and for individuals concerned with the preparation and training of personnel. Older persons can be helped to make a transfer of skills and professional knowledge from previous to new or modified situations, provided there be an awareness of the importance and possibility of such a transfer.

Although Estes' (1973) study is directed primarily toward improving community planning for the elderly, one strongly made point can be used in the present context of continuity of roles and lifestyles. Speaking of programs for the elderly, Estes writes that "the elderly must be involved in defining the problems as well as in planning the strategies to deal with them, and their implementation" (Estes, 1973, p. 183). While the author makes this a condition for successful programming, I suggest it as a means of providing continuity in role and activity for those who have, as a part of their lives, participated in planning and decision-making. In short, greater efforts must be made to discover and then strengthen those facets of older peoples' lives which can continue to bring meaning and satisfaction to them.

Making up for role loss is perhaps more difficult since a kind of personal destruction has taken place already. For the present it requires energetic and creative effort on the part of those working with or planning for the elderly to discover new areas of activities and responsibilities. Although the Pfeiffer and Davis (1971) study suggests that planners be cautious about counting on volunteerism as a major source of activity, such programs as the federally sponsored RSVP* and the efforts of such groups as the Amer-

* Retired Senior Volunteer Program. See the footnote on page 190.

ican Association of Retired Persons† indicates that some help may come from that direction.

In the same study, which points up the work orientation of American society, the pursuit of hobbies ranks fairly low on the list of leisure-time activities. In spite of this fact, efforts to encourage and assist older persons to participate in hobby activities is important. This is especially true of handicrafts, which permit expression of creativity and in many instances provide a source of income. Since productivity is so admired in our culture, status can be enhanced, some independence restored.

Fisher (1973) points out the close relationship between social adjustment and the opportunity for interaction with others. Families, church and civic groups, private and public agencies, must continue to attack the isolation and loneliness which tends to diminish social competence and satisfaction for so many older people.

So much for the ameliorative approach. The discussion is far from complete, but one can hardly deny that programmers, planners, and educators are being challenged to help older people overcome society's pressures.

SOCIETY'S RESPONSE BY MEANS OF PREVENTION

Developing a strategy or strategies by which these social consequences can be avoided or prevented in the future calls for an entirely different approach. While amelioration attempts to compensate for society's failure to make a truly fulfilling life possible for older people, this second approach turns attention to the structure and values of society itself. It calls for an analysis of the social factors affecting older people and a commitment to work for the modification or change of dysfunctional structures and norms. Simultaneously with the ameliorative efforts, the culture and value system creating and/or supporting these structures and practices must be changed.

Generally speaking, education, which is the basic tool, will have two targets. The first is directed to those persons who can be prepared to cope with the social and technological conditions and the factors which present so much difficulty. The second thrust, and undoubtedly the more elusive one, is directed to society as a whole.

The importance of changing our attitudes from an overly work-oriented culture is an example of both endeavors. The future older person needs preparation to cope with the problem, and at the same time society as a whole must give support to the changing value if the individual is to be really free to act upon it.

To be specific, let us examine a situation. We know that working hours will decrease and that the retirement age certainly will not go up. We know that our evaluation of leisure is low (Pfeiffer & Davis, 1971). Yet we know

† 1909 K Street, N.W., Washington, D.C. 20006

that creative use of leisure can be beneficial, socially, especially to older persons. Pfeiffer and Davis state the problem this way: those in middle age will arrive at old age "essentially unprepared for the meaningful utilization of large amounts of free time" (Pfeiffer & Davis, 1971, p. 192). They suggest, therefore, training for leisure in middle age, and an increase of leisure time during work years through longer vacations and fewer work hours.

Thus, by educating for leisure we would lessen the impact of non-work, and provide an additional basis for the continuity of lifestyle. In addition, if, through education, leisure could come to be understood as a gift providing opportunities for serving others and improving oneself, increased opportunities for social interaction would result.

Pre-retirement and retirement-preparation programs are a beginning in this respect, but they reach only a segment of our society. To bring about an understanding of aging and an appreciation of the older person *as* a person, to reduce the stigmatization and isolation of older people, to overcome the expectation, as Seguin (1973, p. 212) puts it, that older people should be dependent and not in charge of their own affairs, requires a much more broadly based educational effort.

Not only must the education be broadly based—that is, reaching across the total or near-total age span of our society—it must also be education in a broad sense. Not only do the formal educational structures need to assume the role of catalysts in this value-oriented approach, but new channels need to be developed to reach the many members of society who remain untouched by formal educational efforts.

One important content area of education, or even of information, is that of the human life span itself. Can we, through the use of the developmental approach, show aging for what it really is, a continuation of the life span, just as infancy and adolescence are earlier continuations of the same span? We have so sectioned our study of the human being that we think of a six-year-old as a child rather than as a person who was an infant and is now a child, and who is in the process of becoming an adolescent, a young adult, an adult, and, in all probability, an older person. Aging really means growth, continued growth.

One of the most delightful, and at the same time profound, articles I have ever read on this subject, deals with this problem of time in relation to our understanding of the importance and role of older people. Dr. Eric Cassell (1972, p. 251) asserts that the role of the aged is to be "symbols of the future" because they provide continuity of the present with the past. Society fails to give this role to them, he says, because of the loss in our culture of the abstract concept of time. One reason for the failure is the current practice of studying a thing by parts. He does not propose the elimination of analysis as an intellectual tool, of course, but he would have it recognized as only one of the tools we should use. Holism and the concept of totalities are equally important intellectual tools.

Other methods of changing society's values in regard to aging, and to the roles assigned to older persons, are available if we are willing to use them; and we can invent additional ones. Isolation of the elderly apparently is seen as a normal, acceptable process by society at large, but as unwanted and undesirable by those working in the field and by many older people themselves. Will we set ourselves the task of breaking down barriers between age groups, and of providing experiences and situations for age-groups integration?

Looft (1973, pp. 6–9) makes an interesting proposal. Referring to a study which he conducted in 1971, he points out that age stratification has so reduced the awareness of the role of older persons in the transmission of information and knowledge to the young that not even older persons themselves any longer view themselves as important in this regard. In consequence of this fact, Dr. Looft proposes the development and advancement of the concept of life-span education which does away with the idea that education is for the young to prepare them to be successful competitive adults. Instead, he would substitute the concept of education as a lifelong process directed not only toward pragmatic ends, but toward continued enrichment and fulfillment of the person. One way of accomplishing this, he suggests, might be the creation of what he calls Centers for Life-span Education, in contrast to age-graded schools for children and youth. The aged might come to a better understanding of youth and their values, and youth might experience the wisdom of the aged.

This paper has been filled with challenges. We must admit, however, that the ultimate challenge of successful aging rests not out there somewhere in society, but right here among us. Are we willing, in whatever way it is given us, to remove barriers, to open new vistas? Are we willing to work to create a society which will make successful aging possible? In the last analysis, I suppose the question is "Are we willing to be catalysts?" This, I believe, is the ultimate challenge.

REFERENCES

Cassell, E. J. On educational changes for the field of aging. *The Gerontologist,* 1972, *12,* 251–256.

Estes, C. L. Barriers to effective community planning for the elderly. *The Gerontologist,* 1973, *13,* 178–183.

Fisher, J. Competence, effectiveness, intellectual functioning, and aging. *The Gerontologist,* 1973, *13,* 62–68.

Inkeles, A. *What is sociology?* Englewood Cliffs, N.J.: Prentice-Hall, 1964.

Kuypers, J. A. Changeability of life-style and personality in old age. *The Gerontologist,* 1972, *12,* 336–342.

Looft, W. R. Reflections on intervention in old age: Motives, goals, and assumptions. *The Gerontologist*, 1973, *13*, 6–10.

Lowry, R. P., & Rankin, R. P. *Sociology: The science of society.* New York: Scribner's, 1969.

Pfeiffer, E., & Davis, G. The use of leisure time in middle life. *The Gerontologist*, 1971, *11*, 187–195.

Rosow, I. The social context of the aging self. *The Gerontologist*, 1973, *13*, 82–87.

Seguin, M. M. Opportunity for peer socialization in a retirement community. *The Gerontologist*, 1973, *13*, 208–214.

Successful Aging:
A Psychological Viewpoint

COMILDA S. WEINSTOCK

Dr. Comilda Sundeen Weinstock received her B.A. degree from Brooklyn College of the City University of New York in 1955; her M.A. from Teachers College, Columbia University, in 1957; and her Ed.D., also from Teachers College, in 1969. At the present time she is Associate Research Scientist in the Gerontology Unit of Biometrics Research, New York State Department of Mental Hygiene; and Adjunct Associate Professor in the Program in Gerontology and Leisure Education, Teachers College, Columbia University. Dr. Weinstock has a long-time commitment both to research and teaching in gerontology, as her current affiliations indicate, and she has published extensively in this field. She is a member of the Gerontological Society and, appropriately, a Member of the Steering Committee for the Establishment of an Association of Gerontological Educators.

If we see aging as a life process, as a cycle of maturation and development from conception through death, then it would seem wrong to speak of successful aging as the ultimate challenge. Psychological development and the course of the life cycle unfold in phases. Each phase may be defined by a set of tasks which must be met and conquered by the individual at that particular time in his developmental career. A number of interlocking factors are central to understanding the meeting of the challenges of life from infancy to old age.

First, physical maturation and the changes which take place in the structure and function of the human body play a major role. No child learns to crawl until the nerve and musculature growth which permit the necessary voluntary discrete movements become functional. No amount of training prior to such maturation will change the normal patterns of such psychomotor development. Once such readiness is established, however, the acquisition of such skills is amenable to and enhanced by practice, training, and opportunity for its acquisition. With such understanding of physical maturation, modern parents provide open spaces, climbers, walkers, and other such opportunities for the enhancement of such simple skills. Likewise, in later life, shifts occur in physical maturation which become a challenge to the developing human being. Adolescence brings internal as well as external physical changes which require adaptation to new ways of functioning.

Secondly, the human being matures and develops within a society. At the earliest stages, the society is represented first by one's parents, then by the extended family, and throughout life by one's peers, and through the roles established for different age groups and developmental periods. The child entering school brings with him his physical maturation, which is put into play with the new set of demands and expectations which define the role of schoolchild. Later in the life cycle, marriage, parenthood, and retirement all provide a subset of society's expectations to which the individual must adapt. New behavior, new abilities, new ways of handling old problems, come at different periods of the life cycle and are largely determined by the specific set of norms established by the social setting in which development is taking place.

Finally, a developmental view of the life cycle must also take into account the changing nature of the individual's mental growth and decline. The challenges wrought by the growing capacity to think, to learn, to interpret life's experience, to communicate, to integrate these abilities into a meaningful capacity, to assume responsibility for one's own actions and feelings, and to direct one's own life, are also part of the life cycle of adaptation.

SUCCESSFUL AGING, PSYCHOLOGICALLY

Successful aging, then, is but a phase in the course of a life which contains a series of crises arising out of the need to meet new physical, social, and psychological challenges common to every man. Overcoming and resolving these challenges determine the future development of the person, ensure his success or failure in adapting to the inner and outer world to which he must adjust, and draw for him and the world a sense of and evaluation of self.

From a psychological viewpoint, then, growing old successfully, means adapting to the changes in structure and function of the human body, to the changes in roles demanded by the social setting, and to the changes which a lifetime of human experience have imprinted on the human mind.

THE ELEMENTS INVOLVED

Earlier papers presented at this Institute have documented fully what the major physical, psychological, and social changes are which present challenges for adaptation for the older person. There is a growing body of knowledge in the multi-disciplinary field of gerontology documenting the variety of declines, both physical and psychological, which affect the everyday functioning of the older person. Older people must adjust to a variety of chronic diseases and failing organ and muscle systems. Older people suffer from declines relative to the middle-aged or younger adult in sensory and perceptual abilities. The average 75-year-old man or woman can see at 20 feet what the younger person with normal vision can see at 70 feet. There is a decline with age in dark adaptation. The ability of the eye to focus on near objects by changing its focal length decreases with age. That is, we tend to get more far-sighted as we get older. Here, the changes which take place, however, are more marked through the middle-aged period as all of you whose arms have gotten steadily shorter holding books or newspapers are aware. There are gradual hearing losses from age 60 upward, particularly for higher frequencies.

Sensory Changes

Other sensory changes include loss of sensitivities in taste and smell, although the evidence is somewhat contradictory depending on who were studied and with whom they were compared.

Tests of strength, reaction time, and sensorimotor coordination all show declines with age, again, when compared with those of younger adults.

Cognitive Abilities

It has been widely assumed that declining intelligence is also typical or normal in aging. However, much of the literature on aging and cognitive behavior has been concerned with describing how older individuals differ from younger people at a given point in time. This is valid and worthwhile if we are interested in the standardization of our measurements or in comparing older with younger persons on a specific measure. But such cross-sectional data tell us nothing about the changes in the cognitive abilities of an individual which take place throughout the life span. Furthermore, given the fact that we know that the older population have been exposed to less education and been away from school for longer than younger people, we are penalizing them unnecessarily by characterizing their performance on measures so closely related to school achievement.

We find that longitudinal studies (i.e., following the performance of the same individuals over time) show a different pattern of cognitive changes with age from those of cross-sectional ones. Longitudinal data usually show a steady increment in cognitive abilities during childhood, slight improvement in middle age, and continued increases in certain tests such as vocabulary, verbal abilities, and general information in old age. One reason, then, why cross-sectional data show declines with age is that younger generations (because of differential socioeconomic and educational factors) start out at higher levels of ability.

Furthermore, the tests themselves have often been developed for, or normalized on, young-adult populations, such as college students or army selectees. The resulting data have serious limitations, then, for an understanding of adult abilities. Observed decrements in test performance noted with increasing adult age may simply reflect the structure of the test. Asking an older adult (who probably has less than an eighth-grade education and who has been removed from any kind of school learning situation for upward of 60 years) to tell you "who wrote *Hamlet*" or "*The Iliad*" is hardly a measure of his cognitive ability. More likely, it is a measure of his exposure to information and of his school experience, and a commentary on the lack of opportunities for continued education through the life span.

Memory

A similar problem arises when we attempt to assess the memory function of older adults. We all know that older people are forgetful; that they dwell on the past, not the present. Most of what we commonly call senility has to do with an older person's inability to remember names and dates, and his tendency to confuse events and people, to reminisce about other times and other places inappropriate to the situation in which he is behaving. When we analyze memory in older people, then, we recognize that their memory for past events seems unimpaired, if inappropriate at times. So, it would seem that what they learned and experienced early in life remains with them through old age. What are the factors, then, which affect recent memory in older persons and cause its deficits?

First, we must hark back to the sensory declines we outlined earlier. Older people suffer visual and auditory handicaps. On a very concrete and simple level, this means that the world in which they are operating is severely limited. Because mental functioning operates on the level of a feedback system, sensory handicaps act to limit the amount and the kind of stimulation available to the individual. If I cannot see clearly and am limited in my vision by the amount of light which reaches the retina, or cannot hear clearly and am limited by my hearing deficit in understanding conversations which go on around me, it is clear that the higher mental processes such as comprehension, storage of information, organization of learned material, and the like, are going to be affected as well.

Furthermore, if my social world is also being narrowed by the loss of its important members (spouse, peers, children), the stimulation from the environment undergoes further deprivation. Therefore, when we draw a picture of a socially isolated, visually handicapped, hard-of-hearing old woman, we are also describing a human being whose information about the world around her has been cut back. Without such information, such feedback, such environmental stimulation, mental functioning suffers. Again, all this takes place in a larger social context where older people are viewed as less able, as non-productive; where the ability to find continued gratification through jobs or voluntary association is curtailed by age; where reduced mobility economically and physically offers restrictions; where the general attitude is that when you are old you are unwanted. The older person would like to continue to participate in everything belonging to society, but society shows a hostile and rejecting attitude toward him.

The Social Setting

This last factor, that of the social setting in which adaptation takes place, often determines, for the older person in particular, the balance between success and failure. We have already noted that optimal adjustment or adaptation for any human being involves an integration of available inner resources within the social system surrounding the person. Social systems which make demands above and beyond the capacities of the individual produce stress and tip the balance in the "failure" direction. Just as stressful, however, are those social settings which offer no expectations, no challenge, no opportunity for use of accumulated individual resources. A situation which has become too familiar, which offers no new roles, may result in adaptive failure as well (Lewin, 1946). The apathetic older person, the older person who seems to show decline in overall psychological functioning manifested by denial of future goals and over-attention to the past, may be reacting to the social setting which represents a sameness of life, a lack of environmental demands. A routine such as is typical in many institutional settings for the aged calls forth little motivation for change on the part of the older resident, and it is reasonable to assume that such drive, and its concomitant behavioral improvement, might be enhanced were the individual offered a more stimulating environment.

EFFECT OF ENVIRONMENT ON COGNITIVE PERFORMANCE

Little direct attention has been given to the effect of environmental deprivation or stimulation on cognitive performance. I should like to report on some of my own studies (Weinstock & Bennett, 1971) which were conducted to determine if some types of social environment are related to the maintenance of a high level of cognitive functioning in the aged. In these studies, attention was given to the relations between cognitive performance and the social cognition, social isolation, age, and mental status in three populations: "newcomers" and "oldtimers" residing in a home for the aged, and a "waiting list" group residing in the community. The major hypothesis was that aged persons within a stimulating social environment can perform at relatively high levels on tests of cognitive ability as compared with their socially deprived counterparts. Age, per se, was not thought to be the factor accounting for poor cognitive functioning.

Sixty persons, over 65 years of age, comparable on background characteristics such as age, sex, education, religion, and place of birth, and differing only as to place and length of residence, were interviewed. Two-thirds were female; one-third, male. More than half of the total sample were in the 80- to 89-year-old range. Oldtimers had a mean age of 83.7; waiting-list subjects, 79.8; and newcomers, 79.3. Of the total sample, 40% had had at least some high school education. Over 40% were native-born Americans. The newcomers had the highest proportion of foreign-born subjects. The sample was divided for place and length of residence as follows: 20 waiting-list subjects residing in the community, 20 newcomers to the home, and 20 oldtimers whose length of residence in the home was more than one year. Newcomers were selected by the investigator and included 20 consecutive new admissions to the home who were English-speaking and could complete the interview. Oldtimers and waiting-list subjects were selected by staff members of the home's social service department according to their estimate of the subjects' fluency in English and intactness.

A standard interview lasting approximately one hour was administered. It contained the following indices:

1. The Adulthood Isolation Index, which is a measure of the extent of lifetime social contacts with family, friends, work, and organizations.

2. Past-Month Isolation Index, which is a measure of the number of social contacts outside the institution in the month prior to the interview.

3. Three Wechsler Adult Intelligence Scale (WAIS) * subtests: Information, containing 20 questions measuring basic knowledge of topics ranging from names of composers to the colors in the flag; Comprehension, containing 14

---

* Published in 1955, the WAIS comprises 11 subtests. Six subtests are grouped into a Verbal Scale and five into a Performance Scale. The three subtests employed in this investigation all belonged to the Verbal Scale.—Ed.

items designed to measure the ability to combine information into new forms; and Similarities, which is a measure of conceptualization with 13 items of paired association.

4. Socialization Index, which is a measure of the amount of information learned about life in the home, consisting of 15 questions about formal procedures and norms in the home such as "what kinds of activities are available during the day?"

5. Mental Status Schedule, which is an instrument containing 350 items worded for true–false judgments of current psychopathology based on data collected during the interview.

The hypothesis that old people involved in a stimulating environment would perform best on tests of cognitive abilities was supported. Residents of the home for the aged obtained higher-mean WAIS total and subtest scores than their waiting-list counterparts. In general, newcomers obtained higher scores than both oldtimers and waiting-list persons on tests of cognitive ability. The home seemed to provide the type of environment which sustained a high level of cognitive performance. These findings seem best explained by a "disuse" model of cognitive functioning which holds that cognitive skills tend to be "forgotten" or are possibly lost unless they are put to use. Opportunities to put them to use in the home were many and varied. Newcomers were introduced to a social setting which required new learning on a daily basis. They were actively involved in the process of learning the role of a new member of the home. To learn this role it was necessary for them to be aware of, and accumulate information about, the norms and expectations of the home. Some of this information was communicated to them through talks with social service workers and through printed material sent prior to entry, as evidenced by the fact that waiting-list subjects knew some of the rules of the institution. In the main, learning about the role of becoming an institutional resident occurred through a process of daily interaction between newly admitted residents and oldtimers within the home. This communication process necessitated continual social interaction with other residents, some of whom acted as role models as well as teachers. Staff members also were in constant touch with newcomers, keeping them alert to expectations for behavior, observing them closely, and repeatedly sanctioning them. Newcomers were seldom left to their own devices or allowed to sit idle; they were constantly active and involved, possibly to avoid rejection by their peers or admonition by staff members.

LONGITUDINAL EXTENSION OF THE STUDY

One year after the initial study, a follow-up was conducted at the same institution. This longitudinal extension tested the general hypothesis that the socialization process is a salient, highly stimulating learning experience which positively affects other cognitive processes. Therefore, we expected to find that a former waiting-list person when interviewed in his new status as a newcomer-resident of the home would show improvement on tests of cognitive ability. We thought former newcomers might show signs of decline. We did not know what to predict for oldtimers grown even older.

The follow-up sample included all surviving subjects from the original sample whose physical and mental condition permitted their participation in an hour-long interview. The survivors constituted a group of 28 females and 12 males (the original sample of 60 had 41 females and 19 males). Mean chronological ages of the groups were 79.1 years for former waiting-list persons, 80.1 for former newcomers, and 85 for former oldtimers.

A standard interview lasting approximately one hour was administered. It was identical to that given to the original sample in the first study.

The WAIS information test scores showed the most stability for all three groups. Similarities scores showed the highest percentage of gains for the waiting-list group, but almost half of both newcomers and oldtimers showed drops in similarity scores. One-third of the waiting-list gained in their comprehension scores in the time they were institutional residents. Over half of the oldtimers, however, showed losses of more than one point on retest. One-half of the waiting-list population showed gains in total WAIS score, and only one-third showed losses. Of the newcomers, 64% either gained points or maintained total WAIS score on retest. However, almost three-quarters of the oldtimers showed losses on total WAIS scores over time. In general, the effects of environmental stimulation seemed most evident for the former waiting-list group who had become newcomers, and least for oldtimers.

It had been hypothesized that a stimulating environment which provides salient new learning situations, and which is supportive through peer and staff social interaction, would positively affect performance on a test of cognitive functioning. This hypothesis was supported. Those individuals who were engaged in the socialization process in order to adapt to the role of newcomer showed gains in cognitive performance on retest. Former newcomers, who were beginning to settle into and accept oldtimer status, showed some signs of loss in cognitive functioning. Of the three groups, the oldtimers showed the greatest percentage of loss in scores on all WAIS subtests. Former waiting-list persons, such as new residents stimulated by new experiences, were socially and cognitively alert. But the old-age home evidently does not continue to provide this stimulation on a long-term basis.

COUNTERACTING DESOCIALIZATION IN THE AGED

Institutionalization affects people differently. After about one year of residence, the transition from newcomer to oldtimer status is achieved, and the lack of challenge and of new roles and relationships becomes evident: newcomer status provides residents with daily stimulation and tangible goals, whereas oldtimer status—although not without privileges—provides fewer incentives since the environment and the residents have stabilized to a great extent. Using a longitudinal design, this study has confirmed earlier findings of our cross-sectional study and those of Lieberman, Prock, and Tobin (1968), and of Anderson (1964). All these studies demonstrated mixed efforts, negative and positive, of institutionalization. However, our longitudinal study has enabled us to pinpoint in time the onset of these negative effects. Presumably, they can be offset with environmental manipulation.

An applicant can anticipate, then prepare for, and finally involve himself in the socialization process—learning and practicing where to go, what to do, whom to meet, when to speak—as a new resident. Performance brings the rewards of acceptance by staff, residents, and family. Once orientation is accomplished, continued daily participation (e.g., volunteering for certain privilege jobs) can help newcomers further establish themselves. However, eventually there fail to be new rewards and experiences to prevent the monotony of passing days and the realization that these days are among one's last. Studies by Lieberman and Lakin (1963) and by Hadley (1963) have stressed the debilitating and deteriorative aspects of the institutionalization of the aged. Programs in institutions seek to introduce work-like recreation activities to attempt to maintain some semblance of former-life patterns. But our data seem to point to the need for some further thought about institutional programming.

If meaningful learning experiences, positive milestones, were provided throughout a resident's length of tenure in an institution, then oldtimers might show fewer cognitive decrements. Furthermore, such deterioration as takes place in waiting-list persons, which seems to be overcome by the initial impact of newcomer status, might be avoided altogether through concerted community effort to provide social and intellectual support and prevent the role loss experienced by the non-institutionalized elderly.

Most important perhaps for the socialization of older people is the basic premiss that most of what is learned from socialization in childhood and throughout life is a series of complex interpersonal relationships. In the life of every person, there are a number of people directly involved in socialization who have great influence because of their frequency of contact, their primacy, and their control over rewards and punishments. We can say that the individual learns the behavior appropriate to his position in a group through interaction with others who hold normative beliefs about what his role should be and who reward or punish him for correct or incorrect actions. When we begin to analyze the social behavior of older people, we begin to recognize that the opportunities for practicing social skills are severely limited by virtue of the ever-increasing losses of social contacts (particularly "significant-others") who have been involved in the lifelong socialization process. There is a decrease in frequency of social contact; there are fewer relationships which are intimate, and therefore fewer people to control, to reward appropriate and punish inappropriate behavior. Therefore, with older people we are often dealing with a phenomenon which may be termed "desocialization"—that is, a loss of social knowledge and skills. Given the assumption that frequency of contact, interpersonal significance, and reward can influence behavior or is the prime mover in the socialization process, then when old people are offered such opportunities, they should be able to relearn what has been lost through disuse and even add new learning for appropriate social roles.

WORK WITH GERIATRIC OUTPATIENTS

From this conceptual framework, we continued our studies (Weinstock, 1971) with a program initiated for geriatric outpatients of a metropolitan hospital to offer opportunities for older people to interact with a group of their peers to modify their social behavior. An ongoing discussion group of patients was organized with the purpose of giving the patients a chance to socialize with peers, to share and resolve common daily problems, and to offer a focus for social interaction other than that of bringing medical problems to the doctor.

With few other roles to play in our society, and with the severe social isolation suffered by this population, at least some of the older persons attended the clinic in a search for social interaction. These patients in part play the "sick role," which is then reinforced by the sympathetic treatment of staff. But if they are given substitute socially interactive opportunities and receive negative reactions to constant physical complaints, their "need" to be sick might diminish along with the "need" to attend the clinic.

Since one of the goals of the sessions was to direct focus away from physical complaints, the group leader attempted to use one of the members as a "solution" model, asking the member to talk about some positive ways to cope with physical ailments and to help oneself. Although surprised that their opinions might be listened to or deemed worthy, the members hesitatingly and briefly offered general ways in which they attempted to cope with some of these problems.

In ongoing sessions, group discussion involved talking about the living conditions of the members, with all expressing their feelings about living alone. Each appeared eager to tell about her own loneliness, the difficulties with shopping, and the fear when she becomes sick and no neighbors are around. When the group leader introduced the topic of living among age peers as opposed to living in age-integrated housing, all but one member appeared to favor living in a mixed community, and all gave cogent reasons.

It became more and more evident as the sessions continued that the group considered social isolation their major problem. Members began meetings telling the group how depressed they were over the weekends or how whole weekends had been spent in bed. These were contrasted to the few experiences of getting out into the world, a Tuesday night Bingo game, for instance, where "there are people, there is excitement, and things to do. That's when I glow . . . not like when you're alone and have no one to talk to." Attempts to counteract loneliness with a pet and stories of the affection they give and the joy they bring were scoffed at by some members who expressed the notion that an animal cannot make up for the desired human companionship.

As the group focused more and more on these problems, they were gradually led to discussion of the possibility of planning activities as a group, going on trips, and the like. Soon after, the members themselves organized a buddy system whereby telephone numbers and addresses were exchanged and group members kept in touch with each other between sessions.

Group discussions began to change not just with regard to content, but with regard to structure and function as well. That is, in the early meetings, the group leader was continually working to focus and refocus the discussions around issues relevant to all; but as the meetings progressed, group members themselves were beginning to orient the discussions in a problem-solving direction. Throughout the sessions, members expressed problems, the group offered solutions, alternate ways of handling situations, and more realistic ways of coping. They respected more each other's ability to offer solutions as they began to recognize the commonality of problems they shared.

The sessions provided them with the kind of normative social feedback which they had all been deprived of prior to these meetings. A setting had been provided in which there were behavioral expectations, some regulation of behavior, in the form of the group leader's structuring of the discussion as well as leader's use of reinforcement techniques, and a group of people with whom to relate.

In summary: the group members had entered this program showing signs of loss of social skills, a verbal focusing on physical selves while behaviorally not attending to appropriate dress or cosmetics, and manifesting grossly inappropriate social behavior. Among the latter, for example, was hoarding when refreshments were served, a lack of concern for another's needs during this time, and interrupting one another or ignoring conversations during meeting time. In other words, social cues, practiced by most adults in order to respond relevantly to others, were ignored by this group. Also observed were memory losses while giving physical histories to the physician, and highly dependent behavior with the nurse and social worker, asking for help with any minor everyday routine. Thus social competence, independent thinking and action were ignored and put to rest, whereas dependency and socially inappropriate behavior had been reinforced prior to our intervention.

After participation in the program, given an opportunity and encouragement by the group leader to voice independent thinking and manifest self-sufficient behavior, and given a socially interactive setting, members began to censure each other's socially inappropriate behavior. They began to show renewed interest in activating social roles, through exchanging telephone numbers and offering suggestions for meeting daily problems. They became less concerned with their own medical symptomotology and more concerned with exploring, though in a limited way, the tackling of objective problems of aging such as housing, transportation, social activities, and finances. Their dress improved. They began using cosmetics. They began meetings with social greetings for each other, showing concern for the way the time between meetings had been spent. They inquired about problems raised in past sessions and their outcomes. In addition, they communicated to members who had missed sessions what had taken place. They proudly cited their competence in handling situations which previously had been left to others to handle for them.

It appeared that the problem-solving orientation of the group became a consistent approach for handling situations which previously had been left to others to handle for them.

THE ELEMENTS OF SUCCESSFUL ADAPTATION TO OLD AGE

It is evident, then, that successful adaptation to old age is dependent on the recognition and implementation of norms and goals which are appropriate to an individual's physical and psychological capacities.

Margaret Clark's (1968) studies of aging in San Francisco have yielded a number of criteria for adaptation used in attitudinal interviews with persons over the age of 60.

> These, in order of their frequency of mention, were as follows: (1) independence, (2) social acceptability, (3) adequacy of personal resources, (4) ability to cope with external threats or losses, (5) having significant goals or meaning in later life, and (6) ability to cope with changes in self [Clark, 1968, p. 438].

She found that those older people who continue to hold to values of achievement, success, individualism, control, and orientation toward the future were those she found to be the most maladjusted aged persons.

> To go a step further in generalization, it seems likely that patterns of value appropriate to the middle-aged in our society are deemed inappropriate (or prove dysfunctional) for the elderly [Clark, 1968, p. 441].

However, adapting to these cultural discontinuities is, as we pointed out earlier, a life-cycle process. That is, throughout human development, social goals, expectations, and value systems change, and these force the individual to change identity. They have their impact on the individual, on his personality, and on his ability to see and interpret events around him. An adolescent must move from the dependent family-centered child to a new sense of self, a sense of responsibility for his own actions, a value system or sense of morality which is his own and with which he is comfortable. This is seen as a crisis in identity which must be resolved before one takes on the developmental tasks of adulthood.

Ruth Benedict (1938) suggested that cultural discontinuities, such as those which accompany adolescence in Western society, are stressful for the individual, but that critical support is offered in other cultures and could be in our own as well by one's social group. We could read Ruth Benedict's observation to mean "the adolescent peer group," "the family," "the older person's significant reference group," etc. She writes:

> Fortified in this way, individuals in such cultures often swing between remarkable extremes of opposite behavior without apparent psychic threat [Benedict, 1938, p. 166].

Clark's (1968) studies give us evidence to support this point. She found that older people living in the community had more social relationships and were more active in their relationships than were those who had been hospitalized for mental illness but were discharged and living in the same community, thus having similar opportunities for social interaction. According to Clark:

> A significant reference group, then, may protect the aging individual against the stresses of cultural discontinuity [Clark, 1968, p. 442].

Another line of research which tends to bolster the developmental framework being put forth comes from the studies done by Charlotte Bühler (1935), who adheres strongly to the notion that adaptation throughout the human life cycle may be studied by examining the individual's motivation for behavior. Bühler documents through collections of life histories a distinct need for continuous "expansion," a future-orientation underlying human behavior. She sees this in terms of a need to occupy significant roles. Kuhlen and Johnson have empirically shown such changes in goals throughout adulthood by asking schoolteachers what they would like to be doing ten years from now. Most notable in the charts developed as a result of this study are sex differences in long-term goals, differences between single and married individuals in their orientation, and evidences of a sequence of goals as life moves on (Kuhlen & Johnson, 1952).

Kuhlen in another article concludes as follows on this point:

> In general, though goals may change, the obviously expansive phase of life is determined not only by a strong desire for achievement and "expansion" but by the increasing competence in environmental manipulation which re-

sults from the growth of mental and physical capacities, the development of culturally appropriate goals, the accumulation of experience and the chronological achievement of opportunity (granted, in a sense by society) to function with relative independence and in significant roles [Kuhlen, 1959, p. 860].

Finally, one last piece of evidence which may be applied by all of us whether we are concerned for our own successful aging or for that of others.

Some years ago, a series of studies were conducted at an all-geriatric hospital by Robert Kastenbaum (1972), and involved the introduction of wine and beer at specified times on the wards. Kastenbaum began with a basic assumption that early in life human beings develop a need for mutual gratification, the need for pleasurable interactions with others. In meeting this need, by the time he reaches adulthood, a person has learned to interact with many others within his life space in a number of different roles prescribed by society. He is a son, a father, a husband, an employee, a friend, a church member, a neighbor and so forth. Through these roles, he has built a picture of himself. Loss of roles in young adulthood tends not to affect the stability of the self-picture because the young adult has many environmental opportunities in which to play out or substitute other roles. The older adult faces a different situation, however. We have noted that role loss is a concomitant of the aging process. Wives and husbands die; children move; the deaths of friends and relatives cause considerable shrinkage in the social world in which the older adult operates. Substitution through other roles is limited either by the environment (i.e., substituting a "job" for the loss of parental role) or by the lack of it between loss and substitution (a new friend for an old). If this is true for the average elderly person, it becomes even more exaggerated for the geriatric patient in an institution. The only role open to the institutional resident is that of "patient."

As Kastenbaum puts it, speaking of the institutionalized older person:

Clearly he is expected to follow, not to lead; to receive, not to give. Just a shade less obviously, the staff is also bolted into position. Most of "us" make a determined effort to be helpful to "them." We do not expect "them" to help "us." Both sides have allowed themselves (ourselves) to be trapped and at least half-persuaded that this is the best, if not the only, possible arrangement [Kastenbaum, 1972, p. 368].

Application of a "mutual gratification" model was proposed to answer the question:

Could staff and patients be enticed to seek each other out not because they "have to" or "should" but simply because the contacts might be enjoyable? [Kastenbaum, 1972, p. 372].

Wine was originally proposed because of the connotative meaning it has for most adults. It arouses thoughts of pleasure in social situations, of family togetherness, of special occasions, of mutual gratification in adult socialization.

The initial introduction of the program took place in a male ward where the patients were among the least impaired in the hospital. As per Kastenbaum's description:

> Medically and mentally, these men were capable of leading relatively normal lives within the protective environs of the institution. In point of fact, however, they tended to constrict themselves to parallel, isolated existence. . . . Clinical experience with these patients indicated that they felt they had little that was worth communicating to each other [Kastenbaum, 1972, p. 375].

Groups were asked to meet every day at 3:00 P.M. in the day rooms. Red port wine was served. A participant-observer from the staff was assigned to be with the group as a group member (not leader) and for record-keeping functions. The major findings were:

> For the first time in the history of the hospital, patients spontaneously formed themselves into groups. The simple beverage-administration situation became elaborated into something of a social club. The "members" increasingly stepped outside of the patient role to function in an equalitarian manner as adults who enjoyed each other's company, the company of the Participant Observer and of those staff members who dropped in from time to time. The daily "club meetings" persisted for more than a year after the termination of the study per se. . . . The group became a place where pleasure and complaints could be aired and shared with little fear of rejection or reprisal. . . . Patient behavior with the group improved markedly—more communication, more positive in spirit, more varied [Kastenbaum, 1972, p. 376].

Despite such positive results, there were disasters, too. An attempt to implement a similar program in an intensive-treatment unit proved to be problematic. Despite some staff resistance, the favorable response of the patients seemed to generate a general acceptance. However, even after it appeared that the project had succeeded with patients, ward staff, administration, and visitors, failure came in the form of the objections from an influential member of the professional staff.

> Essentially his position was that such a development was unprecedented, unnecessary, and improper. There should not be such goings on in a medical setting; it lacked dignity. Furthermore, such a program invited the wrath of relatives, and there were relatives who knew how to make trouble for a public institution if they so chose [Kastenbaum, 1972, p. 384].

Despite some efforts by hospital administration to support the continuation of the project, the ward personnel found it difficult to remain spontaneous and active. No matter what they did, they were bound to incur someone's wrath. The program was terminated for this reason.

CONCLUSION

What was learned from the positive and negative results of the studies which have been described?

First, it is possible to apply what the social sciences tell us about human behavior to action programs. If we acquaint ourselves with an understanding of the needs, the motivations, the foundations, of human behavior and accept them as important determinants for adaptation throughout the life span, we can begin to provide settings for people which are appropriate to the developmental phase being examined.

Accepting a developmental viewpoint about human behavior and acquainting ourselves with the knowledge gathered about the elderly within this framework, we then enable ourselves to recognize the special as well as the universal needs of the elderly population. Like the rest of us, they need a host of interpersonal relationships to maintain their human qualities, and these interpersonal relationships must provide *mutual* gratification. Whether child, adolescent, young or older adult, no human being can develop positively when he is the taker and everyone else is the giver. And particularly when one has spent a lifetime successfully coping with the environment, it must be a particularly defeating notion to accept total dependence on others. However, it is possible to attempt to search for the kind of meanings which are mutually gratifying even in the most limited of environments.

If we accept the premiss that old age and its concomitant limitations are only another phase in the developmental process which calls for maximizing the fit between psychological needs and an arena in which they can be met, we can build programs which are rehabilitative rather than welfare-oriented, which focus on the life-experience skills gained with age, which recognize that old age is part of our own life cycle as well as of the cycle of others. Working with the elderly does not mean separating ourselves from them, but rather allowing ourselves to learn more about how, despite biological, social, and psychological handicaps, human beings continue to overcome.

REFERENCES

Anderson, N. N. Social activity, self-conception, and institutionalization of older people. Paper presented at 7th annual meeting of Gerontological Society, Minneapolis, Minnesota, October 29, 1964.

Benedict, R. Continuities and discontinuities in culture conditioning. *Psychiatry,* 1938, *1,* 161–167.

Bühler, C. The curve of life as studies in biographies. *Journal of Applied Psychology,* 1935, *19,* 405–409.

Clark, M. The anthropology of aging: A new area for studies of culture and personality. In B. Neugarten (Ed.) *Middle age and aging.* Chicago: University of Chicago Press, 1968. Pp. 433–443.

Hadley, R. G. Psychological changes in institutional residents. Research Project,

Domiciliary Psychological Service, Veterans Administration Center, Los Angeles, California, June 1963. Mimeographed.

Havighurst, R. J. A social-psychological perspective on aging. *The Gerontologist.* 1968, *8* (2), 67–71.

Kastenbaum, R. Beer, wine and mutual gratification. In R. Kastenbaum, *et al.* (Eds.) *Research, planning and action for the elderly.* New York: Behavioral Publications, 1972. Pp. 365–394.

Kuhlen, R. G., & Johnson, G. H. Changes in goals with adult increasing age. *Journal of Consulting Psychology,* 1952, *16,* 1–4.

Kuhlen, R. G. Aging and life adjustment. In J. E. Birren (Ed.) *Handbook of aging and the individual: Psychological and biological aspects.* Chicago: University of Chicago Press, 1959. Pp. 852–897.

Lewin, K. Behavior and development as a function of the total situation. In L. Carmichael (Ed.) *Manual of child psychology.* New York: Wiley, 1946. Pp. 791–844.

Lieberman, M. A., & Lakin, M. On becoming an institutionalized aged person. In R. H. Williams, C. Tibbetts, & W. Donahue (Eds.) *Processes of aging: Social and psychological perspectives.* (2 vols.) Vol. I New York: Atherton, 1963. Pp. 475–503.

Lieberman, M. A., Prock, V. N., & Tobin, S. S. Psychological effects of institutionalization. *Journal of Gerontology,* 1968, *23,* 343–353.

Weinstock, C. Development of a socialization program for geriatric outpatients. Paper presented at 79th meeting of the American Psychological Association, Washington, D.C., September 5, 1971.

Weinstock, C. & Bennett, R. From "Waiting on the List" to becoming a "Newcomer" and an "Oldtimer" in a home for the aged: Two studies of socialization and its impact upon cognitive functioning. *Aging and human development,* 1971, *2,* 46–58.

Successful Aging:
A Religious Viewpoint

ROSARIA BUESCHING, O.P.

Sister Rosaria Buesching, O.P., is the Director of the Penafort Program (named after the thirteenth-century Dominican, St. Raymond of Peñafort) for the Adrian Dominican Congregation, Adrian, Michigan. It is a pre-retirement and retirement program. Sister Rosaria holds a B.S. degree from Siena Heights College, and an M.A. degree from the Catholic University of America. She has done advanced study in guidance and counseling at DePaul University, Siena College, and Rutgers University; in theology at Providence College; and in applied social gerontology at Mount Angel College, Oregon. Before becoming Director of the Penafort Program, Sister Rosaria taught high school mathematics and science, was a high school principal, and a guidance director. In keeping with her current position, Sister Rosaria is a member of both the Michigan and the National Gerontological Society, and the National Council on Aging.

In the course of preparing this paper, I have changed my notes many times. Each change was an experience of accepting the unfinished. Of God only can the Bible say that on the seventh day He had completed His work (Gn 2:2). I have made several good friends because of my constant return to the thoughts of Rabbi Heschel (1961), Alfons Deeken (1972), Paul Tournier (1972) and Henri Nouwen (1969, 1972)—a rather ecumenical group, you will agree. Each has offered brilliant crystals of the kaleidoscope which fuse to form a transparent One, who comes into focus through the eye of faith, and hope, and love, dimly at first, "through a glass," but gradually and finally "face to face." I have experienced a deepening of my friendship with the carpenter's Son, Christ Jesus, whose book, the Sacred Scripture, is filled with messages concerning the ultimate challenge of successful aging. These associations may come across to you as male domination in contradiction to the liberation or freedom from oppression which successful aging represents—a freedom, however, of Children of God, heirs of His Kingdom, and therefore both male and female liberation.

I come before you not as a specialist in the field, but rather as one who, in spite of my deepest yearning to be faithful to the best in the process of aging, must say regrettably that the best of Buesching is simply not synonymous with the ultimate challenge in successful aging.

I bring you neither a brainstorm nor a breakthrough, very little that is original, and certainly not the perfect formula for successful aging; that must emerge in the life of each individual. I bring you only a beginning. I can at least share with you my enthusiasm and my conviction that today's accent, Successful Aging, is not unreal, not artificial, but indeed challenging to the ultimate for it forces us to confront our own convictions, our own lives!

My approach to the process from the point of religion considers three realities:

1) the aging person in society;
2) the correlation of religious development with human development;
3) the contribution of religion in the later years, or man in the process of Redemption.

THE AGING PERSON IN SOCIETY

Aging has many facets, and any study of it must acknowledge the complexity of the process. It is usually thought of and described in terms of the biological and psychological or personality changes which develop within an individual during the second half of the life span and which eventually terminate life. Total understanding of older people, however, requires more than a grasp of physical and psychological concepts; it requires that one also see aging persons as members of society and of the various social systems of which society is composed. Men live, grow, age, act, and react within a kinship group, neighborhood, community, economy, cultural system, and society. At every stage of life, men influence and are influenced by these systems in a complex of reciprocal relationships (Tibbitts, 1965).

Social scientists have developed a number of theories relevant to aging and to the structure of society and social change. In recent years two new theories have been systematically investigated and reported. The Disengagement Theory maintains that marked withdrawal from activities is the modal pattern in aging. High satisfaction in aging usually results from the acceptance of the inevitable reduction in social interaction. The Activity Theory, in contrast to the Disengagement Theory, maintains that satisfaction in aging is increased if the individual maintains his interests and activities within the limits of his capabilities. There is much evidence in biological and medical research to support the latter view that continuing activity throughout the life span is beneficial and affords greater satisfaction than the reduction of activity.

One cannot ignore the fact, however, that there are differences in the lifelong patterns of living. Some people tend to maintain relatively high and others relatively low levels of activity. This pattern is usually consistent throughout an individual's life span; consequently, one cannot expect a significant change in the level of activity based on a new view of the advantages or disadvantages of activity as applied to the older person. It does appear, however, that those who reduce their activities as they age tend to suffer a reduction in overall satisfaction (Busse, 1969).

The need for authentic social theories of aging is apparent when one considers that in the last seventy years changes in medical care, food production and distribution, income and housing patterns, coupled with the invention of labor-saving devices, have contributed to longer life for more and more people.

Consequently, social gerontologists are asking significant questions. If for most older people the later years are a time when energy is low, the circle of family and friends diminished, and income is reduced, what is the reasonable expectation for life satisfaction in these years? What is the position of older people in advanced society? Both the gerontologist and older people disturbed by the prospect of a dehumanizing technological culture question how we can enjoy the advantages of a rapidly developing technology without destroying the other values we cherish.

The complexity of the issues of social gerontology cannot be minimized; they encompass the entire human condition. But sociology alone will not provide the answer to the problems of aging. Nathan Shock suggests that the solution to the multiple problems of gerontology will require the application of research techniques of virtually every scientific discipline. He further suggests that the ultimate goal of all research on aging is to improve the performance and well-being of older people. The goal is to improve the "quality of life" in the later years by reducing the incidence of disabilities which afflict many elderly (Shock, 1973, p. 12).

Closely related to the biological aspects of aging is that phase of psychology which deals with the individual's ability to adapt to changes within himself and his environment. Significant to successful aging from the viewpoint of religion is the fact that man's peculiar ability to form abstract concepts, to use these concepts in the solution of problems, and to communicate the solution to others does not diminish appreciably as he grows older.

Through recent research the normal psychology of later life is beginning to be better understood; this leads to expectations for successful adaptation for most persons. As research on the relations of psychological, physiological, and social changes in later life continues, the characteristics which promote optimum adaptation should become better known and be applied to all aspects of life in the later years (Birren, 1964).

Today's gerontologists, unlike the scientists of forty or fifty years ago, are no longer looking for a panacea which will greatly extend life. The Biblical pronouncement that man's allotted time on earth is three score and ten remains a good estimate, despite all the advances in medicine over the last 3,000 years. Gerontology, consequently, is concentrating on making life more livable for the elderly. Ralph Goldman explains this view: "If we attain our goal, life in old age will be healthier and more enjoyable, altogether better, but only a little bit longer" (Boehm, 1965, p. 140).

Significantly, the focus in the scientific world makes repeated reference to improving the quality of life in the later years. Each new reference seems to come close to the heart of the matter. One answer to the question of what is included in the term "quality of life" may, in fact, take the Activity Theory one step further, i.e., to the continued growth process with an emphasis on the intellectual and spiritual development of man. Essential to that process is life, the vital force in which any growth process is encompassed. Life demands greater life, quality life. The whole of Scripture traces humanity's response to God's call to life. Moses challenged the Israelites:

See, today I set before you life and prosperity, death and disaster. . . . Choose life, then, so that you and your descendants may live, in the love of Yahweh your God, . . . clinging to him; for in this your life consists . . . [Dt 30:15, 19–20].

St. John gives us Christ's words: "I have come that they may have life, and have it more abundantly" (Jn 10:10). A recent speaker has given the following specification to the "quality of life" concept:

Quality human life needs meaning beyond itself. To be human is always to be more than human. Quality life means freedom. It means seeking liberation, struggling to break through whatever keeps us from being a whole person. Quality life means shared life; it means brotherhood [Rothluebber, 1971].

Elsewhere in this Institute the sociological and psychological implications for successful aging have been treated in detail. Now it is the intention of this writer to focus on the dimension of religion or spiritual development.

CORRELATION BETWEEN RELIGIOUS DEVELOPMENT
AND HUMAN DEVELOPMENT

In speaking of successful aging from the viewpoint of religion, let us emphasize that there are three phases of life to bring into balance: physical, mental, and spiritual. It is the whole person in the process of becoming. Growth is a continuing journey embracing life from birth to death. Integration of the three aspects of the whole person is not something which happens automatically or merely through physical maturation; it is the individual operating as a unity, maintaining and intensifying this wholeness or integrity. The human personality is dynamic, moving forward, not at random but with direction in the evolution of all its qualities. This is indeed a magnificent responsibility and splendid ambition which is ours, of becoming our own selves. A sound approach to religious development, therefore, cannot afford to overlook the interdependence of religious maturation and psychological maturity of the individual.

One popularly accepted theory of maturation is that offered by Erikson. For the purpose of this presentation, a brief summary, which I shall call the correlative religious manifestations of each age, may serve as a foundation for the years of later spiritual development. The first of the successive stages, infancy, Erikson characterizes as one of basic trust *vs.* basic mistrust. "Trust born of care is in fact the touchstone of the actuality of a given religion" (Erikson, 1963, p. 250).*

The vital relationship which the infant forms with his parents conditions his own relationship with the heavenly Father. Through the feeling of grandeur, of strength, and of power, which his father's love awakens in the child's heart, the father is instrumental in calling forth in him the sense of God who is great and transcendent. The mother, on the other hand, through her goodness, her selfless love, and affectionate presence, awakens in her child's heart a sense of the love of God, of His presence, of being safe with Him (Babin, 1963).

The religious manifestation of the second stage is a consciousness of one's personal value, a sense of reverence. The familiar atmosphere of the home and the mutual affection of his parents create for the young child his first genuinely human and religious values. Following closely upon this are the awareness of God's presence and an early attempt at prayer expressed through the limited vocabulary and naïve imagination of a child. The fourth stage is significant because the eagerness to do good for God and others often leads to an intimate relationship with God in personal prayer which ceases to be self-centered and becomes genuine interpersonal communion.

The social awareness, moral or religious consciousness, and personal

---

* Erikson's developmental stages have been described in the paper on the Psychology of Aging, page 75.—Ed.

attachment of the adolescent to Christ as a friend often provide the deep convictions which can weather the storms of adolescence and provide solid foundation for adult faith.

The adolescent's deep longing for identity with another person in mutual love and his fear of rejection, because of personal failings and inadequacy, are expressed well in the words of a modern youth:

> Jesus Christ is by far my closest friend. He is even my only friend. He is my best friend. I have never been able to lie to Him. It has been possible for me to lie to my parents and to my friends; finally I lied to myself. . . . I knew that Christ was the witness of my life. . . . At first this caused me to rebel violently for I would not accept that gaze of God penetrating into the depth of my soul. When I understood that by delivering myself to Him I had been delivered from my own duplicity, I found that I can say I had never had a better friend [Lombaerts, 1967, p. 714].

The sixth stage (between the ages of 16 and 19) is the least religious time of life in external practice and fidelity to faith-commitment; it is a time of question and doubt. In reality there are often successive conversions before the young adult reaches the point where his life receives "direction and meaning in relation to transcendent values, with a depth of consciousness and decision that put an end to the vacillations of his adolescence and profoundly affect the moral and religious sense of his adult life" (Babin, 1963, p. 60).

The young adult, then, is capable of consistent faith, responsible conduct, balanced self-criticism, freedom in expression, and respect for religious differences. In one way, man has found himself and established his identity, but in a more profound manner he will continue throughout life to search for the truth of his existence; there is no finite answer to the infinite mystery of the person, whose religious attitude must continuously restructure his life in harmony with an ever-deepening relationship with God (Van Kaam, 1968).

The religion of adulthood manifests confidence in acceptance of self and others as worthy of trust; security in self-giving love of God and neighbor; consistent, dynamic, effective conduct in lived relationships; awareness of self-value and consciousness of limitations and value; consistent respect for the sacred in every dimension of life (Mullins*).

By steadfast adherence to God's presence, the autonomous development of human personality is not eliminated but illuminated in the focus of a two-fold fidelity: sustained effort to deepen the bond of divine union and human labor carried out in the confident awareness of his faithful love. Thus we may say with the Psalmist: "I will celebrate your love forever, Yahweh. Age after age my words shall proclaim your faithfulness" (Ps 89:1).

---

* Unpublished paper of Sister Mary Mullins on Faith and Growth, prepared in 1971.

Realistically and humanly speaking, we must acknowledge that the sequential development just described is not the general pattern of spiritual growth. The spirit of man is a mystery, a fragile component, subject to the tide and torrent which threaten to diminish, to arrest, or to crush its delicate growth at any point along the way.

The writer of the letter to the Hebrews encourages us that this need not be the unhappy ending of our story, that it is never too late to remove the barriers, to revive the life and to resume growth. He says:

> If only you would listen to Him today . . . Every day, as long as this "today" lasts, keep encouraging one another so that none of you is hardened . . . because we shall remain co-heirs with Christ only if we grasp on our first confidence right to the end. . . . The promise of reaching the place of rest . . . still holds good, and none of you must think that he has come too late for it [Heb 3:7, 13–14; 4:1].

This message gives us a renewed hope. Development does not always follow the ideal pattern; sometimes it suffers some disruption at an earlier stage. The later years, free of the responsibilities of the middle years, allow man the time to begin again to deepen the dynamic inner search.

THE CONTRIBUTION OF RELIGION IN THE LATER YEARS

Gifted with leisure as a result of freedom from the responsibilities of the middle years, the person of the later years is able to experience a new sense of freedom, a freedom which enables him to "transcend the dimensions of economic and social necessity" in which his life is spent, in order "to participate in some higher realities" (Dahl, 1973, p. 15). A leisure which is more a spiritual condition than an economic, social, or psychological condition is a leisure of a "free spirit." It is a quality and style of life which enables a person to discover who he is and what life is. Leisure liberates man from his illusions of successful ambitions and strivings, liberates him from his myth of technological progress, and frees him so that he can discover anew the presence of grace, joy, and peace in his daily life.

In the context of Christian theology, one could say that a Christian experiences leisure "when he comes into full awareness of the freedom he has in Christ, freedom not only from fear and guilt because of sin, but even more important, freedom to be and become the New Man after Christ's own example" (Dahl, 1973, p. 15). Man in the process of redemption has, in his later years, a splendid opportunity to "grow up fully into Christ" as Paul expresses it (Ep 4:13). However, the reality of the lives of aging persons shows that in many instances this is not the case.

Rabbi Heschel cites the following trials of aging persons:

1) the sense of being useless to and rejected by family and society;
2) the sense of inner emptiness and boredom;
3) loneliness and the fear of time (Heschel, 1961, p. 10).

Alfons Deeken describes the following pitfalls and dangers of the later years as:

1) a rejection of the fact of growing old which causes the person to cling to youth by closing his eyes to the evident facts and pretending he is still young;
2) a resentment or envy toward the younger generation by refusing to let go interiorly of what is proper to an earlier stage of life;
3) an egoism of aging which frequently manifests itself by exaggerating the importance of eating and drinking, of the well-padded bank account, of the comfortable easy chair. This egoism also shows up in a senile caprice and selfishness which is observable in a lust for power, a desire to dominate, and tyrannize over one's own surroundings (Deeken, 1972, pp. 10–18).

Paul Tournier speaks of the pain of the later years which derives from the unfulfilled. One must face the fact that he has left many dreams, desires, and ambitions unfulfilled and that they will not reach fulfillment.

We can readily see, therefore, that aging which presents the opportunity for growth into full personhood through the leisure of a free spirit also presents a major challenge to this inner development. Rabbi Heschel pinpoints the problem when he refers to the cry for relatedness which gains intensity with aging. Such a cry, however, is for a referent which transcends personal existence (Heschel, 1961). One must not forget that man by nature is relational. He relates dialogically both to God and to his fellow-man, but his relation to others is grounded in his relation to The Other. In and through Jesus of Nazareth, God revealed to man the reality that He is tripersonal, that community is of His very essence. In the Trinity of Father, Son, and Spirit, Each exists for the Other in a loving participation of infinite giving and receiving. When Jesus prayed:

> May they all be one.
> Father, may they be one in us,
> as you are in me and I am in you . . . .
> may they be so completely one
> that the world will realize that it
> was you who sent me, and that
> I have loved them as much as you loved me [Jn 17:21, 23]

He brought to all human beings the understanding that they are called to intimate union and life within the Triune God. He brought to all human beings the realization that they are to be in community one with the other. Man by his very nature is other-directed, and he can become fully himself, fully human, only by living in loving reciprocity with others, sharing with them the very life and love which exists in God Himself. Therefore, in speaking of successful aging from the viewpoint of religion, one cannot consider just the aging persons themselves. The actual life-situations must be provided which make the life and love of our Triune God a reality in which the aging person can participate.

A compassionate, listening mind and heart will enter into the trials and provide the healing so necessary for the growth of a free spirit which can enjoy the leisure of the freedom of the Sons of God, and thus create an atmosphere to enjoy and deepen one's relationship with the Triune God who calls each of us to union, love, and life with Himself.

Henry Nouwen beautifully expresses this idea when he says:

> For one man needs another to live, and the deeper he is willing to enter into the painful condition which he and others know, the more likely it is that he can be a leader, leading his people out of the desert into the promised land [Nouwen, 1972, p. 63].

When one man is willing to see his own pain and suffering as rising from the human condition common to all men, then he can enter into the painful condition of another, and his own wounds become a source of healing for the other. And so it is with Christ. He entered into our human condition and shared our wounds. He took upon Himself our sinfulness and the forces of evil, death included, and in Him they suffered defeat. The Father raised Jesus to a new life and in Him pledged to all mankind that entrance into eternal life.

For those who are experiencing the later years of life, Christ holds out the reality of a new life. But His promise is made real only in and through His living disciples who are willing to become "wounded healers" and to minister in His name. Through personal concern, through faith in the value and meaning of life and of hope which breaks the boundaries of death, the "wounded healer" can lead others who are experiencing the trials and pitfalls of later years to a new experience of life (Nouwen, 1972).

Because someone gives his life for another fellow-traveler, he opens the door whereby the other can enter with him in faith, hope, and love to embrace the God who offers him life in His Son Jesus Christ who is the resurrection and the life.

Faith brings a new perspective to life, adds a new dimension to the realities of life. It unifies our fragmented, broken personalities into whole beings. It inspires the searching mind and provides a constant incentive for an ongoing renewal of life (Nouwen, 1969). Faith in Christ and in all that He promises enables an aging person to say "Yes" to the fact that he is nearing a new stage in life and thus he is willing to accept the reality of his later years. It enables him to embrace a broader perspective of life and love, of God and the world, of time and eternity.

Such a view allows for developing a spirit of detachment so that one does not fall into the egoism of aging which exaggerates the importance of material possessions. And such a faith permits the one of leisure years the opportunity to experience aloneness rather than loneliness. The emptiness of being alone

> can open man's heart and make him more perceptive of the presence of God, who likes to speak in silence . . . it can strip man of his masks and force him to confront his real self. Being alone can deepen his faith and inspire him to see a more personal relationship with God [Deeken, 1972, p. 25].

Such a relationship is founded in Trinitarian life. Faith in Christ does not allow the person of later years to say, "I am useless to society," because by his baptism his very life and sufferings are caught up into Christ's supreme sacrifice for all men, and he daily allows Christ to live in his body and plead through him for the salvation of all men.

The sense of inner emptiness, boredom, loneliness, and fear of time must give way when one is consumed with the need to live his life for his brothers and sisters in Christ. These trials of aging must disintegrate when one needs time to be with his Heavenly Father who calls him in Jesus His Son to an intimate friendship through their Spirit. The unfulfilled dreams, desires, and ambitions fade from perspective as one longs eagerly for the fulfillment which looms on the horizon of eternal life in the new creation which God prepares for His people.

The ultimate challenge of successful aging is one shared by all members of all ages of society. It involves the development and growth of man into his full personhood through loving mutual relationship with God and his fellow-man. A person deprived of a loving exchange with other persons is hampered in his search for a loving relationship with God. Conversely, one who is supported by loving relationships with his brothers and sisters in Christ is aided in developing an intimate relationship with God which will sustain him during the final years of his life.

When society is built on the rock foundation of Christian love, it can and will accept the challenge to provide for its aging members the necessary means whereby the person of later years can grow up fully into Christ. However, this is a two-way street, and the aging person must take advantage of the opportunities which are available for him.

Given this condition of loving union, the Father, who loves and calls

each of us to Himself in Christ Jesus, will not fail to supply the divine help
which each one needs to be drawn to Him. Then will be fulfilled the words
of Christ, "I have come that they may have life—life to the full" (Jn 10:10).

REFERENCES

Babin, P. *Crisis of faith: The religious psychology of adolescence.* New York:
Herder & Herder, 1963.

Birren, J. E. *The psychology of aging.* Englewood Cliffs, N.J.: Prentice-Hall, 1964.

Boehm, G. A. W. The search for ways to keep youthful. *Fortune,* 1965, *71* (3),
138–142.

Busse, E. W. Psychologic, psychiatric and social aspects of aging. *Sandoz Panorama,* 1969, *9* (4), 5.

Dahl, G. Towards a theological understanding of leisure. In R. Ochsenrider (Ed.)
Every day a holy day. Nashville, Tenn.: Tidings, 1973. Pp. 9–16.

Deeken, A. (s.j.) *Growing old and how to cope with it.* New York: Paulist Press,
1972.

Erikson, E. H. *Childhood and society.* New York: Norton, 1963.

Heschel, A. J. To grow in wisdom. Paper delivered at White House Conference
on Aging, Washington, D.C., January, 1961.

Lombaerts, H. A church of the poor, the servant of humanity. *Lumen Vitae,* 1967,
22, 693–724.

Nouwen, H. J. *Intimacy.* Notre Dame: Fides, 1969.

Nouwen, H. J. *The wounded healer.* Garden City, N.Y.: Doubleday, 1972.

Rothluebber, Sister Francis Borgia. Religious women in ministry. Address given
at meeting of Interfaith Council on Urban Ministry, Notre Dame University,
1971.

Shock, N. The biologist's view of aging. *NRTA Journal,* 1973, *24* (3), 11–12.

Tibbitts, C. Middle-aged and old people in American society. Paper prepared for
the Training Institute for Public Welfare Specialists in Aging, Cleveland, Ohio,
June, 1965.

Tournier, P. *Learn to grow old.* New York: Harper & Row, 1972.

Van Kaam, A. *The emergent self.* Vol. II. *The self and others.* Wilkes-Barre, Pa.:
Dimension Books, 1968.

ISBN 0–8232–0980–6

AGING:

Its Challenge
to the Individual
and to Society

Edited by William C. Bier, S.J.

The perennial problem of aging has come into even sharper national focus in recent years, with the *percentage* of our population aged 65 and over having more than doubled in this century thus far, while the *number* has increased more than sixfold. These facts are basic, but their implications are manifold, presenting challenges for both the aging individual and for society-at-large.

Number Eight in the Pastoral Psychology Series, this volume points up some of these challenges and, in addition, provides useful and productive responses. Reflecting attention to topics of an immediately current nature, it views the subject matter in an interdisciplinary context.

Aging is first viewed in historical, cultural, and religious perspective. This background is followed by the dimensions of aging as seen by modern science. Focus is then placed on the topic of retirement as

(continued on back flap)

The Fordham Institutes in Pastoral Psychology are held biennially in June. The 1975 Institute will be concerned with the topic "Human Life," and its proceedings will be published as Number Nine in the Series in the fall of 1976.

Photograph by Gregory S. Dinallo